HAROLD BAUER
His Book

HAROLD BAUER

His Book

GREENWOOD PRESS, PUBLISHERS
NEW YORK

Illustrations

[5]

Preface

I NEVER INTENDED TO WRITE THE STORY OF MY LIFE, AND I neither know nor care whether I shall be believed when I say that this writing has been the most abominable and tedious chore that I ever undertook.

What happened is this: my very dear and distinguished friend, the late Carl Engel, president of G. Schirmer, Inc., wished to pay me a compliment on the occasion of my seventieth birthday. Since he had always been amused by my relation of little incidents in my long career, he got me to write some of them down, then put them together with inimitable skill and charm, and published the result in the *Musical Quarterly*.

This created a great deal of comment, and the next thing was that Warder Norton asked me to write a whole book about myself. I rejected his suggestion with horror, but I went to tea with him and his wife, and, as a consequence of their skillful and delicate flattery, I was undone.

Even so, the book would never have been completed

without the gentle and incessant nagging of my wife.

The time has come for me to express my acknowledgments to everyone concerned in this perpetration, and I hereby do so, peevishly, with the fervent hope that they will all leave me alone in future.

It remains only for me to add, now that I notice the curiously abrupt fashion in which this book starts, that I was born near London on April 28, 1873.

H.B.

One

MY EARLIEST REACTION TO MUSIC, AS FAR AS I CAN RECALL, was one of fascinated terror. Even at this far-distant time, it almost makes my flesh creep when I think of the huge faces of adults bending over me, or over one of my sisters, and emitting the strange sound which, I was later to learn, is called singing. The music was not confined to noises coming from human faces, however, for there was also the unforgettable sound—solemn and yet piercing—of the shiny brass instruments played in the street by a group of shabby men called the "German Band." In addition, there was the Italian barrel-organ grinder, accompanied sometimes—oh, bliss!—by a monkey; an occasional violinist; a man who played a bright yellow clarinet; two men in Highland costume, one of whom danced to the playing of the bagpipes (the most exciting sound in the world, I think) by his companion.

Then the music of the street cries ("Chinaware cheap" and "Jubilee Coal Blocks" provided the themes, later on, for a juvenile sonata), and finally, the god of musicians, a glorious individual who went about with a dozen different instruments distributed over his person, playing them all at the same time. That, to me, was real magic; and I longed unspeakably to grow up and conquer my fear of the sounds, so that I could wield the power he possessed—some day!

I suppose it was this mingled feeling of fear and ambition that made me try to find the notes of a tune which had alarmed me to the extent of wanting to hide under the table. After I had picked out the notes, I did not mind it so much. It was the opening of Brahms' piano quintet, and I am still a little afraid of it.

On my fourth birthday, I decided that the time had come for me to do something important, so I composed a polka which contained exactly eight measures—quite enough, I considered, for a beginning, a middle, and an end. How it was that this babyish little thing stuck in my mind I am unable to say, but it came back to me about half a century later, when Ossip and Clara Gabrilowitsch told me almost tearfully that their daughter Nina showed not the slightest interest in music.

"How old is she?" I inquired.

"Today is her fourth birthday," was the reply.

"Nina, darling," I said in my most persuasive tones, "wouldn't you like to hear the piece your Uncle Harold composed when he was four years old, like you?"

"Yeth," she said. (I think it was "Yeth," but it may have been "Yes.")

I played her my polka. She was enchanted.

"Do it again," she said.

"Again"—"Again" . . .

Finally I had to write it out and leave it with her mother, so that she could learn it. Ossip told me later that it was the only music she had ever enjoyed. I do not know whether it opened the way for general appreciation of the art—and anyhow, the story ends there. I relate it only because no composition of mine, as far as I know, has ever had the effect on anyone that my polka had on Nina Gabrilowitsch.

My aunt taught me to play the piano, and my father gave me my first lessons on the violin—a half-size instrument which had a loop of string tied round its scroll, so that it could be suspended from the bell-pull at the side of the fire-place when I was not using it. The bow hung from one of the tuning pegs.

When I was left alone to practice, I used to prop a book on the music-rack and read while going through the motions of the technical exercises I was supposed to master. This was not conducive to the development of good posture as a violinist, although I believe it did no harm—if no good —to piano playing. However, I progressed rapidly on the violin, and before long I started playing publicly in a small way.

Most concerts in London were given at St. James' Hall, an auditorium seating about 1,800, located at the lower end of Regent Street, up one flight of broad marble stairs. Below were numerous shops, and immediately underneath, an-other, smaller auditorium, which housed a permanent troupe of black-faced comedians known as the Christy Minstrels. The same box office sold tickets for the Minstrels and for the classical concerts, and an attendant, dressed in formal clothing with a high silk hat, was stationed in front of this box office for the sole purpose of preventing the "Minstrel" audience from strolling into the classical concerts, and vice versa. "Upstairs for the concert—this way for the Minstrels" —I can still hear his strident voice.

To walk up those marble stairs was an experience. They

were not steep, but they were fairly wide; my legs were short, and even holding tight to my father's hand I was unable to negotiate them otherwise than with two steps to each tread. This was the reason, I felt, that we did not sit in the main part of the auditorium; I was too young and unworthy of that honor. We had to climb up two other flights of stairs—much narrower—and found our places finally on wooden benches. I did not yet understand the difference between stalls—seven shillings and sixpence; balcony—three shillings; and gallery—one shilling. The music was the same everywhere, and all I knew was that my place was on those top benches, whence I could look down on the performers.

There were two sets of subscription concerts during the season, known respectively as the Saturday Pops, afternoons, and the Monday Pops, evenings. I was rarely taken to the evening concerts, because the trip from our home took about an hour each way, the distance being all of three miles; and this in the slow horse-omnibus meant getting home at an unduly late hour. The programs for these concerts generally included a string quartet, some piano solos, some violin solos, some songs, and another piece of chamber music, with piano, to end the program, which lasted at least two hours and a half, and sometimes longer. I do not recall that there was any intermission; neither do I recall any occasion when the hall was crowded, although the number of subscribers alone for each series averaged, I believe, about a thousand, which shows the public interest in chamber music at that period in London.

The works played at the "Pops" were as a rule familiar to me. My father was but one of a large number of amateur musicians who were accustomed to meet regularly at each others' homes to play quartets, and it is to this that I owe my knowledge of chamber music. Frequently, however, the great artists—Joseph Joachim at the head—who took part in these concerts brought out important novelties by the great composers of the day, such as Brahms, Dvořák, Grieg, etc., and these were always occasions for great excitement among the audience.

On the other hand, many of the compositions played were dull and academic, and it is rather surprising to look back to a time when a quartet by Rheinberger, Raff, Rubinstein, Spohr, or Götz was esteemed just as highly as anything in the so-called "classical" repertoire. And, of course, Mendelssohn—any amount of Mendelssohn. Queen Victoria was still on the throne of England, and although the composer had died forty years earlier, he was still looked upon as a kind of Court Musician. How we used to love his quartets! —in fact, all of his chamber music. I learned to play the viola through his A major quintet, because only one of the amateur group could read the C clef, and two violas were required.

When the Octet was played at the "Pops," the newspapers always carried a special advertisement saying that "Mendelssohn's celebrated Octet will be performed on this occasion." The designation "celebrated" was kept for two or three compositions only. One was Bach's "celebrated" concerto for two violins, which Joachim and Madame Norman-Neruda, greatest woman violinist of her time, used to play regularly each season. There was also Beethoven's "celebrated" Kreutzer Sonata, in the performance of which the second variation was invariably applauded so vociferously that it had to be repeated. I am quite sure—and I speak from personal experience—that every violinist confidently expected this tribute to his skill, and would have been intensely mortified if his performance of the "Kreutzer" had not been thus interrupted.

Sometimes a member of the Royal Family announced his or her (generally her) intention to attend a concert. This was advertised with a becoming mixture of humility and pride. It was assumed, I think correctly, that the announcement would attract people who otherwise would not go. Sometimes the concert was delayed until the Royal personage arrived, and sometimes the concert was interrupted when Royalty was ushered in, the performers, as well as the entire audience, rising to their feet at the moment of entrance. I do not remember whether or not I was impressed by this display of loyalty on the part of the audience. It seemed curious and interesting, and I always wondered, when the advertised royal personage had not arrived for the beginning of the concert, if the performers would be able to get through the first movement without being interrupted, or if they would have to stop in the middle to make their obeisance; in which case would they take up just where they had left off, or would they go back to the beginning? One never knew what would happen, and it was quite a nice field for speculation.

On one occasion, the performance of Beethoven's Rasoumovsky Quartet in F major was thus interrupted in the middle of the violin cadenza which occurs at the end of the long slow movement. Joachim could not stop—no artist could possibly have stopped just at that point—and he continued to the trill which ends the cadenza, after which he and his three colleagues rose and bowed deeply, as in duty bound. Then, whispered consultations—where should they begin again? I was breathless with excitement—would he repeat the difficult cadenza? Oh, joy! *He did.*

Joachim's playing meant to me, even as a little boy, the very pinnacle of musical art. I wished, however, that he would play longer pieces at the "Pop" concerts because, to the best of my belief, he never gave any solo recitals during the period I am writing about. So I took the great liberty of writing to tell him that I was a little boy ten years old, and that I should be very much obliged to him if he would kindly play Bach's G minor prelude and fugue as an encore next Saturday, "because," I added, "I play that piece too."

To my astonishment and delight, he answered my letter, saying that he would like to see the little boy who could play such hard things. My mother took me to see him. After hearing me play, he predicted that I should become a successful violinist and offered to place me at the recently established Royal College of Music to complete my musical training.

My father disapproved, I do not remember why, and instead, I became a pupil of Adolph Pollitzer, who at that time was considered, I believe, the greatest violin teacher in London. Under his direction, I learned the entire violin repertoire, and each time I played in public my master lent me his beautiful Joseph Guarnerius violin.

Joachim manifested no further interest in me, and while I keenly regretted that my father's refusal to follow the great artist's advice had cost me a valuable patronage, my feeling was tempered by a secret and guilty sense of relief; for I knew that my new teacher would not require me to follow any longer the Joachim tradition of holding the bow arm tightly glued to the side when playing. There have always been, and there always will be, discussions and conflict as to the proper method of playing on an instrument, but I doubt if any violinist in these times can realize the violence with which players of the Joachim school repu-

My dear "little boy!"

You wrote such a nice
letter, that I should like to
comply with your request about
Bach's fugue in G minor;
only as an "Encore" after the
Tartini it would be hardly
acceptable to the majority
of the public, especially as
the programme is rather long
already. Some other time
I hope! — If you will come
round to the artist room
after the Concert I should
like to shake hands with

you and hear something about
your musical study's; for
if you can really play the
compositions you are so fond
of, you are very far for
your age! Who is your
teacher?

Looking forward to meet
you, my dear little boy,

Yours very sincerely

Joseph Joachim

25, Phillimore Gardens
W.
16th March 1883

diated and denounced violinists who lifted the elbow—and vice versa. In England, where Joachim was a musical god, it was almost a point of respectability to keep the upper part of the bow arm immobile. Raising the arm was just one of those things that "weren't done."

Madame Norman-Neruda, who played with a free arm, and had many admirers, was tolerated, I think, mainly because she was a lady, and perhaps also because of a hazy idea that her womanly figure compelled her to raise her elbow in order to play on the G string. But it was quite customary in London for people ignorant of violin technique to express disapproval of a violinist who, although admittedly a fine performer, lifted his elbow in playing. As a boy, I had the feeling that the practice was almost the equivalent of wearing detachable cuffs or a bowler hat with evening dress, and I considered that the annual performance of Bach's "celebrated" concerto for two violins, wherein Madame Neruda's right arm occasionally hid the view of her right eye, constituted an act of the most magnanimous condescension on the part of Dr. Joachim, whose whole face, including the beard, was never once obscured. Once he kissed her hand before the whole audience after the concerto. How noble! I thought.

At that time of my life, although I went to many concerts, I never met any of the great artists who performed, and I was accustomed to think of them all as superior beings, living apart from the rest of humanity. There was only one thing that brought forth a sense that I might be their equal: that was when they forgot their notes. It may not be amiss to remind my reader that the practice of public performance without notes was only just coming into vogue. Only shortly before, artists who played solos "by heart," as it was called, were criticized openly for lacking in respect both for the

[16]

audience and for the composer by indulging in such theatrical display. Opinion was divided as to the propriety of changing old customs, and, on the whole, the public favored the novelty; possibly because of the element of danger involved—the player might forget, and then what? Sure enough, the player did very often forget, and when that happened, the public burst into applause, as who should say: "Never mind, now, don't get rattled but try again." At these moments, as I said, I felt myself the equal of the greatest. I, too, could break down and begin again.

I was always profoundly impressed by the entrance of the performers onto the stage of St. James' Hall. They came up a small staircase to the left of the piano. First one saw the head, then the body, and finally the magnificent feet which brought them before the audience. I remember noticing that the men performers always looked straight in front of them, while the ladies kept their eyes down, and I thought that must be to avoid stumbling over their long dresses as they came up the stairs. But it was the tops of their heads that fascinated me, and I wondered if some day some little boy would look down on the top of *my* head as I came up the stairs.

I do not think there were very many concerts during the winter. I went whenever I could and very rarely paid for admission. The usher in St. James' Hall knew me and generally passed me in without a ticket. Whenever I could, I took a seat at the side of one of the music critics. There were two reasons for this: First, I knew that they had received two tickets and usually came alone; second, I wanted to listen to what they said about the music and the performance. The critic I liked best to sit next to was an ill-dressed young man with a large red beard. His name was Shaw—George Bernard Shaw. I heard him once utter the word "monkey" when Vladimir de Pachmann was making antics at the piano, and I was deeply shocked. De Pachmann, in my estimation, was a genius to whom everything was permissible, and I could not bear to have him ridiculed. Shortly before, he had made a sensationally successful début at one of Mr. Wilhelm Ganz's orchestral concerts, and everyone was talking not only of his playing, but of the reply he had made to a lady at a fashionable reception. It was customary, of course, to address all foreigners in the style established by Mr. Podsnap, namely, with great emphasis on each word for their better understanding.

"And what," said the lady very slowly and distinctly, "does Mousseer de Pachmann think of London?"

The response was immediate and extremely rapid.

"Zat iss not ze question, Madame. Vot does London sink of de Pachmann? Zat iss ze question!"

What impudence! said everybody. But his fame as an eccentric dated from that day and has always paralleled his fame as an artist.

I paid a shilling to hear the great Anton Rubinstein at one of his historical recitals, waiting for hours with the crowd until the doors leading to the top gallery were opened. This stands out in my memory as a most exceptional occasion. I don't remember any such crowds for any other concerts (this was long before Paderewski had revolutionized the behavior of the English concert-goer). How I wish I could recall the playing of that great man! But alas, only a few scattered impressions remain.

There were two concert grand pianos on the stage. They had come from Russia, made by Becker. I wondered why one piano was not enough, even for the greatest of pianists. But I found out soon enough. Something broke—string, hammer, or key?—under the master's mighty blows, and he transferred to the other. During the intermission a mechanic repaired the first piano, to which Rubinstein returned later, when the second went out of tune. I remember wondering how he could see with so much hair falling down over his face. I remember his impatient gesture as he dashed away a small flower thrown by an admirer, which lodged on the top of his head.

One of the pieces on the program was Schumann's "Etudes Symphoniques," which I remember solely because he failed to turn into the major key at the point indicated on the very last page, and played the major chord only once instead of twice. Was it a lapse of memory, or did he purposely make the change? I shall never know, but the effect is so fine that I have always played it that way.

The rest of the program, for all that I can recall, might have been the celebrated "Valse Caprice" played over and over again. I do not remember anything else. How grand, I thought, to be able to play all those false notes so fast and so loud! Why, after all, should a great artist be under the same rules and restrictions as a common person who, whatever secret ambitions he might cherish, must never play wrong notes? Nothing else remained of that recital except my sense of having participated in a musical experience with one of the Sons of God, and this gave me an extraordinary feeling of exaltation.

I never heard Rubinstein again.

Another of the most distinguished musicians of the day was Clara Schumann, who played many times in London. She was called the Great Lady of the Piano. I remember her appearance, dressed in widow's weeds, a voluminous skirt which seemed to cover a large part of the stage, and a posture at the piano quite peculiar to herself, although imitated by her pupils—bent over from the shoulders so that the head seemed occasionally to be perilously close to the keys and in the way of the hands.

Madame Schumann played a great deal of her husband's music. I remember her performance of the Concerto and the Carnaval without any pleasure. Her tempi seemed too fast, and I do not recall any charm in her tone. She played at orchestral concerts or at the chamber-music "Pops," and I do not know whether she ever gave solo recitals in London. My impression is that she would not have attracted a large public had she done so, for in spite of her great reputation there was nothing in the least glamorous about her.

The exact reverse was the case with the violinist Sarasate. When that man appeared with his glittering black eyes, his mop of black hair, his Spanish mustache, when he advanced to the very edge of the stage and stood motionless with the violin gripped by the body between his two fingers, we were all tense with admiring expectation. There was an indescribable swagger about him. After bowing in acknowledgment of the welcoming plaudits of the crowd, he struck an attitude with his feet spread apart, and looking us over, so to speak, he allowed the violin to slip through his fingers until its progress toward the floor was arrested by the scroll. All this was accomplished with a self-confident nonchalance which was simply irresistible, and the British public came nearer, I believe, to getting a "thrill" than ever before.

Sarasate's playing was unique and unforgettable—a marvelous example of complete union between the player and the instrument such as most of us had never witnessed. It was assumed that those who admired Joachim could not like Sarasate, and vice versa. I admired Joachim and I loved Sarasate.

Possibly few people would have been willing to admit how large a part personal attractiveness played in the career of a musician in England. It is hard to explain otherwise the failure of some of the greatest artists of the day to please London audiences. For example, Hans von Bülow, esteemed everywhere as one of the supreme elect, known by name to every English concert-goer, announced a series of recitals devoted exclusively to the compositions of Beethoven. No pianist had ever before played all the sonatas, and the announcement was in itself sensational. I remember his first concert. He came onto the stage holding his silk hat and his cane, and he drew off his gloves before sitting down to the piano. His playing was deeply impressive—the listeners all felt, I am sure, that they were receiving a message direct from Beethoven himself. But the public did not like the looks of the man, and the audiences grew smaller with each recital. Von Bülow left England in a huff, disgusted, and wrote to the *Times* denouncing the British public, adding that he would never return. The music critic, publishing this letter, thought fit to retort with a quotation from the latest Gilbert and Sullivan operetta, to the effect that "it didn't matter, matter, matter." I think I may have been one of the few people to whom the thought that Bülow would not come again did matter quite a lot.

About that time (it was probably earlier) a young pianist, born in Scotland, whose talent had been recognized and patronized in many ways, created a storm by a letter, also written to the *Times* (the newspaper which still receives everyone's complaints and comments), in which he declared his intention to throw off forever his allegiance to England and to leave a country which was in his opinion unworthy to harbor anyone gifted with artistic talent. I do not think I exaggerate in saying that this letter was greeted with howls of indignation. "Renegade" was the mildest term to be applied to Eugen d'Albert, the young man in question. But he carried out his word all the same, went to live in Germany, and became one of the most eminent and successful of European musicians.

The departure of Frederic Lamond from the country of his birth and education was less violent and sensational. He left England in order to complete his musical education in Germany, and took up his residence in Berlin because he was successful on the European continent, whereas he was never appreciated to any great extent in England. He was Liszt's last and youngest pupil, and when the great man visited London in 1886, Lamond prevailed upon him to come to one of a series of recitals he had announced in Prince's Hall, a small auditorium with a capacity of about 600.

It was announced that the great Liszt would attend this concert, and all the tickets were immediately sold. The concert was transferred to St. James' Hall, with three times the capacity, and all the tickets there were promptly snatched up. We did not care about Lamond, but we wanted to *see* Liszt. The day of the concert came, and the hall was crowded to the last seat. After some delay Lamond came from the artists' room into the body of the hall with the Abbé Liszt leaning on his arm. What a great moment! We all stood up and cheered for ten minutes while the old man bowed. Finally he signed to Lamond to go up the steps to the stage and start the concert. He did so, but the audience would not stop applauding and cheering, and it was impossible for him to begin. "Liszt! Liszt!" We wanted Liszt and nothing else. At last Lamond stepped down again, and after some obvious gestures of reluctance, the great man allowed himself to be led on to the stage. Delirious excitement! There stood this fabulous personage with his cassock and his crucifix, bowing in apparent humility to his worshipers. The noise was deafening—we never stopped shouting and he never stopped bowing. Suddenly a complete hush fell over the assembly. *He had moved a few steps nearer to the piano!* The cheering broke out again with greater vehemence than before.

He is going to play! . . . No, he is not going to play! . . . Yes, he is! . . . Did you see him put his hand on the back of the chair? . . . Hurray! Encore! Bravo! Hurray!

He began to move off. . . . Groans of dismay. He turned again, smiled and bowed, and taking Lamond's arm, went back to his seat in the front row. The concert started. Nobody listened. A number of people left before the end, feeling, I am sure, that they had been swindled. Liszt never appeared in public again; he died a few months later.

The reference to Prince's Hall reminds me of all the concerts I heard there. It was also the place where two or three times a year I gave concerts with my oldest sister, who was an excellent pianist. Once I played with her a sonata I had composed for piano and violin, which was received with applause and praise by the critics. I cannot imagine why they thought it was good, for it was not good. I had never had any instruction in composition, and I cannot honestly say that I even tried to teach myself. My father, who was a public accountant in a very small way, had as his sole assistant a shabby young man who played the organ. He used to get five shillings every now and then for setting and correcting harmony and counterpoint exercises for me. That was all the theoretical instruction in music that I ever had.

One day I was given a ticket to hear the debut of a young Polish pianist who, according to reports, had had a brilliant success in Paris. I saw his head coming up the stairs to the stage in St. James' Hall, and I never forgot it. He had an immense lot of yellow hair, and below that a white face with a desperate expression on it—below that again, a large white silk cravat which seemed to spread all over his chest. When my fascinated gaze finally reached his feet, I saw that he was wearing dancing pumps.

He thumped away most gloriously at Mendelssohn's E minor prelude and fugue (not the one we all play, but the other) and continued to play for about two hours. The audience was deeply impressed, but not particularly enthusiastic. The general feeling was voiced, I think, in the opinion expressed by a young lady as we all walked out after the concert.

"I don't like his playing as well as Stavenhagen's," she said in hushed and awed tones, "but I never saw such an *interesting* man."

Stavenhagen was the most popular pianist in London in those days; however, it was subsequently decided that the young Polish gentleman, whose name was Paderewski, was the greatest pianist in the world.

In comparison with the tremendous activities of later years, musical life in London was sedate, not to say dull. Looking back, it seems to me that people neither expected nor desired to be greatly wrought up by a musical performance. Music was thought of mainly as sweet sound. We did not like dissonances, and we did not want to be "thrilled" (was that word in the English dictionary then?) by anything that savored of dramatic harshness—above all, music had to be "refined." The same taste pervaded the drama, the painting, and the literature of the period.

The great thing was to avoid any reference, oral or optical, to matters which "might bring a blush to the cheek of a decent woman," as the current saying went. Mrs. Grundy not only riveted fig leaves on every sculptured representation of the nude human form to be found in the United

Kingdom, but frequently decreed that the legs of tables, chairs, and grand piano constituted an improper spectacle, and should be swathed in draperies. Shakespeare was played in expurgated versions. Ibsen was taboo, and the eminent dramatic authors of the day, Arthur Pinero and Henry Arthur Jones, became practically the arbiters of public taste in matters theatrical—an honor which they shared to some extent with Oscar Wilde, whose gentle and tedious paradoxes bordered, however, on social questions which were only barely permissible on the stage.

The most popular painters were those whose portraits of society ladies and gentlemen could invariably be relied upon to conceal the slightest blemish of skin or feature— just as, in their allegorical, historical, or theological compositions, one always had the comforting assurance that whatever the subject, the treatment was certain to conform to established standards of propriety. I suppose that the immaculate smoothness of the skin in Sir John Millais' celebrated picture "Bubbles" made this painting so eminently desirable for an advertisement for Pears' Soap, but the use of the picture for this commercial purpose created nevertheless a terrific commotion. "What is the world coming to!" everyone said.

Most of these artists had fine homes and studios in St. John's Wood, not far from where we lived, and as I knew some of the younger members of their families, I visited them sometimes and was awestruck by the evidences of prosperity and success which were to be seen on every side. How I hated their pictures! I could not have put into words the reason for my aversion to these slick and inane productions, but I think my main exasperation may have been due to the cocksure manner with which they succeeded in persuading the public and the art critics that their superficiality was related to artistic creativeness. I often wondered what became of the innumerable pictures annually exhibited at the Royal Academy, although I knew that rich people paid very high prices for a good many of them. Years later, I saw them all—or so it seemed to me—in art museums of the principal cities of the British colonies. So that is where they finally went! What a curious age it was! Everything apparently ruled by a complacent British spirit which had decided that civilization and culture had reached its zenith, and that change or progress at the close of the so-called Victorian era was neither to be expected nor desired.

Since childhood I have owned a set of *Illustrated Handbooks of Art*, published in London under the editorship of one of the most eminent authorities of those days, Sir Edward Paynter, R.A. From the preface to the volume on English Painters, I quote the following: "Hogarth came, followed by Reynolds, Gainsborough, and Romney. Art has year by year progressed, till now English painters have become a recognized power in the State and contribute in no small degree to the enlightenment, pleasure, and refinement of the age." And again, at the end of the volume: "During the past decade, Art has advanced with steady progress, and we can confidently say that at no time have the ranks of the Royal Academicians and the two Water Color Societies been filled more worthily than at the present day. The last quarter of the nineteenth century is likely to be a golden era in the history of British Art."

A golden era it certainly was, if one considers the very large earnings of the fashionable painters. But . . . the first President of the Royal Academy was Joshua Reynolds. In my day the post was occupied by Frederick Leighton, a courtly gentleman, a favorite with Royalty, and an immensely popular and prolific artist, whose pictures were sold for very high prices. It is probably fair to say that only a few people now living have ever seen one of his pictures, which an unkind posterity regards as artistically worthless.

$\mathcal{T}wo$

MY MOTHER AND MY AUNT TAUGHT ME READING AND WRITING and the elements of music. My father taught me a little arithmetic, and twice a week two gentlemen, one French and the other German, came for an hour or two to give us (my sisters and me) some "simple notions" of history, geography, and the languages. They were poor teachers, and I was a worse pupil. I hated both them and the tasks they left me to perform, which I did badly and unwillingly. Nevertheless, I did want to know something about the world and natural science, and I remember begging my father frequently to tell me about what I called the "ologies," and hoping that he would bring me home one of those little primers over which I loved to pore, even though I understood them only partially. I had the usual boy's interest in mechanics, and sometimes, when I took a clock or some other article apart, I succeeded in putting it together again. As time went on, I became a little more proficient in such things. I made telephones, electric batteries, and other apparatus, and amused myself in countless ways, frequently imagining that I made a scientific discovery, and invariably finding out that what I thought was new had been known for at least half a century. All this play—or was it work?—led me nowhere and served no purpose. The one useful thing that survived from this mechanical dabbling was my acquisition of the principles of musical-instrument making, and I have always been glad that I learned how a violin and a piano were constructed.

I have regretted all my life that I was not sent to school, because I believe I should have acquired habits of mental discipline and concentration which would have led me further than I have been able to go. It is no pleasure for me to confess that I have never mastered any subject to which I addressed myself, but such is the unfortunate truth. I am unable to say why, with my ambition and my determination to work, I always stopped short of the goal, but I dare say that the absence of school discipline had a great deal to do with it.

This lack of education and the infrequency of contact with boys of my own age prevented me from absorbing many of the principles and theories with which young English children grew up. For example, the prevailing conceptions of nationalism and patriotism were never conveyed to me, and I cannot recall having had at any time a feeling of attachment to the country in which I was born. I was totally ignorant of the meaning of politics, foreign relations, and statesmanship, and my ideas of government hardly went beyond a hazy understanding of the policeman's duty to keep order and arrest criminals. The Army and the Navy, I knew, belonged to the Queen and to the Lord Mayor, whose grand annual pageant on the ninth of November was one of the great treats and events of my childhood; for

I was taken to see this wonderful show from the windows of my father's little office in Newgate Street. Queen Victoria, I knew, kept her soldiers and sailors in her palaces to play with, just as I played with my tin soldiers and toy boats. There were two kinds of war, I learned—foreign wars, which were always criminal folly, and wars waged by England for the benefit of humanity. The Houses of Parliament were intended for people to make speeches in. These people were divided into groups consisting of Lords and Commons, and Conservatives, Liberals, Tories, and Radicals. They all hated each other, and my father, I think, hated them all alike; although he respected Mr. Gladstone because of his advocacy of Irish independence.

I think we were all acutely conscious of class distinctions in those days. Apart from Royalty, there were three main divisions—namely, the Aristocracy, the middle class, and the working class, and everyone was supposed to know his place and keep to it. This was not always easy, because of the numerous subdivisions and borderline overlappings, and it was embarrassing if one did not know what manner to adopt toward the person one was addressing—differences of rank being usually expressed by subtle vocal inflection rather than by servility on the one side or arrogance on the other. It was just as improper for the upper classes to be familiar with their social inferiors as for the lower classes to be impudent to their superiors. The system was complete, and I dare say it may have had its good points, for it seemed to be unchangeable and eternal, and doubtless gave us a certain feeling of social stability. At any rate, it enabled us to accept with perfect equanimity the most glaring contrasts between squalor and wealth, nowhere more apparent than at Covent Garden Opera House, which was situated

Harold Bauer at the age of ten

The "Paderewski" picture

Concert announcement of Nikita's Russian tour with Harold Bauer as pianist

in the midst of one of the most hideous and obscene slums of London.

The class to which my family belonged could be roughly defined as "lower middle class," although—make no mistake about it!—we were a social step higher than the small shopkeeper, who in most cases was far better off in the world's goods than my father, considered a "professional" man because he had an office and did not sell things over the counter. The struggle to keep up appearances and make provision for old age was cruel, and in most cases futile, for the members of this "superior" lower middle class, one of the largest of England's social groups. In theory, a man should have been able to bring up a family on a small earned income and put aside enough money to live on at the end of thirty or forty years of unremitting work. In practice this was only very rarely possible. The margin was too narrow, and besides, prudence and custom alike forbade the investment of savings in anything less secure than government 3 percent bonds, known as "Consols." Speculation and dealings in stocks and shares were matters reserved for those living on a higher economic level.

In the case of my father, earnings were inadequate to permit of any savings, and we lived in respectable poverty, practicing the strictest economy. Living was cheap and simple enough in many respects. Many things which today are considered indispensable and are cheerfully paid for had not yet been invented or were luxuries in the hands of the wealthy. Most fair-sized houses had one bathroom, but the general practice was to wash in individual tubs. This is why most of the middle-class people used to smell of soap. They never had extra water to wash the soapsuds off their bodies. The one bathroom was usually provided with a large sponge used by the entire family. Central heating was unknown. There were gaslights in some of the bedrooms, and candles were used elsewhere. Electric light had not come into general use, and the street gas lamps were turned on each evening by a man carrying a long pole with a lighted torch at its upper end. The incandescent gas mantle was a great innovation. There were no telephones, no radios, no fountain pens, no typewriters, no electric domestic appliances of any kind. We made toast over an open fire with a long toasting fork. Laundry was done mostly at home. There was a mangle over the washtub, and I used to turn the handle. Meat was roasted in front of the open kitchen fire, turning round and round on a spit revolved by clockwork which I was permitted to wind up. Cakes were usually made at home, as there were very few bakers' shops in the vicinity, and the cakes made there were both poor and expensive. The muffin man, carrying his wares carefully blanketed on a shallow tray balanced on the top of his head, went his rounds on late winter afternoons, ringing a bell, just as in the time of Dickens.

The milk cart, heard in the early morning, rattled a good deal on account of the number of cans it carried on the floor of the low vehicle, raised only about a foot from the ground. The driver's strident cry of "Milk-O!" was intended to bring his customers running out of the house to obtain their daily supply. If they did not appear, it was he who dashed out, seized the quart- or pint-size pewter milk can which had been hung out on the iron railings of the house, filled it rapidly with a long dipper from the large supply cans, re-hung it on the rails, and drove off to the next house. The butcher came for orders at about eleven o'clock in a small cart with two very high wheels and drawn by an incredibly swift pony. The orders were taken at the kitchen door, and the driver said "Hup!" to the pony, which immediately started to trot off, but was overtaken by one single stride of the driver, who leapt easily into his place on the top of the cart. In fifteen minutes he was back with the meat, bringing it into the house on a curved, four-handled tray which he carried easily on his right shoulder. All butchers' boys seemed to take great pride in their ability to hop on and off their little carts, and to drive their ponies with extraordinary skill and speed. If they were not circus-trained lads before being butchers' boys, I feel sure they must have joined the circus later on in their lives.

I cannot remember whether or not the baker or any other tradesman delivered goods regularly at the house, but if there were any such calls or deliveries they were certainly not as exciting as those of the milkman and the butchers. In London, nobody of the middle class knew anything about refrigerators. Ice, whenever used, was obtainable in small quantities from the fishmonger, whose supply was drawn from frozen rivers and lakes. The ice was kept in large store-houses, buried in sawdust. Ice cream (called "ices") was an expensive rarity and came from the confectioner. It was hard to keep food for any length of time during warm weather, and it was generally placed in the coolest part of the house, covered with wire gauze to keep off flies. I recall the small barrel of beer which rested on trestles in the cubbyhole known as the "larder." When the barrel was delivered, my father and I used to knock out the bung with a hardwood tap from which the beer was drawn off, as required, in jugs. It was bitter, flat, and tepid. To give it a "head" of froth, one poured it from a height into the glass, thus obtaining some air bubbles. I shall never forget the taste of sharp Cheshire cheese on a crust of fresh English bread with a glass of "bitter" to wash it down.

[33]

People talked a good deal about the typewriter, which was going to revolutionize clerical and secretarial work. I do not remember ever seeing a typewriter or a typewritten letter, however, in those days. There was considerable opposition to the idea of writing letters "by machinery." It would be cheap and undignified, they said, besides being harmful to the personal relation which was considered as important in business matters as in private life. When my father took me to the City as a special treat, one of my favorite occupations in his little office was to participate in the process of making copies of his handwritten letters with the copying press and book. The letter was first dampened and then pressed onto specially prepared thin sheets of paper which were bound in the book. I still remember the feeling of triumphant accomplishment with which I pulled round the levers of the small iron press, using all my force. I knew what the important result would be.

I well remember seeing a fountain pen for the first time. "Where is the cork?" I asked, and was laughed at for my pains. But the question was not so stupid after all, for very few men who used this newfangled writing tool could boast of a vest pocket free from inkstains. My mother, like many of her day, wrote with a feather quill pen which required constant trimming. Somebody once offered to give me a penknife. "I don't want it," I said. "I want a *knife*." The two things were entirely different in my mind, and I had no use for the little one-bladed instrument that served only for trimming pens and pencils.

There were, of course, no automobiles, and it took a long time to get about the city in the conveyances then available—namely, horse omnibuses and cabs, the underground railways, steam-driven and smelling horribly of smoke, and an occasional surface tramway which never seemed to go in any direction I wanted to take. The safety razor had not yet been invented, and I am sure that many men wore beards because they did not wish to take the trouble to shave. It was surprising how many beards disappeared later, although the Prince of Wales (afterward Edward VII), who set male fashion in many respects, never took *his* beard off. It was understood that Queen Victoria did not approve of cosmetics; consequently very few ladies used paint or powder on their faces. The staining of fingernails was regarded as an oriental practice which could never conceivably be tolerated in a Christian country.

I, like everyone else, had to conform to prevailing fashions and customs, and after growing out of the sailor suits of my childhood, I was put into starched shirts with stiff collars and cuffs. How awful I thought they were! And how hard it was to hold the violin against a stiff collar! But bad as they were, the stiff collars were comfort itself compared to the hard stiff shoes of the day. That was real torture until the feet had been "broken in." They talked of "breaking in" the leather, but I knew perfectly well that it was the skin that had to give way. And as for hats—I cannot recall that there was such a thing as a soft hat in those days. People called "bounders" wore caps; except for uniformed men, the rest of the world wore stiff headgear—silk, felt, or straw. My father, who, as I have said, was a radical—that is to say, an extremist—wore turned-down collars, low shoes with elastic sides, and a felt hat with a square top exactly like the hat that Winston Churchill has made famous. He seemed comfortable in his clothes, but as far as I was concerned, everything I wore was too hard, too tight, or too warm. I never could understand how a violinist could hold his instrument against a high stiff collar, but I noticed that those who wore turned-down collars developed sore places

from the rubbing of the violin on the side of the throat—
life would be too easy, I said to myself with some bitterness,
if one did not have to struggle against difficulties and suffering.

There was, in fact, a horrid specter which seemed to
loom over me constantly with the threat and the warning
that my ambitions toward a public career would never succeed unless I could conquer it completely. This was an in-
veterate propensity to seasickness. Every form of travel in
any kind of conveyance—even if it were no more than a
mile or two in an omnibus or a cab—was a misery to me.
It seemed clear that I must try to overcome this illness if
I intended to go about the world with my violin, giving
concerts. I determined upon a heroic treatment. One summer, having been sent to the seashore with another boy,
I spent my small savings on the purchase of a season ticket
on one of the excursion steamers plying daily up and down
the English Channel. For two horrible weeks I went on
those trips twice daily, invariably returning to land ill with
exhaustion from the seasickness which refused to be cured
by any such treatment. My heroism and my suffering were
completely wasted.

Later in life, I tried every conceivable remedy, but none
of them gave me the least help. On one occasion I bought
a special kind of belt which was "absolutely guaranteed" to
prevent seasickness. It was furnished with a triangular-
shaped pad made to press tightly against the solar plexus
by means of a thumbscrew which passed through a metal
plate attached to the leather belt. I put it on one day between Calais and Dover with a fairly uncomfortable sea
moving underneath the steamer. I screwed the pad in tight.
It felt good. "Is it possible that I am *not* going to be seasick?" I thought. "How marvelous! The man who invented

this is certainly a benefactor to mankind." Half an hour later I felt ill, but still grateful to the inventor. Fifteen minutes after that I realized in a flash of horror that the claims advanced by the inventor were absolutely true. The belt absolutely prevented seasickness . . . but what if one *wanted* to be seasick? That thumbscrew with the triangular pad digging into me . . . should I loosen it? "Never!" I said. "It would be utter cowardice—besides, there are the cliffs of Dover, and in another twenty minutes" . . . Just then the steamer gave an awful roll and I was panic-stricken with the realization that my insides, tightly screwed up, *had not moved!* "I don't care," said my better self, "it must and shall be endured. . . . Courage!" With that I revolted in rage and agony. . . . "Enough!" I shrieked (internally), "I will no longer be a slave to will power. Here and now I release myself!" . . . I loosened the screw. . . . Five minutes later the steamer glided to the quay in the smooth waters of Dover Harbor.

I never overcame seasickness, although, thanks to larger steamers with stabilizers, improved roadbeds for railroads, and more smoothness with modern road travel, I no longer suffer as I used to; but nothing would ever induce me to travel by air. That, I know, would be to begin the agony all over again.

Traveling in those days was uncomfortable, dirty, and tedious, hot in summer and cold in winter. Lighting arrangements in the trains were very poor, and this was a great inconvenience when the days became short. Each compartment was provided with a round oil lamp, set into an opening in the roof. When the oil was exhausted, these lamps were replaced and refilled by trainmen who walked over the roofs of the cars to perform the operation. The light was unreliable and insufficient, and many travelers carried small lanterns with them for additional illumination and reading purposes. When I first went abroad, my father gave me the lantern he had been accustomed to use in traveling. It was a fairly flat receptacle about six inches high, containing a candle and provided with a lens and a reflector. Sharp hooks on the outside permitted the lantern to be pinned to the upholstery of the railroad carriage at a convenient height for reading.

Later on, gaslights replaced the oil lamps, the gas being carried in tanks underneath the cars. These lights being quite brilliant, shades were provided which could be drawn over them by passengers who wished to sleep. For most people, however, the experience of spending a night in the train was one to be avoided, if possible. If one could only lie down, it was not so bad in spite of the hard seats, and provided that the regulation stiff pillow and equally stiff blanket had been hired before leaving. But one could never be sure. Four people in a compartment were enough to spoil everyone's rest, for this number prevented anyone from lying down, and each passenger spent the night as best he could, tightly wedged into his corner.

Early morning or late evening arrival at London or any large British city was generally a gloomy experience. I always felt tired and hungry, and the sight of the dirty railway stations and the shabby people there depressed me. I wonder why so much poverty and squalor seemed to gather around these London terminals. Even now, it wrings my heart to recall the "cab-runners," those destitute men constantly on the watch for a cab loaded with a trunk or two issuing from the station. If "cabby" were kindly disposed, he would tell them where he was going, and, if the destination did not exceed a mile or so, they would run the whole distance behind the vehicle in the hope of receiving sixpence (that was all one paid, as a rule) to take the trunks down from the cab roof and carry them into the house at which the passenger alighted. Those men were half starved, breathless, and ragged. It was assumed that the few pennies they earned would be immediately exchanged for gin. "What is the use of trying to help people like that?" was the usual comment. But nobody did try to help them. They slept on doorsteps and under bridges near the railroad stations in full view of the passers-by. Sometimes they were found dead there.

Another failing that threatened my hopes of a career was timidity. I was a painfully shy and reticent boy and had very few friends. It was an ordeal for me to attend any kind of social function. The idea of contest or competition was always abhorrent to me, paralyzing me with nervousness to such an extent that I became completely indifferent to the outcome —success or failure. I decided that it was my duty to overcome this absurd weakness.

There were certain open competitions established at that time in London—I believe by the County Council—with the object of encouraging independent study among school children. I entered my name in one of these contests. The subject was plane geometry, in which I thought I might pass, having studied it from textbooks and being fairly conversant with Euclid. But when I found myself seated in a classroom with the examination paper before me and heard the busy scratches of pencils wielded by students all around, I was seized with trembling; cold perspiration ran into my eyes and dripped over the paper, and my brain refused completely to work. After a few vain attempts to write the answers to at least some of the questions, I gave up in despair and sat there helplessly until the end of the period, when, filled with shame and fury, I returned home.

I suffered similarly whenever I played chess or whist, which excited me so terribly that I always had nightmares from the thought of how I *might* have played. Finally I had to give up both these games. I do not know what has enabled me to withstand the terrible nervous strain of a public career for so many years, for I can honestly say that I have never in my life walked out on the stage without the feeling that I was undertaking a tremendous adventure in which my whole being was concerned.

Comparing notes with my colleagues, it seems to me that while I suffered less from actual stage fright than many of them did, they had, on the other hand, certain compensations which were denied to me. I never found in any performance an occasion for feasting and rejoicing after it was over, but they did. It is true that some of the experienced and older artists went soberly home and to bed after a performance which to them was just part of the normal day's work, but I was unable to do that, either. On the whole, I experienced very little satisfaction from my public appearances. If I felt that I had failed to do my best, I was wretchedly unhappy for days and nights following. If, on the contrary, I felt that I had played well, any pleasure I might have had from praise and applause was invariably soured by the thought that I had only succeeded on that one occasion by a stroke of luck which would never occur again. It was very rare indeed for my judgment of my own performance to correspond to the judgment of the public and the critics as evinced by applause and written articles. I always thought that my own judgment was infinitely superior and that I frequently received praise after having played badly; nevertheless, I had a very decided feeling that a certain amount of praise was my due, and I was bitterly disappointed and discouraged if I did not get it.

One day I read the line: " 'Tis not in mortals to command

success, but I'll do more: I'll deserve it." I thought that was a marvelous idea and that it corresponded exactly to my own thought. I knew, or thought I knew, perfectly well that a good performance could not possibly be anything but a happy accident of fate; yet I needed to receive credit for conscientious work and sincere endeavor, even if I failed. It was certainly not a happy state of mind. During the six years preceding my departure from England—that is to say, up to my nineteenth year—I used frequently to envy the pianists, whose instrument seemed so much easier than my violin. But when I tried the piano, I disliked the sounds I made, and the technical problems of controlling and directing the fingers of both hands seemed insuperable, so I went back to the violin with indescribable relief.

I thought of this a good many years later at a supper party in London, given by Eugène Ysaÿe after a performance of Beethoven's "Fidelio," which he had conducted without much success at Covent Garden. He made us a little speech, holding his beer stein in one hand and his enormous Belgian pipe in the other. "My friends," he said, "it has happened many a time that I have looked out of the corner of my left eye at the conductor of the orchestra while I was playing a difficult concerto, and I have said to myself: Oh, the happy man! He has not a preoccupation in the world—no capricious squeaking instrument which goes out of tune, nothing but his baton with which he obtains perfect performance. God, what a happy man! and what would I not give to be able to exchange my violin for his baton!"— Then a long pause. The master took a drink and sucked at his pipe. Finally he said with a sigh, "Tonight . . . if I had had my old violin and if I had been playing Brahms or Beethoven, I would have given up my baton very gladly. I would have been the happy man . . ."

I have often thought that the price paid by artists for the doubtful and evanescent satisfaction of public applause is far too high. The greater the talent, the more rigorous and relentless is self-criticism, and this at times becomes so painful—and so tedious—that any momentary escape from it will be welcomed with the irresponsible enthusiasm of a child. One is apt to praise this kind of childlike naïveté without stopping to think what it conceals.

I remember finding Paderewski one morning at his home, sedulously practicing a passage for the left hand in Beethoven's Sonata, Opus 31, No. 3, a piece which he had probably played a hundred times in concert.

"Master," I said very respectfully, "why do you give yourself so much trouble with a passage which everyone else simplifies—and it sounds just as well, if not better?"

He looked at me furiously. "I practice it for my personal satisfaction," he said. But his face was worn and haggard as he spoke. Does he really believe it essential? I thought— and I never knew. He and Ferrucio Busoni were the only artists I ever knew who had the force of character to practice *after* a concert, believing that the powers of self-criticism were keenest at that time. Busoni used to sit at his piano all night sometimes after a triumphant public success, reviewing, criticizing and practicing the program he had just played. Perhaps that was one of the causes of his commanding eminence among the great artists of the age. I wish I had possessed some of his concentration and energy.

About this time I founded a string quartet, playing of course the first violin. My second violinist was a young American named Carl Engel, who had studied in Berlin and London with the great violinist Emile Sauret. My viola player was Emil Kreuz, leader of his section at the Symphony Concerts at the Crystal Palace, and my cellist was

Herbert Walenn, member of an unusually large and musically gifted family, who subsequently became one of the
leading teachers of violoncello at the Royal Academy of
Music. John Barbirolli told me nearly fifty years later that
he used to take his cello lessons under the photograph of
my quartet which hung in Walenn's studio, and his teacher
was accustomed to refer to the quartet as an example of
conscientious study. We certainly practiced a great deal,
and we became thoroughly familiar with the whole literature of chamber music for strings. We had very few public
engagements, and those poorly paid; but that did not matter
—it was a wonderful training, and I have often thought that
the understanding of musical phrasing which I acquired
thereby was infinitely superior to anything I could have
learned as a solo player. To this day, having relinquished
my violin for the piano half a century ago, I find myself
influenced by habits of phrasing derived from the violin
bow and from the feeling of the interweaving of separate
parts which I gained from my practice of ensemble music,
and I know that I should have been a totally different kind
of musician if I had not been for so long a violinist.

One day I went to Prince's Hall to hear a young American
conduct an orchestra in conjunction with a fairly well-known
soloist. I mentioned this recently to Walter Damrosch, and
he said: "Yes, that was my début, and the performer was
the violinist Ovide Musin."

"No," I said, "excuse me, it was the pianist Madeleine
Schiller."

Neither of us could produce any corroborative evidence,
so the point remained unsettled.

This concert stands out in my memory, first, because to an
English audience it seemed almost unbelievable that anything artistic could come out of America, and second, be-

cause any orchestral concert was something of an event in London in those days. The Philharmonic Society gave only three or four concerts during the season, and there was a short series organized and conducted by Wilhelm Ganz, whose principal claim to attention lay in his talent for arranging pleasing programs wherein brilliant if unknown artists were introduced to a sparse but appreciative audience. I doubt if he succeeded in filling the hall on any single occasion during his annual series of concerts, although he was well liked by everyone and had many friends who gave financial support to his enterprise.

Many years later I took part in a benefit concert arranged for his relief, for the old gentleman had become very poor and in addition was crippled by the loss of one of his feet, amputated following a case of blood poisoning. Many well-known artists, all old friends of his, played and sang to an audience of about five thousand in the Royal Albert Hall. Madame Adelina Patti sang "Home, Sweet Home" twice over, and the celebrated actor Beerbohm Tree acted as master of ceremonies, introducing each artist as he or she came on the stage. I do not recall what he said about the other artists, but I was startled when he referred to me as one of the many artists who had been introduced to the English public by Wilhelm Ganz. It was not true, for I had never played at his concerts and I did not even know him until long after these concerts had been given up. But what did it matter, I thought. The poor old man was dying, unaware of the affectionate solicitude of the friends who had gathered together in order to express their sympathy in practical fashion, and he never knew that the only large audience which his name had ever attracted was fully aware that he was not going to conduct on that occasion and that he would never be seen again. I remember that many flowers were handed up to the stage in his honor, although it was known that he was too ill to attend the concert, and I particularly recall that one of these floral tributes was in the shape of a giant boot filled with enormous lilies. The sender doubtless intended to indicate in this delicate and tactful manner his knowledge of Ganz's crippled condition.

William Ganz's orchestral concerts were vastly important to me, inasmuch as I became familiar with symphonic music through them. There were no other regular orchestral concerts in London during the winter, and, most important of all, I could always get in without paying. The Richter concerts, which took place in the spring or early summer, were fashionable and highly successful events, and it was only once in a while that I was able to get a ticket to them. It seems strange that the only stable and regular series of orchestral concerts was not to be found in London proper but in the suburb of Sydenham, several miles away, at the Crystal Palace, an enormous glass building built for exposition purposes and used for general public entertainment. August Manns, the conductor, who was in charge of all the music there, has never received, in my opinion, the recognition and the credit which is due to him. In addition to his daily musical duties, he organized a first-class orchestra and gave weekly subscription concerts through the winter. His personality was striking and unforgettable. Long white hair, a tremendous mustache, and a rather abrupt manner combined to give him almost a ferocious aspect, but this belied his warm and generous nature. Everyone loved and admired him, and I used to look forward with eagerness to my rare visits to the Crystal Palace, where I was always kindly greeted by the conductor, who invariably kept me in his private room while he changed his black velvet coat for his blue velvet coat and put on a clean flowing necktie just before the concert.

Both my sister and I played under his direction. She played the St. Saëns Piano Concerto in G minor and I played Vieuxtemps' Fantasia Appassionata for violin, considered in those days a very important piece. I cannot imagine, however, why a more classical work was not chosen, for I played the Mendelssohn, Beethoven, and Mozart violin concertos in other places. When I played again at the Crystal Palace, Mr. Manns asked me to play Vieuxtemps' Concerto No. 4 in D minor, which I did. About that time, Eugène Ysaÿe made a sensational début at the London Philharmonic, and also played the Fourth Concerto of Vieuxtemps, in which, to my utter amazement, he started the first note up-bow instead of down-bow. This was something unheard-of. My amazement later gave way to admiration. I realized that Ysaÿe was not only the greatest violinist I had ever heard, but also a revolutionary and an innovator. A good many years later, I asked him if he thought that my feeling had been due in part to boyish reverence for an older man.

"Certainly not," he said, "there is no special reason for youth to respect age—the reverse is probably more justifiable; and, for my part, the greatest innovators that I have known among instrumentalists are the two youngsters, Fritz Kreisler and Pablo Casals."

Before leaving the Crystal Palace, I must speak of the Handel Festival; for nothing was more representative of English musical taste of the period than these stupendous choral performances which took place every two or three years. My recollection of the "Messiah," with over three thousand individuals singing and playing in the orchestra under the direction of the tiny, white-headed figure, August

Manns, apparently miles away from me, is as vivid today as it was fifty years ago. I know I shall never again be moved by such sounds, rolling as they did through the echoing spaces of the enormous glass building. The spectacle, too, was unlike anything I have seen before or since, and although the effect of the orchestra and of the solo voices was thin and puny, and a great deal of the musical detail was lost, the sheer impact upon the ear of chorus and organ was literally overwhelming in its power and majesty. I had a confused feeling that the Hallelujah Chorus was something like a challenge to the angels in heaven to do better if they could.

Perhaps it was because of the supremacy of England in this special branch of music that vocalists had a far better chance of making a good professional career than instrumentalists. Naturally the language had something to do with it. Back of the snobbishness which inclines to attribute superiority to the imported article, be it food, clothing, or music, there is a secret desire for the plain things of home life. People really do like to understand the words of a song, even though they may be taught to believe that an opera is not an opera unless it is sung in a language entirely strange to them. In England, oratorios were invariably sung in English and opera was invariably *not* sung in English.

There was no reason for us to be consistent. But of course we had to have English singers for the oratorio performances, and these singers, their reputation once established, were in great demand at the so-called "Ballad Concerts," organized by the two great music-publishing firms Boosey and Chappell, to bring forward and popularize drawing-room songs composed to sentimental words which were turned out in incredible numbers by a class of musicians who never composed any other kind of music. I knew several of these composers in London: Lady Arthur Hill, best known as the writer of "In the Gloaming"; Luigi Denza, who was famous all over the world as the composer of "Funiculi, Funicula," and a dear kind man he was too; Tosti, the aristocrat of the group; and one or two others. Of course, they had talent. They invented tunes which, whatever one may say of their innate artistic value, are as alive today as the melodies of Schubert, Mozart, or Brahms. But their ideas of musical composition were primitive, not to say stupid, and I never in my life had a more tedious and dreary experience than sitting through a Boosey Ballad Concert one afternoon with an old lady who had invited me, and whom I had not the courage to risk offending by leaving before the end.

It was due to these two factors—namely, oratorio and ballad—that a good English singer was able to make a highly prosperous career which lasted because of the notorious fidelity of the British public toward established favorites, until the voice had dwindled to the feeblest of croakings; and even then enough old people to form a respectable audience were still willing to buy their admission tickets in order to be able to say tearfully, "Ah, you should have heard him/her when . . ."

I do not intend any particular irony in thus commenting upon the English singers' opportunities for a career in those days. My concern with this exceptional state of affairs was purely egotistical. There were no such opportunities for me, and as far as I was able to judge, no instrumentalist born and brought up in England had the slightest chance of achieving success as a public performer. I found, however, that a number of young artists in my position were building their hopes of a public career upon the patronage of private individuals who were believed to be influential in high society. If So-and-So could be prevailed upon to come to my concert (so ran the argument) I should sell more tickets, and perhaps I might get some private engagements. In most cases, I think, these hopes were doomed to disappointment.

Others have described better than I can that fringe of the aristocracy composed of impecunious female members of great families who derived a handsome income from chaperoning and introducing wealthy young women (particularly Americans) into high society and arranging for their presentation to Royalty at the functions known as "Drawing-Rooms." These ladies conducted a regular business with considerable skill. They gave large parties at their homes and they were able to convince may ambitious artists, both English and foreign, that the way to fame and financial success was through these parties, where, however, they must give their services for nothing, because this unquestionably would "lead to something," as the current phrase went. There was this much truth in this scheme, that wealthy aristocrats paid large fees to well-known artists who performed privately at their houses. But I never knew of any artist unknown to the public achieving success or financial reward through this frightfully undignified and snobbish submission of his talents. Yet to this day, or perhaps I should say, until yesterday, any person connected, no matter how remotely, with British royalty had only to express the wish for musical entertainment, and a hundred aspiring performers would clamor for the privilege of laying their artistic wares, gratis, at the feet of the distinguished personage I always considered this kind of transaction as shameless exploitation on the one side and disgusting snobbery on the other.

Perhaps I should not have felt so strongly on the matter had there been the slightest compensation in the way of artistic satisfaction, for it is worth a sacrifice to play to an audience of the élite. But unfortunately there was nothing of the kind. Music at these large social parties was simply a background for conversation and nobody listened to it, no matter who the performer was. As a small boy, I used to be taken sometimes to play at these parties in the hope that they might "lead to something," but they never did. Later on, when I was prevailed upon to give my services once or twice at such receptions, I feared that something awkward and resentful might creep into my manner, and that this would militate against any future advantage, even if the fable of "leading to something" had been true. I shall never forget the sight of a violoncellist bending over his instrument while playing, and being gently but firmly thrust aside by an aristocratic old gentleman on the way to greet his hostess.

Returning one day in a state of great discouragement from one of these social functions, I called on my old violin teacher, Pollitzer, and told him of my experiences, my doubts, and my dislike of the means which seemed to be necessary in order to make progress. What to do?

"It has always been like that in London," said the old gentleman, philosophically smoking his pipe, and he told me the story of Ernst, the great violinist, through whose influence he had come to settle in England thirty years before. Ernst's Elegy was one of the most popular and successful pieces of music of the day. Its vogue, I think, was like that of Paderewski's Minuet or Rachmaninoff's Prelude later on. The great violinist was engaged to play a reception in a private house, "and above all," wrote the lady who was giving the party, "please do not fail to play your divine Elegy."

The concert started with a crowd of people talking at

the top of their voices. Ernst played his Elegy and nobody listened or applauded. After a suitable interval, he appeared again, and as there was no change in the attitude of the crowd, he said to his accompanist: "Nobody heard me the first time. Let us have the Elegy once more." The result was the same. At the end of the program, the lady came to compliment him and said, "Now, Mr. Ernst, after all this lovely music you have played so superbly, will you not favor us with your divine Elegy?"

So that, I thought, is what a musical career in England means. It has not changed. These were miserable thoughts, and they made me despondent and melancholy. I wondered what my future would be. I confided in my young friend Leopold Godowsky, whose extraordinary gifts were never recognized in London as they should have been. We used to play violin and piano sonatas together. He understood my feelings exactly and said with simple directness: "Why don't you get out of England?"

These words seemed to burn their way into my brain. I could not follow the suggestion, for I had no money, and my small earnings were needed for the family exchequer. But the thought remained and gnawed at my very vitals. Some day I might escape. I do not remember complaining openly about what I thought was my completely thwarted life, but I suppose that everyone of my acquaintance finally got to know that I was pining to leave England and to try my luck somewhere else on the European continent. If my friend Leopold Godowsky could choose his field, why could I not do the same, as he had advised?

One day the miracle happened. The postman brought me a registered letter in which I found banknotes to the amount of fifty pounds, with an unsigned note saying that this money was "to be used to go abroad with." I thought

[51]

122887

I must be dreaming. At first I simply could not conceive who had done this extraordinary thing for me, but after some reflection it became clear that it must have been not one generous donor, but two, middle-aged ladies who had considerable means and who had shown kindness to me and my sisters ever since we were small children. I was not mistaken, and I thanked them, quite inadequately, I am sure, for it was impossible for me to express what the thought of release meant to me.

"Where shall I go?" was the next thought. There was no immediate hurry, and I waited. During the winter months I was engaged for a few violin concerts in the provinces and in Scotland. I made the acquaintance in Glasgow of a piano teacher named Graham Moore, and he became a good friend to me when, shortly after, he established himself in London as professor at the Royal College of Music. He had been a pupil of Kullak in Germany, and from his residence abroad he had become acquainted with many foreign musicians, Paderewski among the number.

Moore took me to one of Paderewski's recitals and, after the performance, went to greet him in the artist's room. Paderewski invited him to dinner.

"Soll er mit?" (Shall he go along?) said Moore, motioning toward me.

"Certainly," said the great man, and I had the pleasure of taking a meal with these two old friends who had much to tell each other. Moore told Paderewski about me, and the great pianist expressed interest, inviting me to go and play to him the following day. I did so and also played something on the piano. He pulled me by the hair, saying,

"Sie müssen Klavier spielen—Sie haben so schönes Haar." (You must become a pianist—you have such beautiful hair.)

He ought to know, I thought, contemplating his yellow mane with respectful awe.

Perhaps it was on the strength of this facetious remark by the great artist that his manager, Daniel Mayer, decided that I should be included, sooner or later, on the list of professional musicians whose affairs he directed, and therefore, that I must be helped in my career. Mayer was not only the most enterprising and important concert manager in England, but in addition was director of the London branch of the Erard piano manufactory. Paderewski formally opened a small recital hall in the Erard building in 1892, and Mayer arranged for me to give a piano recital there in November of the same year. I had expressed hesitation about the wisdom of displaying myself as a pianist, considering that my career up to that point had been based on the violin; but my objections were overridden and I finally prepared and played the following program, to which I look back with real amazement, for I cannot imagine how I was able to play such difficult pieces:

Toccata and Fugue	Bach–Tausig
Sonata, Opus 101	Beethoven
Air de Ballet	Gluck–St. Saëns
Feux follets	Liszt
Allegro de concert	Chopin
Valse poétique	Graham Moore
Légende	Paderewski
Characterstück, Op. 7, #4	Mendelssohn
St. Francis Walking on the Waves	Liszt

A remarkable feat, even if I do say so, for a boy of my age who was devoting his energies to making a career as a violinist. I daresay the performance was very poor. It attracted no

[53]

attention, and I have no record of any comment made upon it in any newspaper.

Later, when I played the violin again, Paderewski said, "If you ever come to Paris, I should like you to study with my friend Gorski, who is the greatest living violin teacher." He added that I could also play the piano for him sometimes, and that he would interest himself in my future musical career.

That was enough for me, and there was no more cause for hesitation. I left shortly afterward for France, arriving in Paris on a fine spring morning in 1893. The horse chestnuts were in bloom, and the smell of fresh roasted coffee was in the air. I was in heaven.

Those fifty pounds, I said to myself, must last forever. I shall never live in England again. They did, and I did not. Paris became my home for the next twenty years.

Three

MY ONLY FRIEND IN PARIS, MONTAGUE CHESTER, MET ME ON my arrival and took me to a small hotel near the Avenue de l'Opera. After he had left me for his business occupation (he was cashier in the Paris branch of an English bank) I went for a walk and soon lost my way. I approached a policeman and said, very carefully, "Où est l'avenue de l'Opéra, s'il vous plaît?" But he did not understand me because I pronounced the word "Opera" as an Englishman would. I persisted, however. He listened patiently and finally caught on. "Ah," he said, as if suddenly stung by a bee, "Avenue de l'O—pair—rah?" "Oui," I said.

That was my first French lesson. I think it brought me some little insight into the French national character, as well as the French language, in which all syllables are supposed to be equally stressed. Clarity is the key to both. It is neither customary nor desirable in France to leave anything to the imagination. Essential things are done and essential thoughts are expressed in the simplest and most direct fashion, but always with a certain urbanity.

Politeness is more important than candor, says the Frenchman. Rudeness is preferable to untruthfulness, says the Englishman. The Frenchman is "enchanté" the first time he meets a stranger; the Englishman makes no attempt to disguise the caution (not to say suspicion) with which he regards anyone who says "good morning" to him without a prior introduction. He seems to fear that anything which might convey the impression that he is interested in a casual acquaintance would compromise him. He is anxious to make it clear that there is no reason for any subsequent meeting. The Frenchman, rightly or wrongly, considers this kind of indifference discourteous. The expression "au revoir" has no equivalent in the English language. You may call a Frenchman a sort of a cow, a sort of a camel, or even a sort of a pig (there are plenty of insulting names, most of them comical), and in the course of time such expressions, uttered in anger, may be forgotten. But accuse a Frenchman of lacking in politeness and, in my honest belief, he will never forgive you. To say that a man is a "goujat," which means an ill-bred person, is to set him outside the pale, and constitutes the supreme affront.

I am not expressing any opinion as to the relative merits of English and French national behavior; but I cannot refrain from touching upon the subject, for the reason that the unexpected courtesy I met with on every side in those early days acted as a salve to my shyness and a stimulus to my ambition, and thereby created a love for Parisian life and customs which had a lasting influence upon my life and character.

Were all these thoughts derived from the correction of my pronunciation made by the polite policeman? Probably not, but I insist that it was he who gave me my first French lesson, and with that lesson a glimpse into the national character.

The rates at the Hotel des Etats Unis, where I spent my first night, were far beyond my means (about seventy-five cents in United States currency); so the next day Chester took me to the Latin Quarter across the river, and there in the rue Royer Collard I engaged a furnished room for 30 francs a month. The place was dirty and ill-smelling, but nothing mattered. My quarters were large enough for a piano, and the first thing was to try to get one there—for nothing, if possible.

I had letters of introduction to the directors of the two great piano manufacturing firms, Pleyel and Erard. Both received me most kindly, but I accepted the spontaneous offer of Mr. Blondel of Erard's to send me a piano forthwith; and this was the beginning of a long and most precious friendship with that aristocratic house, whose pianos I subsequently played not only in France but in England and other parts of the world.

I have never been as happy as I was during those first weeks in Paris. Perhaps I should say that I have never known that particular kind of happiness either before or since. It was French. It was "joie de vivre"—sheer love of life. It seemed that I had nothing to do but work steadily toward a goal that was in sight; namely, the successful career as a concert violinist which had been predicted but denied to me in the country of my birth. I practiced with tremendous energy and enthusiasm, and since I had all the time in the world at my disposal, I practiced the piano as well as the violin.

Paderewski was away, and I hoped, when he returned home to Paris, that he would carry out his promise to recommend me for engagements at the various musical societies. I called on his close friends, Mr. and Mrs. Gorski, and was invited to their home, where I discovered that they were taking care of Paderewski's afflicted son, a boy about 15 years old and an incurable invalid.

I had a few other letters of introduction and made a number of friends. Chester seemed to know everybody and became my closest intimate. He was a remarkably well-educated man, schooled in almost every subject except music, which was his greatest passion in life. He had taught himself to read orchestral scores and possessed such an extraordinarily retentive memory that he was able to sing (in the most discordant voice) operas, symphonies, and quartets practically in their entirety. As a musical amateur he was unique because he could play no instrument; and I have never known anyone, professional or amateur, who knew as much music as he did, or whose judgment on musical matters was more sane or reliable. Truly a most unusual character. I believe he was on familiar terms with almost every prominent musician in Europe. Without being a first-rate linguist, he could converse freely in several languages besides French and English, and the fact that he was an accomplished chess player brought him into contact (through the international chess clubs all over Europe) with some of the most distinguished personalities of the day.

I lived with the greatest economy, for I was determined that my fifty pounds should carry me through, and as yet no other money was in sight. My meals, taken outside in small neighborhood restaurants, cost me on an average two francs fifty per day. Breakfast, consisting of café au lait and a roll, 25 centimes; table d'hôte lunch was 1 franc 15, and dinner 1 franc 25. I found that one could get eleven meal tickets for the price of ten, and this 10 per cent represented the waiters' tip, so the saving was appreciable. Very often I dined more cheaply at a wine shop, one of the many establishments known as the "Rendez-vous des cochers," frequented mainly by cab drivers. There I got one dish of meat and a large piece of bread for about 60 centimes, so I saved money even if I indulged in the luxury of a cup of coffee to end the repast. These cheap meals were better than anything I had been accustomed to in England.

I walked all over Paris, and became fairly familiar with its monuments and its museums. Chester introduced me to the composer Fritz Delius, then totally unknown to fame, who lived not far from my lodgings, and we became very good friends. He told me that he was living in the strictest economy on an allowance of ten pounds a month, and I remember the curious feeling of shyness (or was it stupid pride?) which prevented me from telling him that a sum of that magnitude represented unheard-of wealth to me.

I did not care very much for the compositions he showed me, for I found them loose in construction and deficient in contrapuntal writing. We discussed these things very frankly, and he criticized my attitude as being unduly academic, saying that he was not interested in writing in the style of the ancients. This did not mean that he disliked the music of any one of the great composers; on the contrary, his tastes in art were as wide and liberal as could be imagined; but he had the strongest feeling that the first duty of any artist was to find ways in which his own personality could be expressed, whether or not the process conformed to traditional methods. "An artist," said Delius, "will finally be judged by that and nothing else. He must have"—here he hesitated and finally found the expression of his thought in French—"une note à lui."

We talked of many things besides music, and I enjoyed being with him, for he was a highly intelligent and original thinker. Later on, he married a talented painter, Miss Rosen, and lived at Grez-sur-Loing, where I used to visit in the summer, and we played tennis together every afternoon. When I came to the United States in 1900, I brought the score of his symphony "Leaves of Grass" to submit to Mr. Gericke, conductor of the Boston Symphony Orchestra, who did not like the work. I do not know if it has ever been played in America.

Paderewski, whose great success had kept him in England through the summer season, finally came home to Paris and sent for me. At his suggestion, I left the Latin Quarter and hired a room in the apartment occupied by a lady who used to give English lessons to him and to Mrs. Gorski. The apartment was in the rue de la Pompe, not far from the Avenue Victor Hugo, where the Master had an apartment on the ground floor. I did not enjoy living with other people, and I felt that I had lost some of my precious freedom; however, it was convenient for me to be near enough to respond without delay to the Master's call. For I never received any advance notice, and it was his custom to send his valet to notify me whenever he wished to see me.

He was wonderfully kind to me in many ways, and occasionally let me play the piano for him after he had worked on the new concertos he was studying, in which I accompanied him on a second piano. I learned a great deal from my temporary association with this great man, although, just as a matter of record, I feel I should state that he was in no way responsible for my change from violinist to pianist.

He told me once that he believed I might make a unique career as a performer on both instruments, but at no time did he suggest that I should give up the violin. He recommended me as a violinist, in fact, to many people, but nothing came of it. I discovered to my bitter disappointment that there were many difficulties in the way of obtaining engagements in Paris. It seemed to me that only successful pupils of the Conservatoire had any chance.

This was so far true that students who received the First Prizes at the annual examinations were automatically offered appearances at the Colonne and Lamoureux symphony concerts, which, like the Conservatoire, received government subsidies, and consequently had certain working relations with each other. But it was not the whole story by any means. The violin classes at the Conservatoire were exceptionally brilliant at that time, and each year several particularly gifted young violinists were launched upon their careers, after receiving their awards at the great institution.

Only a few years before, a young boy named Fritz Kreisler, one of the last pupils of the great Massart (teacher of Henri Wieniawski, Pablo Sarasate, and many other great ones) had stepped from the doors of the Conservatoire into world-wide fame. Massart was followed as a teacher by Marsick, another of his pupils, whose success almost equaled that of his glorious predecessor. Every year, great violinists came out of the Conservatoire. In my time, I think the two greatest may have been Jacques Thibaud and Henri Marteau, but there were many others of brilliant gifts.

The truth, as far as my career was concerned, is that I could not hold a candle to any of these great violinists. I was not good enough, and I knew it; nevertheless, my ambition was by no means dampened, although I was bitterly disappointed not to have any opportunities of playing in public. Early in August of the following year, Paderewski told me that he was going away for the rest of the summer and that he expected to see me toward the end of September. I decided to visit my family in London, but before leaving Paris I arranged with Chester to take an apartment with him on my return. In the meantime he left the bank and had a position as advertising agent on the staff of the *Galignani Messenger*, then, as in the time of Thackeray, the only English-printed newspaper on the Continent. I became acquainted with many people in the journalistic world in consequence.

The editor in chief of the *Galignani Messenger* was a young man called Ralph Lane, who had just written a small book on international relations entitled *Europe's Optical Illusion*, under the *nom de plume* of Norman Angell. The book created a sensation and was expanded into a larger work called *The Great Illusion*, which brought such fame to the author that he was induced to leave journalism and to enter upon a career as lecturer, political adviser, and authority on international affairs, in which he achieved great eminence. I often think of him with admiration mingled with a kind of regret, for I feel that if he had been gifted with the *something* which makes leaders of men, he might have helped to save the world from the horrors into which he saw it drifting. He was among the very few who seemed able to understand the fundamental causes of war and to suggest means for dealing with them.

One day Paderewski said to me, "I have an old friend who is looking for a young violinist to play with him. He is a very kind man and I think you can earn a little money with him. Shall I tell him that you will go to see him?" I said, "Yes, by all means." I went to see this old gentleman, who lived in a large and extremely shabby apartment, and I was ushered into a living room where the curtains were drawn and candles were burning, although the sun was shining brightly outside. My host, who had the title of

Harold Bauer, Fritz Kreisler, and Pablo Casals

Harold Bauer and Ossip Gabrilowitsch

Paris, 1912

Medal of the society "La Trompette"

Marshal, came from another room and greeted me, and I explained as well as I could in my broken French that I was the boy sent by Paderewski to play the violin with him.

The old gentleman was the nephew of the Abbé Alexander Jelowicki, the priest who had attended Chopin on his death bed. Because of this connection, he had inherited a good deal more than the usual Polish reverence for Chopin. The way our conversation started was by talking about that composer. The Marshal asked me to play a Beethoven sonata with him; I opened my violin case and we began. In my wildest dreams I could never have conceived of anyone's playing the piano as badly as he did, but since I knew all these sonatas by heart, I was able to follow him, even when an outburst of enthusiasm for some particular harmony led him to shout to me, "Stop! Let us play this chord once more —it is too beautiful." So we played that particular chord over and over again until his aesthetic sense was satisfied and he was willing to go on to the next measure. We went through a vast quantity of music in this way, playing all the classical sonatas and sedulously avoiding anything that had a flavor of modern music about it, because, as the old gentleman repeatedly said to me, "Music came to an end with Chopin." A little later, however, he became acquainted with some of the piano music of Brahms, and he said to me, "Brahms got this from Chopin—it is beautiful music."

At my first meeting, we played in this fashion for about an hour, and then, as we came to the bottom of a page, the old gentleman abruptly stopped in the middle of the phrase. He heaved a sigh and said, "We must take a rest." He gave me a cigarette and invited me to lunch. As I had not been at all impressed by any manifestation of affluence because of the almost incredible shabbiness, not to say dirt, I thought, "Poor old man, he thinks he is obliged to ask me to lunch," and I said, as firmly as I could in my weak French, "It is not necessary to invite me to lunch. I thank you very much." As I was preparing to leave, he laid hold of me and, as though I had not said a word, led me downstairs, holding on to my arm. Then he said, "Please call a cab for me." I thought this was unwarranted extravagance, but it was none of my business, so I hailed a passing cab. My companion, however, refused to get into it, saying, "Did you not notice his number?" "No, what was the matter with it?" He said, "760!" Added together that made 13, and he would not get into a cab the number of which added up to 13. So we found another cab and drove off. I was aghast when I heard him give our destination to the coachman, for it was one of the most expensive restaurants.

As we walked in, the proprietor, together with a whole body of waiters, congregated around the Marshal and began bowing to him and evincing every possible obsequiousness, addressing him as "Monsieur Theodore." We were led to a very large table which was set for about fifteen people. We sat down, all alone, and he began to order a most elaborate luncheon. During this process a number of people came in —all Poles—who kissed him on the shoulder and sat down at the table. I did not understand what was going on, but in the course of time I learned that he was a very rich man who was in the habit of living in the squalor I had seen and who kept open house in the most expensive restaurants in Paris, to which all his Polish friends were invited to come.

This was the beginning of an association that lasted for several years. The old gentleman was the most original, generous, kindly, and—on the whole—the most intelligent human being that I ever met, in spite of his narrow-mindedness on certain subjects.

On one occasion I went to a recital with him, given by

one of the most famous young pianists of the time, Ferrucio Busoni. He was particularly interested in this concert because of the celebrity of the performer, and also because the whole program was to be devoted to the works of Chopin. At the beginning of the concert he sat with an air of humble concentration, with arms crossed, as in the presence of a great master. He sat motionless during the performance of the first piece, one of the Ballades. Then he turned to me and whispered in my ear, "Ce n'est pas cela!" As he listened to the second Ballade—there were four—he uncrossed his arms and put his hands on his knees; in the middle of the Ballade he pinched his lip and said, "Ce n'est pas cela— trop vite!" At the third Ballade he got restless. He whispered to me several times, "What is he doing? It is an outrage. But no!" Before the fourth Ballade, he said to me with determination, "My friend, I cannot sit here any longer. I must leave." I begged him, "Please do not leave. It will make a terrible impression. You are so well known." He consented to stay. After the fourth Ballade Busoni left the stage and was recalled with great applause. The old gentleman said to me, "I am going to leave. I will not hear any more." I said, "I shall leave with you. I am sorry." The applause died down. The old gentleman, deathly pale, turned round to the public from the front seat and said in a broken voice, "In the name of Chopin, I protest!" and he dragged me out with him.

One of the means by which I made a living was playing accompaniments. I was asked one day to accompany a singer at a private house and received a small fee. After this private concert was over, a man came up to me and said, "How would you like to go to Russia and make a tour with a singer, playing her accompaniments?" I agreed immediately, because at that time I would have said yes to any proposition. So he said, "Well, come and see me tomorrow." I went, and I then learned the singer's name, Louise Nikita. That year—1894—she had made a successful debut at the Paris Opéra Comique. But I knew nothing about her. (She was a native American, and her real name was Nicholson.) The man who offered to engage me as her accompanist was her uncle and manager. He told me: "We are going to make a tour in Russia, where this lady is a great favorite, and she cannot sing all evening. You will have to fill in the program by playing piano solos." I said, "I do not know if I can play well enough for that, because I am a violinist." He said, "That will be splendid. You will play accompaniments for her and then play the violin." I asked, "Who will play accompaniments for me?" He said, "In all the places we are going to there are excellent musicians, and I will get accompanists for you in Odessa, St. Petersburg, and so on." He engaged me consequently as both pianist and violinist to fill in the program on the understanding that an accompanist would be provided for the violin solos. I was engaged at a very modest salary to go on a tour of uncertain duration.

Four

I JOINED THE PARTY IN BERLIN, FOR THE PURPOSE OF REHEARS-
ing Nikita's repertoire. While we were there, the Emperor
Alexander III died (November 1, 1894). The news was
immediately received from Russia to the effect that no
public performances would be allowed during the period of
court mourning (five or six weeks). Apparently the tour
could not be made. But the impresario was a man of considerable resource. He thought it might be possible to reorganize the tour so that it could be made privately by holding
the concerts, during the period of court mourning, in closed
clubs in the smaller places of Russia. These clubs were a
great feature of Russian life—"halls of the nobility." The
smallest towns of Russia had such buildings, which included
restaurants and ballrooms. People came to them from miles
and miles away. The whole district converged there. In the
large cities the concerts would not have been possible, for
there the halls of the nobility were open to the public,
whereas in the small towns they were a closed circle. A num-

ber of telegrams were sent out to various towns, and these elicited most enthusiastic responses. Everywhere we were assured of a warm reception.

We set out on the tour, visiting only these smaller cities in Russia. It was immediately apparent that nobody could be found in these places who could play accompaniments for the violin. So I had to play the piano to fill in the program, whether I wanted to or not.

At the end of the period of court mourning we went into the large cities. The manager refused to engage an accompanist for my violin playing on the grounds that I played the piano well enough for him and he saw no reason for the additional expense of an accompanist. The tour continued and finished in this way.

I have just come across a photograph which dates from this time. It shows me with a mustache and a flowing white tie. The mustache was about the same color as Paderewski's, and that, of course, was as it should be. I hoped to grow a little tuft of hair under the lower lip, like his, and was greatly disappointed that it did not sprout properly and only made my chin look dirty. But all the same, there were quite a number of people in Russia who said I looked like Paderewski, and that made me very proud. I felt that it seemed to set me on the way toward playing as well as he did and becoming correspondingly famous.

However, the mustache disappeared before the end of the Russian tour, and it has never returned since. SHE did not like the mustache and kept worrying me to shave it off. I paid no attention to her remarks; I considered that it was none of her business, and I told her so. But one day I fell asleep in the train, and when I awoke I discovered that SHE had trimmed off one side of the mustache very neatly, leaving the other side untouched. SHE had the impudence to ask me which side I preferred. I was furious and she was delighted. Having neither razors nor scissors with me at the moment, I was compelled to ask her to cut off the remainder before we reached our destination so that my appearance should not be too grotesque. I always maintained that SHE had ruined my looks, and I remember distinctly Paderewski's remark, delivered with a sort of chilly disgust some weeks later when I was back in Paris: "Vous avez l'air d'un acteur." I don't know why this should have seemed so devastating, but it did.

The flowing white tie of the photograph was, unlike the mustache, really Paderewski's. He pretended, one day, to get very impatient with me, saying that the formal black bows I always wore gave the impression that I spent all my leisure time going to funerals. "Why don't you wear something different?" he said. I had a reply quite ready. "The main reason, dear Master," I said, "is economy. Black silk bows don't show the dirt and the wear as others do." Paderewski smiled and said he would give me a new idea. With that he went into his bedroom and returned with a handful of flowing white silk ties of the kind he wore all his life. "You can try these," he said, "and at least they won't look so funereal. Besides, they can be washed, and you can get the same kind of thing in any color, even black, if you *must* have black."

In the end, I left the party at Odessa, and came back alone. On the boat from Odessa to Constantinople I was robbed of every cent I had. When I arrived at Constantinople I went to the best hotel and sent off appeals for help, which brought me enough money for the trip back to Paris.

The death of Alexander III of Russia proved to be the cause which ended my career as violinist, for when I reached Paris and saw old friends and again made efforts to start playing the violin, I was laughed at because it was known that I had been playing the piano in public for several months. I was engaged to accompany several singers and instrumentalists, and finally some of my friends thought I had made sufficient progress to guarantee the expenses of a piano recital. I had become a pianist in spite of myself, yet I had no technique and I did not know how to acquire it.

In the midst of this perplexity, I went one day to a private house to see a young woman dance. I paid no attention at the time to her name. She went through a lot of gestures and posing to the strains of classical music familiar to me. It was unusual. I had never seen anything like it before. I noticed that she was using gestures that seemed to illustrate all the dynamic variations of the musical phrase. Her movements fascinated me with their beauty and rhythm. Every sound seemed to be translated into terms of motion, and as I watched her carefully, the idea crept into my mind that this process might conceivably be something like a reversible one. I said to myself that as long as a loud tone apparently brought forth a vigorous gesture and a soft tone a delicate gesture, why, in playing the piano, should not a vigorous gesture bring forth a loud tone and a delicate gesture a soft tone? The fact that this was precisely what had always taken place did not occur to me. It seemed to me that I had made a great discovery and, looking at the dance, I imagined that if I could get my hands to make on a reduced scale certain motions that she was making with her whole body, I might perhaps acquire some of those fine gradations of tone which, to me, represented the most important qualities of piano playing. At any rate, I was desperate and I determined to try. I started by making angular and ridiculous gestures at the piano in a way no human being had ever done before. Any other pianist seeing me practice might have doubted my sanity. I persisted, however. There was the preconceived idea of a certain kind of tone, and it was necessary to find the gesture that could produce it.

This eluded me as a rule, but once in a while tone and gesture seemed to belong together, quite unmistakably, and at such moments I saw a ray of hope that I might be on the right track. Right, that is to say, *for me*, at that time, because my main idea was that if I could give an expressive sound to my performance on the next Saturday night, when I hoped to earn fifty francs, the audience might tolerate, to some extent at least, my lack of fluency and mechanical skill. This way of practicing, first dictated by necessity, later on became a habit of both mind and muscle, from which I never subsequently departed.

Thirty years later I gave a recital in Los Angeles at which my old friend Eugène Ysaÿe was present. He came to see me in the artists' room after the concert with a lady who was a perfect stranger to me. He said, "Of course you know Isadora." "Isadora who?" I asked. He said, "Isadora Duncan." I said I did not know the lady, but should like very much to meet her. He presented me to her. I said, "Miss Duncan, I must tell you the story of my life, because you are certainly unaware that you have had greater influence on it than anyone else." The result was that we gave a very remarkable concert together which we rehearsed in the most painstaking way. The whole program consisted of pieces by Chopin. One of the pieces was the Etude in A flat (Op. 25, No. 1), in the course of which the melody rises to a dramatic climax and then appears to diminish to the end of the phrase. As we were rehearsing, Isadora said to me, "You are playing that wrong. The crescendo must continue until the very end of the phrase, and you can soften it later." I was somewhat nettled and replied that the music clearly indicated the phrasing I had employed. "I can't help that," she retorted with superb egotism. "The music *must* go that way, otherwise there would be nothing to do with my arms. Besides," she added obstinately, "you are quite mistaken." We had a long discussion, and I finally gave in for the sake of the dramatic gesture that she considered indispensable. The end of the story is that I have played the piece her way ever since, for I discovered that Chopin's manuscript bore the precise dynamic curve which she had instinctively sensed and which had been subsequently altered.

Shortly after my return from Russia in the late spring of 1895, I found myself estranged, as the result of some irresponsible gossip, from the Polish social group of which Paderewski was the center. Although it was distressing to me to lose the friendship of the great artist, this incident would have no place in these pages were it not for the fact that my withdrawal from what some people called the Polish sphere of influence opened new doors to me in musical circles which were either opposed or indifferent to it. I did not meet Paderewski again until he came to hear me play some ten years later at a concert in Boston.

In the fall of that same year (1895) Paderewski's London manager, Daniel Mayer, who had always shown confidence in my ability to succeed as a pianist, arranged two concerts in Berlin for me at his own expense. At the first one I played Beethoven's Emperor Concerto, St. Saëns' Concerto in G minor, and Liszt's Hungarian Fantasia, accompanied by the Philharmonic Orchestra—a thoroughly conventional program, typical of those days. I had a great success and was engaged by several symphony orchestras in the larger German cities for performances later in the season.

I had much less success at the solo recital which took place a week after the orchestral concert; and, rightly or wrongly, I have always attributed this in large measure to the fact that this recital program included a number of less known and less effective pieces. It seemed necessary, in order to receive the stamp of approval, or even to be classified at all by Berlin concert-goers, for newcomers to perform the same music on which the success of others had previously been based. Perhaps it was not a bad plan. It certainly facilitated comparisons, but I did not realize its importance.

My time was free during the week between the two concerts. I went about Berlin and made a number of friends. One day, as I sat at Bechstein's large warerooms, trying the concert grand on which I was to play, I heard a stealthy footstep behind me and suddenly felt my eyes covered with two hands. "Who is it?" said an unknown voice in German. The hands were removed. I turned in great surprise, and there stood a little bearded gentleman dressed in a very tight frock coat. He bowed. "De Pachmann," he said. That is the way I met this eccentric genius whose acquaintance I kept although I saw him only seldom.

My meeting with Moritz Moskowski, to whom I had a letter of introduction, was totally different. I called at his house, and when he received me with the simple cordiality which was part of his character, I conceived an immediate affection for him. I feel proud to say that a friendship grew up between us which lasted until his death. He came to live in Paris the year after I first met him in Berlin.

Robert Strakosch, the nephew of Adelina Patti and the son of the celebrated impresario Maurice Strakosch, was my manager in Paris. His devotion to my interests was unlimited, and I was sorry that he never reaped the reward his labors merited. Because of the connections he had established through his father's managerial career with famous artists throughout Europe, he directed my affairs successfully (although quite unprofitably) for several years. In spite of his efforts, and in spite of the fact that I was beginning to be recognized everywhere as a respectable and worthy artist, I never attracted large audiences, and consequently my fees for engagements remained very small.

One of my first engagements as a bona fide pianist was for two concerts with a symphony orchestra in Madrid. This was in the autumn of 1895. I left for Spain with tremendous gratification. Concerts were given in a theater (subsequently destroyed) which had formerly served as an arena. After my performance of a concerto by Liszt, many people in the audience thought the proper way to acknowledge their appreciation was to send their hats spinning to the stage, and for the ladies to throw their bouquets, in the same way as the feat of a toreador is acclaimed in the bull ring. The following week in Madrid I had nothing to do. My success at the first concert gave me a feeling of delirium, and I thought I had reached a pinnacle. One day a gentleman called on me at my hotel to ask if I would give a recital in Bilbao, the largest city in the northern part of Spain. I pretended that I must consult my agenda to see if I was free, and then told him that I was happy I could accept. This recital was scheduled for the day after my final appearance with the orchestra in Madrid. I had a long and uncomfortable journey to Bilbao. After attending to the various details, such as the hall, the piano, etc.—there was much to do—I finally got back to the hotel at six o'clock, completely exhausted and feeling that I could not possibly play that evening unless I took a strong stimulant. I ordered a small bottle of champagne, which I drank, and had a few oysters. In my state of fatigue, I became completely intoxicated. I was taken to the hall and sat down to play the Moonlight Sonata with the feeling that God was helping me by sending the keys up from the piano to bang against my fingers. I was recalled to life after my first number by discovering a small bottle of ammonia in a cupboard in the greenroom; this made it possible for me to finish the concert. I went back to Paris quite crestfallen. I then proceeded to Holland.

The fees earned in Madrid had been pre-empted to cover recitals which I was to give at my own expense in Amsterdam. On my arrival there I called upon a very phlegmatic concert manager who told me that Amsterdam was the most difficult place in the world in which to succeed. Many people, he said, had done as I was doing, giving up later because the public response was unfavorable. So I started my concert, and I thought after I had played the first group that the grim prediction of the manager had been completely realized because, instead of the approval I had earned a few days before in Spain, I heard only the faintest rustling of applause in the audience; in the intermission, when I came off the stage and found my manager in the artists' room, I said, "Well, perhaps I had better not give the second concert after all, because I cannot please the people here." He said, "You have had a great success," at which I was so furious that I asked him to leave the room and let me alone in my misery. But strange to say, his prediction proved true, because Mr. Mengelberg, the conductor, was in the audience, and he had told the manager that he wanted me to play at his very next concert, he was so pleased with my recital. This started my career in Holland, which for years afterward provided the main source of my income. I was most successful there.

In the summer of 1896 I was engaged to play at a festival given in honor of St. Saëns at the great Trocadero auditorium in Paris. After the concert was over, I received praise from the composer for my playing of his G minor concerto.

James Huneker introduced himself to me, and we went off together. "What was the trouble between you and Little Poland last year?" he suddenly said. I looked at him in great surprise, wondering how or why this silly old story had reached his ears after so long a time. "I'm damned if I know," I said shortly. "Well," he said, not at all abashed, "I was told . . ."—and thereupon he proceeded to reel off a comical tissue of disconnected tattle and rumors faintly reminiscent of the incident in question. It made me laugh, and at last I broke in, "That certainly makes a good mystery story." "So it does," he said slowly, as if struck with an idea. Sure enough, he did write an ingenious and quite incomprehensible story based upon the fragmentary stuff he had heard, and this was published, I believe, in both the *Musical Courier* and a collection of short stories. Nobody ever knew what it was all about, but it made amusing reading.

The St. Saëns Festival at the Trocadero reminds me of another story. Some years before, a group of friends and admirers of Anton Rubinstein had organized a festival devoted entirely to compositions by the great artist, who came especially to Paris to conduct his orchestral works. The triumphant success of this festival surpassed all expectations, and Rubinstein was acclaimed by the whole world of art and culture as one of the greatest of composers. In a word, it was an event of historic importance.

Rubinstein, walking toward the Champs Elysées after the Trocadero concert, was hailed by a voice behind him. He turned and saw his old friend St. Saëns. "Rubinstein!" said the latter. "What a surprise! What on earth brings you to Paris?" . . . The story ends there, and I do not vouch for its truth.

St. Saëns was a man of genius and infinite though cruel wit. He was very friendly to me although I met him but seldom. I

used to play his G minor and C minor concertos quite frequently, and I think my performance of the latter work at
an orchestral concert in Kharkoff in 1894 was the first time
I played a piano concerto in public. The great composer
once said to me: "I suppose I ought to thank you for playing two of my concertos so often. But don't forget," he
added, "that I have written five . . . five concertos!" he
repeated, holding up his hand with fingers outspread. Unfortunately the other three concertos never achieved popularity. I studied them, but never played them.

St. Saëns was a marvelously gifted performer on both the
piano and the organ. I used to enjoy hearing him play Bach
at the Madeleine, and his interpretations seemed absolutely
perfect. As a pianist, he generally played with excessive
speed, although he constantly criticized others for playing too fast. He was present one evening at a reception given
by Madame Madeline Lemaire, a fashionable painter who
knew everyone in the Parisian world of culture and was
greatly admired and liked by all. She used to attend my
recitals regularly and frequently engaged me to play for
her guests. On this particular evening, I was to play, as one
number on the program, St. Saëns' sonata for piano and
violoncello with the celebrated cellist Joseph Hollman, a
great friend of the composer. St. Saëns sat at the piano to
turn pages for me. When we came to the last movement
he said, "Everyone plays this too fast, and I am afraid you
are going to annoy me. Let *me* play it and you can turn
the pages."

"Now," said the composer, "here is the correct tempo,"
and he started very slowly. Hollman looked at me and
winked—I could not imagine why. But the master's fingers
began to run away with him, and long before the movement was ended he was playing faster, I believe, than any-

one had ever played that piece. He looked at me comically and, I thought, perhaps a little ruefully. "You see," he said, "I am a musical pig like all the rest of you."

Joseph Hollman was another good friend of mine, and we gave numerous concerts together in France and in England. At this time (around 1896) I was living near the Place de l'Etoile with my friend Chester, in an apartment consisting of three rooms and a kitchen on the ground floor giving onto a courtyard, for which we paid 35 francs a month— an economical arrangement for us both. We furnished it with the barest necessities. My Erard piano was in my bedroom, which opened onto the remaining room, where we had our meals and received our friends. I was the cook and housekeeper, and we shared the work of keeping the rooms in order—a task we both resented, as it took up time which we could have employed far more pleasantly in other ways. Besides, as Chester justly observed, "The rooms are so dark that nobody, not even we ourselves, can tell whether they are swept and dusted or not, so what is the use?" I heartily concurred—with a result that needs no comment.

The house was modern; that is, water and gas were available in each apartment. Both were in the kitchen and nowhere else. The gas company, wishing to accustom people to cooking by gas, provided a small cooking-stove free of charge. This was connected to the main pipe by a piece of rubber tubing and placed on top of the regular kitchen range, which was reserved for more elaborate meals, when the gas stove was removed and laid aside. There may have been a gaslight in the kitchen, but I am not sure. For other lighting in the apartment, we had one kerosene lamp and two or three candlesticks.

I often think of the vast changes in lighting nowadays, and wonder how on earth we got along as well as we did with dark houses, dark streets and shops, and even dark public buildings, theaters, etc. Imagine what the light of one thousand candles means! How many places could there have been which had this amount of illumination? Yet it means no more than ten small electric bulbs of today. It seems to me that human eyesight must have deteriorated enormously. I used to practice in the evening by the light of a single candlestick provided with a shade, which illuminated the music on the rack quite sufficiently, and I read in bed very comfortably with one candle which I used to extinguish when ready for sleep by throwing a book or a magazine over it.

Chester was inordinately proud of me and never missed an opportunity to talk to his friends about my musical abilities. As he had a very large circle of friends and acquaintances, and introduced me everywhere, my life became very interesting; for through him, either directly or indirectly, I came to know most of the important musicians of Paris, as well as many people distinguished in other fields of art, science, and literature. I was delighted to meet so many accomplished people, and I wished I had as much leisure as they seemed to have, so that I could cultivate a closer acquaintance with them. But I never seemed to get through with my work as they did with theirs. They had time to spend an hour or two every day at the café, which constituted the social club of the group to which they belonged, and it was only rarely that I was able to do this; for I felt that I was very backward and that I needed all my time for study and practice. I worked very hard and gradually mastered a large repertoire, setting myself the task of preparing an entirely new program each time I played in public, whether in Paris or elsewhere.

This was contrary to the prevailing custom among young

musicians, who generally worked up one or two programs until they could play every piece impeccably. My method had the advantage of forcing me to learn a great deal of music within a specific period, but it was by no means an unmixed success; for, as I later discovered, it deprived me of the benefit of applying the experience of first-time performance toward improvement, and as a result my playing, although musically expressive, was always lacking in finish. Had I kept my repertoire within smaller limits at that time, I should probably have played better all my life. My attitude was in reality that of the amateur, not of the professional, and in making this confession, I should add that while amateur performance was in early life a thing of impatience and dislike to me, I felt as time went on that I grew closer and closer to the person who says, "I don't know anything about music—I only know what I like!" Finally I realized that this, fundamentally, was my own attitude. The more I studied, the less I seemed to understand of the mystery and the magic of music. The unsophisticated amateur, unconcerned with questions of brilliancy and material success, frequently gave me more pleasure and conveyed musical thought and expression (the only thing which mattered to me) more convincingly than the trained virtuoso. Did that mean that study could lead nowhere beyond the sterile regions of technical display? There was no answer to this, and I had to go on working just the same, hoping with a kind of superstitious frenzy that somehow and sometime I might catch a glimpse of the truth and grasp a part of that superior and transcendental power which would stir the imagination and arouse the emotions of those who listened to my playing.

All these perplexing thoughts, doubts, and hopes were not conducive to systematic study, and I know that I wasted a great deal of time which I could have employed more pleasantly and more usefully in cultivating friendships with the gifted people I met. But I could not adjust myself to the manner in which others worked, for all my previous experience had been based on the method of trial and error, and it seemed absolutely essential for me to experiment with matters which lay outside any of the rules and traditions by which most young musicians seemed to be governed.

I fared very little better when I tried to form my taste upon the opinions I heard expressed by the great musicians who were then living in Paris. While they opened new horizons to me in many respects, I was frequently shocked and repelled by the intolerance of their attitude toward many of the things which I had been accustomed to hold in reverence. How can they be so sure? I thought, bowing mentally at the same time before their superior gifts and accomplishments. Many of these men were engaged in writing music criticisms, their opinions being considered, quite properly I suppose, as matters of public interest. These criticisms, confined to opera performances and symphony concerts, were always serious, frequently witty, and sometimes devastating. Since I heard many such judgments delivered in private gatherings, I could not help being struck by the fact that the written criticisms were not quite as violent and uncompromising as the spoken ones—a very natural thing, of course, but it sometimes gave the impression that the *viva voce* pronouncement was a kind of dramatic rehearsal for the public performance. I wonder if these published criticisms, splendid as they often were as literary compositions, as logical expressions of faith, and as personal revelations, did very much to influence public opinion.

I have never been able to see in what way music critics have contributed to cultural progress; although on the other hand, there is no denying that their writings have frequently delayed it. An example of this, from my Paris days, is that none of the celebrated critics ever had a good word to say for the music of Brahms, which the public nevertheless insisted upon enjoying whenever it was given the chance; and that same public, in the face of the growing recognition in high quarters of Debussy's genius, persisted in saying, "Anybody can write stuff like that."

Debussy, by the way, was the most violent of all the critics I ever met, in spite of his enthusiasms and the delicacy of feeling he seemed able to express as well in words as in music. He satirized Wagner, he despised and detested Brahms, and he attacked Beethoven with such bitterness and sarcasm that it made one's blood boil. Once, in my hearing, he mentioned that he had "escaped" the previous evening from a concert where a Beethoven quartet was being played, just at the moment when the "old deaf one" ("le vieux sourd") started to "develop a theme." There was something so hateful in the tone of his voice as he said this that I rose up indignantly and denounced him for his disrespect to the name of a great genius; and the result was, I regret to say, that our relations were broken on the spot and not renewed for a number of years.

My friend Ravel was not nearly so violent when he said quite seriously that he loved the elegance of Mozart too much to be able to accept the coarseness and vulgarity of Beethoven. Ravel, although he esteemed me sufficiently to dedicate his very best piano piece, "Ondine," to me, was unsparing in his criticism of me for being, as he said, a disciple of Schumann, who, *"just because he was a genius,* had been able to poison general musical taste with his sickening sentimentality." But this was just private friendly talk, not intended for publication!

It was much more important to learn, as I did one day with great concern, that students at the Conservatory were not allowed to study Brahms' music in the ensemble classes for the reason that the director did not like it. But, of course, nothing could be done about that.

Reverting for one moment to the attitude of the amateur which, through all these experiences, was my own, I cannot refrain from quoting a few words written by the celebrated New York critic Lawrence Gilman, in an article entitled "The Amateur," which appeared twenty years later in the *New York Herald-Tribune*. He referred to me as "one of those rare professionals whose point of view toward their art is that of the accomplished craftsman who combines with the equipment of the expert the disinterested passion of the amateur." Nothing that was ever written about me, before or since, has given me so much satisfaction.

Because of Chester's departure on business, I was now living with a violinist, Achille Rivarde. Our housekeeping continued to be of a very sketchy kind, and as we both practiced during the same hours in our small apartment, the neighbors strongly objected and we had difficulties with them. He went to America on a concert tour, but because of his ignorance of money values there (compared to values in France) he earned little more than enough to pay his expenses and came back as poor as he went. The tour, however, was an artistic success and brought him engagements in various parts of Europe on his return. Looking back, I cannot understand why we gave so few concerts together, for our association, both personal and artistic, was most congenial. We met on one occasion in Berlin, he coming from the south and I from the north, and had a happy reunion with our mutual friend Fritz Kreisler. Rivarde and I played together in London in 1911, and he later became professor at the Royal College of Music, a position he occupied for the remainder of his life. My household being once again disorganized, I determined to live by myself in future.

I found suitable quarters in a large apartment house where my friend Joseph Salmon, the well-known violoncellist, also lived. We had many friends in the musical world and gave many concerts together. We used to take our meals in a pension near by, and I frequently found myself the table-neighbor of an attractive young woman who was studying singing and who afterward became celebrated at the Opéra Comique and elsewhere. Her name was Mary Garden.

Salmon asked me to go to his apartment one day to meet a young Rumanian who had come to him with a letter of introduction from Princess Bibesco, one of the leaders of Rumanian Paris society. This boy, then seventeen years old, literally amazed us with his musical genius. He played both piano and violin magnificently, and had already composed several important works in various forms which placed him among the greatest of contemporary musicians, not withstanding his youth. We became great friends, and I have always felt proud and happy to know Georges Enesco.

Rumanian society has always been deeply rooted, I believe, in those aristocratic traditions which gave an especially exclusive character to certain Parisian circles, and I never felt, as I did with groups of other nationalities, that the Rumanians formed a separate colony. They seemed, in fact, sometimes more Parisian than the Parisians themselves —"plus royalistes que le roi," as the saying goes.

Salmon and I used to play every two weeks at the house of

a wealthy Rumanian widow, Mme. Emmeline Raymond, who was owner and editor of a periodical devoted to fashion and women's interests. Her home, with its elaborate eighteenth-century furnishings and decorations, recalled descriptions given in Balzac's novels, and the ladies and gentlemen who came to her receptions seemed in dress as well as in manner to belong to the same period. The hostess herself, wearing a large wig with ringlets, might have been King Louis XIV dressed as a woman. We played sonatas for piano and cello and solos for each instrument. The music was punctuated by murmurs and remarks of approval, that being the fashion of the time. Madame Raymond always spoke of us both as "mes musiciens," exactly as if she had been a great personage of a bygone age holding court in her palace. My concerts were invariably reported in her paper in the most flowery and complimentary manner, for she had quite made up her mind that I was one of the great ones, and I believe the criticisms always came from her own pen. On one occasion the enthusiasm went a little too far. She said in her paper that no difficulties existed for me because I "suppressed" them. ("Pour lui, les difficultés n'existent pas. Il les supprime.") My friends, reading this ambiguous statement intended by the writer as the greatest possible compliment, were quick to seize this opportunity of teasing me and besieged me for months afterwards with touching appeals for assistance in doing away with technical difficulties.

All France was living in those days under the shadow of the Dreyfus affair. The dramatic story of a Jewish officer in the French army, wrongfully condemned for treason, took possession of the public mind in a manner and to an extent of which nobody, I venture to say, without firsthand experience of life in Paris during that time can form the

[85]

least conception. It was like a civil war, with this difference —that the two opposing parties could not get far enough away from each other to draw up regular battle lines. "Are you for or against?" was in everyone's thought on meeting in the street or in any other place. The world was not large enough for both Dreyfusards and anti-Dreyfusards to live in. The talented Russian cartoonist known as Carandache (Russian for "pencil") drew two pictures for *Figaro*, which summed up the situation to perfection. The first of the two cartoons represented an elegant hostess whispering to each new arrival: "It's understood, isn't it, that nobody will mention it?" The second picture—the dinner table—showed the guests in every conceivable attitude of uncontrolled fury: men pulling each others' noses and gouging each others' eyes, ladies clawing at each others' faces and hair, all the dishes toppling to the floor, and a little dog running away with a fork sticking in his hindquarter. Caption: "It was mentioned, after all!"

The weekly household dinners at Madame Raymond's (to which "her musicians" had a standing invitation) were no longer unconstrained. They became more formal than before, and in spite of the fact that no serious doubts as to the loyalty (i.e., the reactionary spirit) of anyone present were entertained by the hostess or her guests—still, who could tell? Constraint and reserve hung in the atmosphere; the more so, perhaps, because of the expressed determination that nothing could possibly be allowed to happen which would in any manner upset the existing order of things. Therefore, all the aspects of the "affaire" must by all means be discussed or at least touched upon at the dinner table.

Finally, the blow which was feared by everyone fell. One of the guests, warming to a discussion which that evening turned upon the word of one man against that of his superior officer, said with a shrug, "We must not forget, after all, that either or both of these men might be traitors." The lady of the house flushed deeply, clenched her fist and struck the table, rising as she spoke: "Monsieur," she proclaimed with great vehemence, "anyone who holds such opinions should not remain one day longer in France." And with that she marched out of the room, leaving us all in consternation. The party broke up and, needless to say, the gentleman in question never returned to the house. This was an instance of the kind of thing that was taking place every day. The question of a miscarriage of justice was only one side of the "affaire," and sometimes it even seemed the least important side, awful though that was. But the fanatic intensification of national feeling, expressing itself in fear and hatred of the foreigner, the unexpected and violent outbreak of antisemitism in its most intolerant form—these were things which seemed to isolate Paris from the world which had always regarded it as the center of culture and enlightenment ("la ville lumière")—and this was worst of all.

The world of music was affected like every other circle. In the midst of all this turmoil we read one day that Fanny Bloomfield Zeisler was engaged to play at one of the Lamoureux concerts, and that she was going to use a Steinway piano. Here was stuff for an explosion. A German artist, Jewish to boot, was to play an American piano in one of a series of concerts subsidized by the government ostensibly for the protection of French interests. To cap the climax, she was to play a concerto by St. Saëns, who had become exceedingly unpopular with a large section of the public because he refused rather contemptuously to become the president of the recently established Musicians' Union. The hall was filled, and when the artist appeared she was greeted with yells, catcalls, and whistles. She started the concerto, and the noise increased so that she was compelled to stop. Finally, after about ten minutes of pandemonium, Lamoureux turned to the audience and, when they had quieted down sufficiently for his voice to be heard, he said very composedly: "You may as well stop shouting now, for we are going to play the concerto." On that the audience started to laugh, and Mrs. Zeisler played her piece through under the derisive comments of those members of the public who could not be restrained. Mrs. Zeisler, recalling this scene years later, said: "Where did the legend arise that the French people were polite?" It was hard to answer her, although I knew and she knew that in all such disturbances, a great deal of the noise is made by those who try to obtain quiet.

Similarly, many people had nothing but condemnation for France during the Dreyfus affair, saying that it could never have occurred in any but a totally corrupt civilization. The answer to that accusation might have been that the turmoil was caused by those heroic Frenchmen who were resolved that no sacrifice would be too great for them to make and no labor too arduous for them to undertake, if an evil could be remedied and an injustice righted. Where else in the world, it might have been said, were so many private individuals to be found ready to rise up and fight, with their closest friends if necessary, in defense of their principles?

I shall always be happy to remember that the greatest hero of the Dreyfus affair, Colonel Picquart, was a good friend of mine. He was an excellent amateur musician and had fine artistic taste, besides being a man of splendid and lovable character. His residence was very near mine, and as we were walking homeward one evening after visiting some

mutual friends, I asked him to explain why that curious expression "conspuer" (applied to everything and everybody
out of favor with the French mob) had been attached to
the tune of a mazurka. He did not know, but he was obliging
enough to dance and sing, very gracefully, in that quiet
midnight street, some measures of the mazurka applied to
his own name:

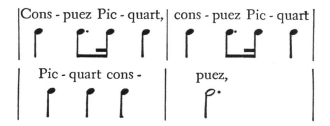

| Cons - puez Pic - quart, | cons - puez Pic - quart |
| Pic - quart cons - | puez, |

with which a number of his enemies were entertaining themselves at that time. I wonder if the unconquerable Gallic
sense of humor will prove the salvation of France in God's
own time?

Five

ONE DAY I RECEIVED AN INVITATION WHICH FLATTERED ME immensely. It was from Monsieur Emile Lemoine, founder and director of a musical society known as "La Trompette," asking me to take part in one of the bimonthly concerts and to play a piece of chamber music with the Quatuor de Paris, as well as some solos. This musical society had a most interesting origin. It was founded in 1861 in the Ecole Polytechnique by Lemoine, a distinguished mathematician and a musical amateur, whose friends included the greatest musicians of those days. The purpose of the society was to bring these musicians together in order to perform their respective compositions informally before a group of friends who subscribed to pay the expense incurred in the rental of suitable premises and the printing of programs. The enterprise attracted so much attention that it was enlarged, and gradually it changed in character. This was unavoidable, since new compositions were not continually forthcoming and it was essential to provide at least a nucleus for the programs by enlisting the services of an established string quartet. A small fund was created for this purpose, but there was no money to pay other fees because no tickets were ever sold. Mr. and Mrs. Lemoine received their friends and their friends' friends at the entrance of the auditorium, and there was never the least suggestion of a public concert, although the audience at times numbered many hundreds and completely filled the hall.

The artistic prestige of the "Trompette" was immense. The name was derived from a septet written and dedicated to Lemoine by his old friend St. Saëns, who was one of the most faithful of the many distinguished supporters of the society. Approximately twelve regular concerts were given during the season, and each year on Shrove Tuesday (Mardi Gras) there was a special concert to which every composer was expected to contribute a comic number. The most important of these contributions was unquestionably St. Saëns' "Carnaval des Animaux," written especially for the occasion but, in spite of the amusement and enthusiasm excited by its annual performance, prohibited from performance elsewhere and, by strictest injunction of the composer, not published until after his death.

I once took part in one of these annual performances. Everyone who participated had to wear a pantomimic make-up representing the animal whose music he was supposed to be playing. Taffanel, the great flutist, conductor of the Conservatoire concerts and the Opera, had a cardboard head showing him as a nightingale. The cellist Delsart was seen through the neck of a very flabby swan; the distinguished string players of the string quartet were shown as donkeys of various breeds. St. Saëns and I were the two pianists—he made up to look like our host Lemoine, and my head furnished with a wig and beard which refused to stick on, supposedly disguised as the great composer himself. The two pianists were provided with immense cardboard hands and feet that were clipped off at the moment of performance, which was extremely hilarious.

I forget what other numbers appeared on the program, although I recall my own contribution—a short set of waltzes on themes taken from Wagner's operas, which amused some people and shocked others. During the years of my residence in Paris I played frequently at "La Trompette" and finally received the distinction of a medal which had been struck in honor of its founder.

Emma Nevada, the well-known opera singer, who was then living in Paris, wrote me that she wanted me to meet a young Spanish cellist in whom she was interested. This was Pablo Casals. He called upon me, and we immediately became great friends. I was tremendously impressed by his playing, and suggested to him that we might give concerts together. He cordially agreed and we at once set to work, he in his own country and I in other European countries (for I had played a great deal more than he had) to arrange tours. We were highly successful and played together for a good many years in various parts of the world whenever our other engagements permitted us to join forces. Our joint concerts in Spain created so much interest in the provincial towns where musical events were rare that a chain of musical societies known as Philharmonic Clubs, which gave an annual series of concerts on a co-operative basis, was established as a result of our visit.

I have always felt that the unusual enthusiasm manifested in those days by Spanish audiences was very closely related to their almost total lack of musical education. They had never been taught to regard so-called "classical" music as something which could be appreciated only after passing through the tribulation of study. Music, thought these poor people, was like painting, sculpture, and architecture—something beautiful which belonged to all the people. Here is an example of that attitude: Casals, at one of our concerts, was playing an unaccompanied suite by Bach, to which I was listening backstage, together with several idle stage hands. One of them said to me with a knowing look:

"Señor, the composer of that music is Verdi."

"Of course it is," said I, "doesn't it say so on the program?"

"I have nothing to do with programs," the man replied, "for I cannot read. But I know it is Verdi's music, for that is the only music that always makes me weep."

This was quite touching, but I could not help recalling the comical paraphrase: "Nur Verdi Sehnsucht kennt," of Goethe's well-known line. Anyhow, my story is true and it seems to me as characteristic of Spain as the incident I shall now relate, which could hardly have occurred in any other country.

During this early period of my career I was singularly fortunate in having the active and friendly interest of the great French firm Erard. There were very few concert grand pianos available in Spain at that time, and Erard generously provided not only instruments sent expressly from Paris, but the services of an experienced tuner as well. The tuner always traveled with me and took charge of forwarding the pianos so that they would arrive at their respective destinations in time for the next concert. For this, two pianos were needed, since it was not practicable for the instruments to be repacked and sent off as expeditiously as I had to travel myself.

On one occasion when I was concertizing alone, things went wrong. Toward the end of my tour, my tuner fell ill and I had to leave him behind. The business of forwarding the pianos devolved upon me. I had a concert in the city of Coruña, following which it was necessary to travel clear across Spain for the next concert, which was to take place in Tarragona. One of my two pianos had been shipped a few days earlier from another city, leaving ample time, as I hoped, to arrive in Tarragona for the concert. I finally reached this city, after a long, tiring journey, on the morning of the concert. The president, vice-president, secretary, and treasurer of the Philharmonic Society were at the station to meet me.

"Is the piano here?" I inquired anxiously.

"Everything is in order," said the president. "We sent for the tuner from Barcelona, and the piano is on the stage ready for the concert this evening at seven-thirty. The hall will be full and everybody is looking forward with greatest pleasure. Now you come to the Club for lunch, then you go to the hotel to rest, and we will call for you this evening."

I was relieved and greatly cheered by this kindness and hospitality.

It did not occur to me to go to the theater, since nothing, apparently, had to be done; besides, I was too tired after my long journey to think of practicing for the concert. So after depositing my baggage at the hotel and removing some of the dust which had accumulated on me during the trip, I went with my friends to partake of a copious lunch at the Club, after which I returned to the hotel and slept soundly until the evening. I dressed and was driven to the theater, which was filled, as predicted, to the last seat. The curtain was down. I walked onto the stage to see that everything was in order. The piano was there. It was standing on its side in the packing case from which it had not been taken since its arrival three days before. Immediately a terrific commotion arose.

"What does this mean? Where is the tuner? Who said that everything was in order? How shall the piano be taken out of the box? Is there anyone here who can fix it? What is to be done?"

The president raised his hand to impose silence and said with dignity, "Clearly, there is only one thing to do. Señor Bauer, are you at liberty tomorrow evening?"

"I am," was my reply.

"Then," continued the president, "the curtain may be raised and I will explain the matter to the public."

And so he did. It transpired that the orders to take the piano out of the box and set it up had passed through so many hands that they finally went astray. The tuner, coming from Barcelona and finding the instrument boxed up, had made some fruitless efforts to deal with the situation and had finally gone home.

The public received the news of the postponement of the concert with good humor; the tuner returned the next day; and I played that evening. My time in the meanwhile was profitably spent in driving around Tarragona, certainly one of the most interesting cities in the world from the standpoint of archeology.

The following summer I spent several weeks at San Sebastian, where my old friend Enrique Fernandez Arbós was conductor of the symphony orchestra at the Casino. This was composed of the best elements of all the Spanish orchestras, musicians who appreciated the opportunity of playing under the direction of a distinguished artist as much as they did that of securing a good summer engagement at an attractive holiday resort. Daily concerts were given under the direction of the assistant conductor, and regular symphony concerts, at which I was soloist during my visit, took place twice a week, conducted by Arbós.

On Sundays, no concerts were given, for everyone went to see the bullfights. Having witnessed a "corrida" once in my life, I never attended these spectacles, and there was a standing arrangement between me and my friends that we should all meet on the Casino terrace at the hour of the apéritif, after the return from the arena. It was my usual practice to play the piano in the deserted concert auditorium at these times.

One fine Sunday afternoon, I sat on the terrace awaiting the return of my friends, and as they appeared, singly instead of in a group according to their custom, I was impressed by their gloomy looks. They were all silent, and they all seemed morose. It was clear that something had happened to upset them all. I waited for someone to speak, but nobody broke the melancholy silence. Finally I asked if anything was wrong.

"No, no, it is all right."

"But," I insisted, "why are you all so gloomy? Was the corrida a poor one? Did anything happen?"

One man heaved a deep sigh, got up and walked away.

"What is the matter with him?" I asked. "Why don't you say something?"

Another man leaned over the table, his face working with emotion.

"Friend," he said, "let us speak of something else. It is better to ask no questions."

This of course increased my curiosity, and I begged to be enlightened.

"Was somebody killed or hurt?" I inquired. "Why should you not tell me?"

A man who had not spoken before said solemnly:

"Let us tell him."

The first speaker drew a long breath and started.

"Today's corrida," he said, "was one of the finest ever witnessed here. The bulls were magnificent, the horses not too worn out and the whole troop splendid. At the last session they brought out a bull . . . What a bull! Madre de dios! What a superb animal!"

There was a chorus of assent, together with melancholy shakings of the head. The narrator then entered into certain technical details which, in my ignorance of the sport, I will not venture to transcribe here. He was describing the manner in which the bull is tantalized by the toreador, who twirls a red cape in front of his nose.

"Well, and then?" I asked rather impatiently.

The speaker looked at me with a lackluster eye.

"And then," he said heavily, "the bull . . ." he choked and was unable to proceed.

"The poor animal," said someone else, softly and solemnly, "made a rapid twist toward the toreador which caused it to slip, and it fell down. . . ."

There was a dead silence.

"Well?" I asked.

"Its leg was broken," said somebody, almost with a sob.

Another silence.

"And then?" I inquired.

"They killed it!" said several voices simultaneously, almost as if the speakers were glad to be able to terminate this dreadful tragedy.

I played frequently in Spain and also in Portugal prior to my tours with Casals. In Oporto, engaged for a recital by a musical club, I was greatly impressed by the personality of its president, a gentleman named Moreira de Sá, whose talents in many fields were truly remarkable. He was a mathematician and an authority on methods of education, and the primers he wrote were in use in most of the public schools of Portugal. He was a classical scholar and an excellent linguist, a gifted musician with an unquenchable thirst for knowledge, not only in his own especial activities but in all other subjects; finally, a merchant and the owner of a music store—the most important of the district—and to end, a delightful human being.

It was the custom at the music club which he headed to introduce the artist who gave the concert. This was done with a short complimentary speech, following which the president retired to the background and returned, preceding the performer but walking backward, applauding as he came. There was a large armchair in the middle of the stage, on which the president sat during the concert, accompanying the performer back and forth at each intermission. The auditorium, a large ballroom, had no greenroom for the artist, who was led to a seat of honor in the front row, while the public, discreetly disregarding his presence in their midst, kept their eyes fixed upon the stage and continued to applaud. My recital was considered a great success.

The following season Casals gave a recital in Oporto under the same auspices and was similarly honored. Moreira de Sá, knowing that we had played a great deal together, asked Casals to arrange with me to make a tour in Brazil under his direction. We agreed and in due course (the summer of 1903) set out for Rio de Janeiro, and gave a successful series of concerts there and in other Brazilian cities. Moreira de Sá played occasionally in a trio with us (he was a good violinist) but as a rule Casals and I gave the concerts by ourselves. Our European engagements compelled us to return in August, but before leaving, Casals and I arranged to return the following year for a more elaborate South American tour. One week before our departure from Rio, Moreira came to us with tears in his eyes. "My dear friends," he said, "I shall not be able to return to Lisbon with you. An important affair compels me to remain here until next month. Just imagine," he continued with enthusiasm, "the ambition of my life is to be fulfilled. I have always been anxious to learn the technique of Japanese lacquer, and I have found a man who has undertaken to teach it to me. I am sure you understand that I could not possibly forgo such an opportunity." A few days before that, our friend had shown me the notes he had prepared for a series of lectures on pragmatic philosophy to be delivered at the University on his return to Portugal. (He had, in fact, introduced me to the works of William James.) In relating this little incident, I feel that I have given the portrait of this unusual and gifted individual.

When Casals and I returned the year after to Rio, we met Ernest Schelling, who had come to South America on a tour with the celebrated dancer Loie Fuller. The tour had broken up, and Schelling was giving solo recitals wherever he could arrange them. It was not long before two camps headed by the musical critics were formed, one proclaiming the artistic superiority of Schelling, and the other that of Bauer. It was ridiculous but amusing. We decided to use this conflict of opinion to our mutual advantage, if possible; so, together with the great local musician Arthur Napoleao, a splendid pianist, we announced a monster concert to take place at the Opera House, an enormous building. There had never been such a musical event, and there never was such a program, in Rio or anywhere else.

We had engaged the entire Opera orchestra, and each of

us played and conducted alternately, using every possible combination of duet and trio throughout the evening. All the tickets were sold and it was, in a word, one of the greatest shows ever witnessed in the Brazilian music world. At a certain moment in Casals' performance of the St. Saëns Concerto, which I was conducting, loud voices and scuffling sounds were heard behind the scenes. I do not think this was particularly noticeable to the audience, but Casals and I exchanged glances, wondering what had happened.

After the piece was over, we found our friend Schelling with his clothes in disorder, reclining on a couch with his nose bleeding profusely into a basin held by one of the stage hands. "For heaven's sake, what has happened?" The explanation was simple. Two gentlemen of the press, one a "Schelling-ite" and the other a "Bauerite," had come to blows following a violent discussion. Ernest had bravely thrown himself between them and, as is quite usual in such cases, was the only one to receive any damage. I am glad to say that he recovered sufficiently to take part in the final piece, Bach's concerto for three pianos accompanied by Casals conducting the orchestra. We had a grand supper after the concert and did not get back to our hotel until the early hours of morning.

I had been given the responsibility of looking after the receipts of the concert—quite a large sum, which, in the form of very dirty banknotes, mostly of small denominations, had been crammed into a small suitcase. What to do with all that money? Everyone in the hotel had gone to bed, and it was impossible to get to a safe at that hour. Casals and I shared a small apartment of two rooms, and we decided there could be no risk in keeping it there until the time came for the bank to open, so we went to bed and slept soundly until nearly noon. Casals awoke me asking the time.

"I can't find my watch—where is yours?" We got out of bed lazily and found the room in disorder—everything strewn about and the door wide open. Good God! A burglar! The money! There was the suitcase with a shirt lying on top of it. It had not been opened, and the money was there, untouched. But our watches and purses were gone, studs removed from shirts and the cello case thrown wide open with the instrument, unharmed, on the floor. We raised an outcry, everyone came running, the police were summoned, and following investigation, two arrests were made. But nothing was proved and the incident was closed. We never knew what had happened, but Casals and I thought that the robber had watched us and, believing that we had this large sum of money, had made careful and elaborate plans to appropriate it. We also believed that he had succeeded in stupefying us with some drug or chemical when he entered our room, for we felt extremely sick the whole day. Of course, that might have been the effects of the wine we drank at supper!

Ernest Schelling and I became close friends as a result of that, our first meeting, and when chance brought us together again on the return voyage homeward, we thoroughly astonished the passengers by the magnificent duets we played upon any and every musical instrument obtainable on board the ship.

Our second South American trip was interesting but uneventful, and on the whole unprofitable. Our concerts were artistically successful and attracted people who were cultured, but the public at large did not take to us. We both enjoyed Montevideo more than Buenos Aires, which at that time presented the aspect of very superficial culture in the midst of great wealth. I hesitate to make this criticism, if only on account of the impression I received on visiting the palatial building of *La Prensa*, which, even then, was undoubtedly one of the greatest newspapers in the world; but I think that my feeling of the absence of substantial culture in that immense metropolis may have been due in great measure to the manner in which music was taught. There must have been fifty or more so-called Conservatories of Music in the city of Buenos Aires. I am sure that Casals and I visited over twenty of these establishments, every one of them showing unmistakable signs of success and prosperity. But as far as we could judge, the standards of education were of the lowest degree. Teaching was confined to a few easy pieces on the piano, the violin, the guitar, and the mandolin, and vocal study involved little more than the learning of a few Italian arias and some Spanish popular songs. Of fundamental training in musical art there seemed to be no trace. At the request of the editor of an English periodical published in Buenos Aires, I wrote an article before my departure which I entitled "Conservatropolis," referring with more irony than courtesy, I fear, to my musical impressions of the city. It was very stupid of me and doubtless proved one of the reasons why I never returned to the great city which has since become one of the most important centers of world civilization and culture. A lot of progress can be made in forty years.

On arriving in Lisbon—(what a relief it was to get off that stuffy cockroach-infested French liner!)—Casals and I were summoned to the royal palace ("palacio dos Necessidades," which seemed a curious name) and were informed by the Master of the Household, an amiable gentleman with a very gaudy uniform covered with decorations, that the Queen would like us to come to tea and to give an informal concert for her guests. The King, it appeared, was temporarily absent in England.

The aspect of the palace was shabby, and the general impression, emphasized by the carelessly indolent attitude of all the Palace guards, was one of formal untidiness. We sat chatting with the major-domo until our conversation was interrupted by a woman's voice coming from the adjoining room: "If you gentlemen have finished your cigarettes you might come and have a cup of tea!" It was the Queen herself, the lovely Amalia of Portugal, who, when I saw her, made me think that there might be something good in a monarchy after all if queens were as beautiful as they used to be in fairy tales. Alas! Queen Amalia was the only good-looking queen I ever saw. Some people said she was too tall, but I do not believe she stood over six feet three inches. Anyhow, she was not only beautiful, but extremely pleasant and friendly, and she handed round the cakes with her own royal hands. Casals and I played a great deal of music for which she asked by name, and had I only found a good piano there I am sure I should have enjoyed my visit very much. The large concert grand in the drawing room was unfortunately out of tune and so much in need of regulation that I had to use all my agility in lifting up the keys which stuck so as to prepare them for the next blow. I never saw such a grand-looking piano. It was an Erard, the case covered with paintings and bas-relief carvings brightly gilded in every possible way. Following the concert, the Queen presented me with the Order of Christ, saying that she wished me to remember my visit to the Court of Portugal. The recommendation was superfluous, for the visit was unlike any Court reception I ever attended in other courts of Europe. I saw the Queen only once again after that day. She came to a recital I gave in 1935 at the San Carlo Opera House in

Naples. The Court of Portugal no longer existed, and she was on a visit to the Queen of Italy.

Casals and I, having arranged to stay together until we reached Paris, then proceeded to Madrid, where we gave several very successful concerts. There, too, we were invited to play at the Court. This time, I knew two things in advance: first, that the concert was a really formal event, and second, that the piano at the palace was very old and worn. I made arrangements, in consequence, to have my concert piano taken from the theater to the palace. On the day of the concert I received a message from the local piano store telling me that I was not to worry. I went to the telephone. "Why should I not worry?" I said excitedly. "No, no, Señor," came the answer, "do not worry. It will be all right. I am at the theater in person." I went round to the Comedia theater immediately and there, issuing from the back door of the stage, was the strangest sight: my piano, hoisted on the shoulders of about twenty porters, looking for all the world like a gigantic coffin, but with three legs and the pedal lyre attached. The piano dealer rapidly explained that no regular piano movers were available, so this was the only way. "But the traffic—the palace doors," I gasped. "Do not worry, Señor, the police will conduct us and all the palace stairs and doors are of ample width." Sure enough, that was the way in which my piano came to the royal concert. And what is more, it went in at the front entrance; we, the humble musicians, were taken in by the back door.

The concert was full of incidents. King Alfonso was then a little boy, his mother, Maria Christina, being Queen Regent of Spain. Court etiquette was very rigid and the little boy was active and mischievous, constantly running about and occasionally causing considerable embarrassment. As the Queen Mother was talking with Casals, whose cello and bow were on the chair next to the piano, I saw with horror that the boy had taken up the bow and was running his fingers over the horsehair apparently amused by the stickiness of the rosin. I could do nothing and Casals was turning his back to the young King. At last the Queen Mother saw and said "Alfonso!" with some impatience. The boy dropped the bow on the floor and moved away. I heard Pablo give a frightened groan; but fortunately no harm was done, and after a good rubbing on the rosin box, the bow bit the string again.

The Queen wanted the entire program we had played at our concert the previous day, but as there was no special reason to follow the order of the pieces as printed, we played them exactly as selected by her Majesty. The first number, I recall, was Chopin's Nocturne in E-flat played by Casals, as usual, with inimitable refinement and expression. The next number was Beethoven's Appassionata Sonata, which the Queen asked me to play from the music, "in order," said her Majesty, "that I may sit next to the piano and follow the performance with the notes." "Yes," interjected the Infanta Isabella, sister-in-law of the Queen, "and I will turn the pages." Gracious heavens! What an awful experience that was for me! The two ladies, both short-sighted and holding lorgnettes to their eyes, crowded me so closely that I hardly had room to play. Nor was that all. They talked all the time. "How like Wagner!" said the Queen. "Yes, Ma'am," I said without stopping. "This reminds me of Chopin," said the Infanta, turning the page at the wrong place. "Yes, Ma'am," I said, continuing to play. And so it went to the end of the last movement, when both ladies bent over the keyboard so far that I had to play the final chords "tenuto" instead of short as is customary. I was glad when it was over.

It was a pleasure to return to Barcelona, where we had announced a series of concerts for cello and piano. Pablo's family lived there, and I was glad of the opportunity to see all the kind friends I had made on previous visits. Chief among these was the composer Enrique Granados, one of the most lovable men I have ever known. I enjoyed every moment that I ever spent with him, and I liked his music as much as I liked every one of his incalculably changeable moods, for he was melancholy or gay, serious or trivial, credulous or skeptical in turn, always humorous and sometimes completely irresponsible as, for example, when once dining at a restaurant with some less lively friends, he attempted to break down the formality of the occasion by balancing a fried sardine on the tip of his nose. And succeeded. Don't tell me that this was not funny. It would only prove that you cannot conceive the effect of this performance by the great artist, the refined, melancholy and witty gentleman who was Enrique Granados.

My affection for him and for many other musicians whose acquaintance I made during these years must not prevent me, however, from saying something of the close and loving friendship which had grown up between Pablo Casals and myself. We were comrades in the best and most complete sense of the term. Our tastes were similar in everything that pertained to daily life in the course of our numerous tours together, and there was never a dull moment. When we rehearsed works that we had never played before, the correspondence of our musical intuitions as regards matters of tempo and phrasing was so exact as to startle us both very frequently.

Because of this almost invariable resemblance in points of musical interpretation, two exceptions stand out vividly in my memory. We were reading through Brahms' F minor sonata for piano and cello for the first time, and as I started the second movement marked "allegro passionato," Casals said: "Why don't you play it in the proper tempo? That's much too slow!" I was surprised, and explained why, in my opinion, it should not be played any faster. Pablo looked over the piano part for several minutes in silence and finally said, with a gesture of impatience, "But of course! Let us begin again." I never saw him more vexed. His intuition had betrayed him for once. Most cellists have yielded to the aspect of the page in this movement, which at first glance suggests a rapid tempo and a light bow. Casals never allows the bow to leave the string during the initial phrase, and rapidity of tempo is confined to the motion between the middle and the point of the bow, used for each individual note. The effect of this is truly impassioned and impresses the listener in a manner which few artists aside from Casals have ever been able to achieve.

The other example of our failure to correspond in tempo was due to a little stage fright which overcame me on one occasion of performing Brahms' G minor quartet. I started the theme much too fast, but realized what I had done before I had played two measures. It was too late to make a sudden change, and I could only hope that the tempo would imperceptibly adjust itself in the course of the performance. To my utter consternation, Pablo, entering with the same theme on the ninth bar, took the true tempo without the slightest compromise. The effect was awful. I could hardly believe my ears. That Pablo should do this to *me*, exposing my weakness in public! It seemed incredible. At the end of the first movement, when we all arose to bow, I looked at him with fury; I could have murdered him. He looked at me with an expression I could not fathom and slightly shook his head. The rest of the composition went well and the public applauded with enthusiasm.

As soon as we reached the artists' room, Pablo threw his arms around me and there were tears in his eyes. "Forgive me, Harold," he said, "I tried to follow you, *but I could not. C'était plus fort que moi.* My fingers and my bow would not respond at that tempo." What he said was, I knew, the absolute truth. His perfect integrity, no less pure in his human relations than in his art, did not admit of the slightest compromise. Like Martin Luther, he could do no other than obey the dictates of his conscience, and it is that that has made him the unique artist, beloved and admired equally by his colleagues and the public.

Apart from these two exceptions, our sense of tempo was, as I have said, strangely identical. We invented a little parlor trick with which we mystified our friends. Standing opposite each other, one of us would announce, after a few seconds, the name of a playing card which had been privately communicated to the other by one of the spectators. We pretended this was telepathy, but it was nothing of the kind. We simply counted mentally the beats of any composition on which we had previously agreed. Four slightly different positions of the feet indicated hearts, diamonds, spades, and clubs respectively, and the counting started at the instant of taking one of these positions. Counting stopped at any prearranged signal, imperceptible to the audience. Try it yourself and see how you come out with the king of spades, for instance. Possibly you may find it easy, in which case your ensemble playing will be just as good as ours was.

Apart from mere accuracy in matters of tempo, our ideas of ensemble playing differed, however, in certain respects, from generally accepted principles. It seemed to us unnecessary, and in most cases undesirable, in the interpretation of a sonata, to give the impression of a single performer playing on both instruments. This was, nevertheless, usually regarded as the ideal result to work for. Instead, our rehearsals were directed toward the preservation of our respective personalities to the full extent practicable within the limits of a musical conception of the work as a whole which we shared in common. The result was a kind of dialogue between two performers, in complete agreement as to tempo, dynamics, and rhythm, but differing in accordance with their individual temperament in the more subtle details of phrasing.

It is my belief that the variety thus obtained was the prime cause of the artistic success of the many concerts we gave together over a period of nearly twenty years. However, such is the perversity of human nature (dare I say, that of professional music critics in particular?) that we were generally praised for doing the very thing which we had taken the greatest pains to avoid: "They play as one," was the usual verdict.

Two methods of ensemble playing have always existed: the first involving a submersion of each performer's individuality in order to reach an ideal unity, and the second, something which might be called the "conversational" method, as above described. It would be folly to assert that one of these methods is good and the other bad. Pablo and I had our preference, and a certain kind of performance was the result. Although it was definitely understood that no attempt was to be made to make piano passages sound like cello passages, or vice versa, there were many times when I longed unspeakably for the power to reproduce on the piano that inimitable tone of his, and it was a poor consolation to tell myself that the nature of my instrument totally precluded anything of the sort.

This much I gained, however, from my constant efforts to give emotional significance to my tone: the understanding that a single note on the piano, unlike a tone produced by the voice or by any other instrument, has no aesthetic value whatsoever. It may be loud, soft, long, or short, but no one of these characteristics is beautiful in itself, nor can it create an effect of beauty except through contrast. In a word, I found that the unit of musical expression on the piano must be sought in the relation of one tone to its neighbor and that no conception of tonal beauty applied to the keyboard instrument could have any meaning unless based upon this very simple fact. Again and again, scientists have come forward with the clearest demonstration of this elementary principle in which acoustics, physics, and aesthetics are equally bound up, but as a general rule the facts have been denied and the conclusions opposed by pianists, great and small. Yet it needs no extraordinary power of discernment to perceive that a single tone produced by someone who has never before touched a piano is in no sense less "beautiful" than a single tone produced by the greatest pianist in the world.

I do not for one moment suggest that it is essential to be aware of this fundamental difference between the piano and other instruments in order to be an accomplished pianist. I merely say that it was of considerable value to me, since, having no traditional rules as a background for my study, anything upon which I could build a formula was most welcome.

Six

ON MY RETURN TO PARIS, I RECEIVED AN INVITATION FROM THE distinguished composer Gabriel Fauré to serve as a member of the jury at the public examinations held annually at the Conservatoire, of which he was the Director. I felt deeply honored by this invitation and accepted it at once. These yearly events took place in the concert hall of the Conservatoire and were eagerly anticipated by the Parisian public, who clamored for admission tickets (which were not for sale) long before the dates were announced sometime in June. Members of the examining boards, known as the jury, were selected from among the best-known artists, resident or otherwise, and invited personally by the Director, who presided over the examinations and subsequent deliberations. Separate juries were appointed for each of the following divisions: composition, organ, wind instruments, stringed instruments, voice, piano, harp, and finally, the art of acting. I believe it is not generally realized abroad that the Conservatoire, whose full title is "Conservatoire National de

Musique et de Déclamation," is as much concerned with the drama as with music, practically every French actor having been a pupil at some time of the great national institution.

Public interest in the annual examinations was naturally intense, if only for the reason that tuition at this state-supported institution was entirely free and the taxpayer was curious to see if his money was serving the purpose of producing performers and composers of distinction.

In the course of time, the concert hall of the Conservatoire proved too small to accommodate the crowds who wished to see and hear all the young performers, and the examinations were transferred in consequence to the theater of the Opéra Comique. Very frequently the public disagreed with the verdict of the jury and showed its displeasure in such violent fashion that on more than one occasion I have seen it necessary to summon the police in order to protect members of the jury from actual physical assault when, at the end of an exhausting day, they left the building. I use the word "exhausting" advisedly.

Berlioz gives, in his memoirs, a vivid picture of one of these piano examinations when, after listening to the same Bach Prelude and Fugue played thirty-seven times by thirty-seven pupils, the members of the jury staggered out of the hall, completely worn out, into the adjoining room for deliberation, only to realize that a thirty-eighth candidate had apparently been overlooked, for the Prelude had started again. Everyone rushed back to the empty hall, where, to the general amazement, the piano was playing by itself. "This must be stopped," said Monsieur le Directeur. Yes, but how? Finally, the only solution was to take the piano into the courtyard of the Conservatoire and chop it into pieces with axes, on which the separate notes of the Bach

Prelude and Fugue flew out and were dispersed amid the surrounding roofs and chimneys.

The Conservatoire was so conservative that all old traditions had to be preserved at any cost. The boys and girls were heard separately. They never took part in the same examinations, nor did they have the same teachers. All the boys played the same piece, selected for them six weeks in advance of the contest, and all the girls played another piece, similarly selected. The average number of candidates was between twenty and thirty, but sometimes there were more.

After all the pupils in succession had performed the prescribed compositions before jury and public, they were locked up in a large room some distance away. The sight-reading test was to follow, and none of them could be permitted to hear a single note of the manuscript piece, written especially for the occasion, which awaited them on the piano desk. One by one they were released from the locked room and brought back to the stage for this test. It was curious and sometimes pathetic to observe the manner in which they approached the task. A few of them came up quite jauntily, confident of their ability to make a good showing. Others, on the contrary, were hesitant and nervous, walking as slowly as possible toward the piano, their eyes protruding, and obviously hoping to get some idea of the music at a distance before sitting down to the instrument. For these uneasy ones, anything that could serve to delay the actual moment of starting to read was resorted to, some of the devices being so ingenuously transparent as to cause laughter, which was sternly repressed by the little bell agitated by the director. The piano stool was too high or too low, the music rack was too close or too far away, those who wore eyeglasses had to wipe them, collars or sleeves had to be pulled up or pulled down. The sight of all these manipulations, with the eyes

of the unhappy pupil glued to the manuscript to be deci-
phered, was irresistibly comical, yet pathetic as well, for so
much depended upon the result. It should be said that the
average ability for sight-reading was very high at the Conservatoire, thanks to the intensive training given in solfège.

Teachers at the Conservatoire were appointed either to the
class of girls or to the class of boys. They never taught both
sexes, although they were free to do what they liked outside
the institution. It seems strange to realize that such a man as
my old friend Isidor Philipp should have been known in
Paris as "professeur de piano (femmes)" at the Conservatoire, whereas he was equally famous all over the world as a
teacher of men. Another of the rigid and unchangeable traditions of the Conservatoire was the practice of grouping harpists and pianists for examination by the same jury. This occasionally caused some confusion, for the pianists knew
nothing of the technique of the harp, while on the other
hand the repertoire of the piano was practically a closed
book to most harpists, whose studies had been primarily
directed toward obtaining a position in a symphony orchestra or an opera house. By way of illustration of the difficulty
confronting this mixed jury, I may mention the case of a
young harpist whose performance was praised by every member except one, a pianist, who asserted that the performer
"used the pedals to excess."

The verdict given by the jury, entitling the candidate to
one of four awards—namely, first or second diploma (accessit) or first or second prize—was in any event arrived at
only after the most serious deliberation. When I recall the
fact that the award of a "premier prix" to a young man, in
those days, relieved him of an entire year of military service
(reduced from three years to two years) I can hardly imagine how any one of us could have had the heart to send

any pupil away from the Conservatoire without this distinction. Horrid visions of talented young musicians in military uniform used to pursue me. Their eyes seemed to say reproachfully, "But for your vote, I might now be a successful concert pianist!"

It was a relief when the term of compulsory military service was reduced by the government from three to two years for everyone, no exception being made for winners of first prizes at the Conservatoire.

Following my first experience, I was regularly invited each year to serve on the Conservatoire jury, and I continued to do this during the entire time of my residence in Paris. This brought me the friendship not only of Fauré but of his successor, Henri Rabaud (who, years later, came to America to conduct the Boston Symphony Orchestra for one season), and of many other distinguished musicians.

One hot summer's day (the examination always took place in June) I found myself in the jury box sitting between Moritz Rosenthal and Vassily Safonoff. We had to listen to over thirty performances of Chopin's A-flat Ballade played by perspiring and nervous students. Relief came at noon after hearing about one-half the number, and we all went out as usual to lunch. Safonoff turned to me and said, "Can you do this?" moving the fingers of his right hand in a peculiar manner which showed unusual muscular control. My effort to imitate him failed completely, and he then stated sententiously but humorously that nobody who could not make those motions had any title to consideration as a pianist. "Ask Rosenthal if he can do it," I suggested. "Nonsense," said Rosenthal, "that has nothing to do with piano playing." But he could not force his fingers to move in that independent manner, and the annoyance this caused him totally spoiled his lunch. We returned to the opera house;

it was hotter than ever, and Safonoff dozed off after the seventeenth performance of the Ballade. The eighteenth student appeared and started the Ballade. Rosenthal, who had not said a word since we had returned from lunch, suddenly whispered in my ear: "Tell Safonoff one hundred and twenty-six with my compliments." I delivered the message. Safonoff, now wide awake, whispered back. "What on earth does he mean?" Rosenthal, who had been busily scribbling in the meanwhile, passed me the paper and looked off into space. He had written the following: "Does his High Excellence Mr. Safonoff consider that a man who is unable to recognize the tempo of a performance by its metronome equivalent is competent to direct a symphony orchestra? Does he know, or does he not know, that the tempo we have just listened to is much too fast?"

There were plenty of other incidents at these Conservatoire examinations. It was pathetic as well as dramatic to see one of the candidates (an American boy, by the way) fall from the piano chair in a dead faint from sheer stage fright before he had even begun to play. He was carried off the stage, automatically eliminated, of course, from the contest, which proceeded without him. Toward the close of the day he sent a humble message to the Director, begging respectfully to be permitted to play after the other students had taken their turn. The Director, finding no precedent for such an irregular procedure, submitted the matter to the jury, who voted unanimously in favor of giving the boy his chance. None of us expected very much from him, however, and we were all tired out when he appeared. Sensation! He played better than anyone else and his sight-reading was also better. He was given a first prize amid the acclamation of the public. The happy ending of the story is that he returned to the United States, where he was engaged as head teacher in an important college, a position he still occupies with honor.

Before leaving the Conservatoire I must not fail to mention a colorless and insignificant personage named Moreau, whose duty it was to announce the names of the candidates as they appeared in turn on the stage for their examinations. Many of the pupils were quite sick from stage fright, and indeed it was a terrific ordeal. Moreau, after announcing the name, returned backstage and held the door open for the advancing candidate. He was kindly but firm, and the pupils looked upon him as a sort of benevolent executioner. All the girls kissed him and all the boys solemnly shook hands with him before marching on to the stage. It was hoped that this would bring good luck. When I was invited some years later to play with the Conservatoire orchestra and found myself following in the footsteps of all the young people who, for over a century, had trod those venerable boards with their hearts bursting with anxiety and ambition—when I thought of all the great ones who had crossed that threshold in the pride and fullness of their glorious career—I had a moment of indescribable panic and anguish. Moreau was there, holding the door for me to enter. I stiffened myself and said with a wry smile: "Moreau, do you expect me to kiss you?" He bowed gravely and replied: "Monsieur, cela n'a jamais fait du mal à personne." (It never did anyone any harm.)
I did not kiss him. Silently, I walked out on the stage.

I have often wondered what the net effects of the Conservatoire method of education were on French musical culture. It was very thorough. It was tremendously serious. It exacted from the students a terrific amount of application and industry. Given the ability to pass the entrance examinations, the final result seemed almost a foregone conclusion.

Every student, even those whose modest gifts could not carry them beyond the "deuxième accessit" with which they were discharged, acquired a solid technical foundation, an ability to read music properly, and a certain kind of understanding of the principles of composition. The students cultivated reverence for the art of music, and they certainly enjoyed music. What was it then that seemed rather rigid and rather dry in the whole thing? What was it that gave the impression that really great talent bloomed and developed not because of the training it received at the great institution but almost in spite of this training? What gave rise to the feeling that original artistic impulse was stifled rather than encouraged, and that aesthetic judgment was considered good only when based upon standards of the past, which to some were not merely outmoded but quite obsolete? To say that the Conservatoire had failed on many occasions to recognize true genius was no refutation of the undoubted fact that the majority of great French musicians —composers as well as performers—and great French actors had received their training at their national conservatory. There was something—what the French call a "je ne sais quoi"—in this strictly academic education which   their productions and their performances in such un   k-able fashion that the listener can assert without possibility of error that "this is French."

But, says the captious critic, is this enough? Where is the aesthetic thrill, the life substance, the irresistible creative urge? Perhaps we have to look elsewhere for the reply.

Let us say first that the above-mentioned stamp of nationalism surely means something quite important. To some, indeed, nationalism in art is a *sine qua non*, the equivalent of a holy patriotism, lacking which, a composer is anathema:

"For him no minstrel raptures swell,"

and he may well die

"unwept, unhonored, and unsung."

It is undoubtedly true that many great artists have found in the love of their native land the source of their inspiration and power of invention. It is also true that other great artists have not displayed in their works any evidence of the derivation of the creative spirit from this source.

A dispassionate critic is scarcely likely to do much more than attach a label to those works where strongly national characteristics have made themselves felt. Not much more, but perhaps a little more. If these national characteristics can be known to contain elements that are universally recognized as worthy and desirable in themselves, the impulse to translate and project them into art forms will receive special praise.

It would lead me too far to offer instances of this process, nor do I consider myself competent to analyze and discuss it fully. Let it suffice to say that certain characteristics of French nationalism are carefully cultivated in the musical education of that country, and these characteristics, universally appreciated for their intrinsic value, are to be found in the work of French artists.

What are they?

The reply is: clarity, elegance, proportion, logic. To these we may add such factors as fluency, wit (in the French sense of "esprit") and, above all, order.

The whole world will agree that these are all intrinsically

valuable and desirable. They are more apparent in French national culture than in the culture of other European countries.

It would not be difficult to show that each of these characteristics may contain seeds of weakness and that the nation, taken as a whole, may display "les défauts de ses qualités." It is possible that clarity may sometimes be opposed to imagination, that elegance may be antagonistic to sincerity, that academic canons of proportion may be cited to defeat the advancement of learning. Fluency may easily become triviality, wit may prove destructive of emotional depth, and, while we all admit the essential need for order, it is obvious that a desire to have everything in its proper place may easily degenerate into futile fussiness.

Originality, profundity of conception, and independence of ideas are unlikely to flourish to the best advantage in an academic environment, unless the possessor of these qualities is an individual of unusual power. On the other hand, nothing more favorable than strict academic training could be devised for the purpose of developing to the fullest extent the capacities of an earnest, docile, intelligent, and totally untalented student.

If, therefore, we find in France evidences of preponderance of skill over original artistic talent, we should first, I think, attribute this to the insistence on technical proficiency which stems from French academic tradition; and second, we should guard against the conclusion that superior genius has been stifled in the process. It is surely a truism to say that France has produced just as many great artists as any other country. It may be that she has also produced more mediocre artists than any other country, and it would not be unfair to suggest that this may be due to national educational methods. In any event the mediocrities are what one might call first-rate second-raters, the kind of individuals who, though unfitted for positions of distinction, play their part in maintaining the general level of musical culture.

To the best of my belief, every one of the French musicians I knew in Paris had been educated at the Conservatoire. There were many foreign-born Conservatoire students too, and some of these rose to positions of great honor, even in the Conservatoire itself. My circle of acquaintances was large, and I made no attempt to discriminate between genius and mediocrity, for everyone seemed extraordinarily gifted besides being musically educated in a manner of which I had had no previous conception. I refer now to the amazing facility that came as a result of intensive study of solfège and also to the fact that all these people, whatever their main subject—with the exception, naturally, of singers—seemed to possess a good technique for composition and instrumentation and were perfectly competent to conduct an orchestra.

I repeat that I made no effort to evaluate their respective talents. Had I done so, my judgment, immature though it was, could hardly have shown less perspicacity than they showed themselves in criticizing each other. I was filled with amazement and admiration for the incredible speed with which an apparently penetrating analysis of a composer's talent was made, exposing with cruel humor every weak point. Favorable verdicts were delivered with equal rapidity and, I should like to add, with equal frequency, for there seemed to be no lack of the capacity for appreciation of another's work.

But the sum total of this kind of snap judgment was zero. It was impulsive, biased, and worthless. And this kind of impulsive, temperamental partiality being generally recognized for what it was, it was only rarely that criticism did any permanent damage to the thing criticized.

Still, the absence of definite standards of artistic value in these circles was sufficiently serious to cast a certain doubt upon an educational system which seemed so precise and exact and yet afforded no guidance to the determination of such values. Looking back, I can now see how often the artists, the public, and the critics were hoodwinked and deceived by sheer charlantanry and imposture. Nor was this imposture confined to the world of music alone. The art of painting lent itself even more freely to shams, practical jokes, and swindles. Who, living in Paris at that period, can ever forget the colossal hoax that was perpetrated on the public, the connoisseurs, and the amateurs of art at the so-called "Salon des Indépendants"?

A manifesto signed by the name "Boronali" appeared in one of the principal daily papers, stressing in high-flown terms what is now known as "abstraction"—namely, the elimination of representational procedures. Attention was particularly called to a picture then exhibited at the Salon des Indépendants, the work of the writer himself. The public, always in search of new sensations, was impressed by the article, which was rapidly circulated through Paris, causing comment in all circles. Naturally, everyone went to see the picture. Some observers, frankly bewildered, confessed their total inability to understand it. The prevailing verdict, however, was that it showed striking originality and talent, and there were not lacking those who unhesitatingly used the word "genius." It was the rage of the season. Finally the exhibition was closed—and shortly afterward came the exposé.

This took the form of a "procès verbal" drawn up by a "huissier," (one of the public officials of the French law courts), which, in dry legal terms, set forth the account some-what as follows:

On such and such a date we were summoned to the studio of Monsieur X, artist painter, and were then requested to take note of the facts, deeds, and occurrences herein related. Primo: The aforesaid studio is located on the ground floor and gives onto a small garden. Secundo: Our attention was drawn to an artist's easel with a clean white canvas stretched over it. In front of the easel a kind of wooden structure resembling the shafts of a cart mounted on upright posts had been erected, and was solidly nailed to the floor.

Monsieur X then exhibited various large-sized containers of paint of various colors. He then proceeded to open the door to the garden and led into the studio an animal, to wit, a small donkey. "This is my friend Aliboron," he said. "Aliboron is a great artist and is going to paint a picture for us." With that, Monsieur Aliboron was backed into position between the shafts and attached thereto by means of leather straps.

"Bear witness, Monsieur l'huissier," Monsieur X proclaimed, "these colors will be mixed and applied by no other than the artist Aliboron. No human hand will be employed in the composition of the picture."

He then produced several vegetables, namely, four large carrots, a small cabbage and two turnips, together with one apple. First, a carrot was offered to Aliboron, who, eagerly accepting it, communicated motions to his caudal appendage, namely, his tail, thereby dipping it into the pails of paint and splashing the contents thereof onto the white canvas. Following this, an additional course of turnips, cabbage, and apple was presented to Monsieur Aliboron; and after close inspection, Monsieur X declared himself satisfied with the result. Aliboron was then reconducted to the garden.

"Now, Monsieur l'huissier," said Monsieur X, "you will kindly affix your official seal to this box wherein, as you see, I am enclosing the picture. After delivery to the exhibition, I shall again request your attendance in order to break the seal. You will then furnish me with a procès verbal, testifying to the fact that the painting you have seen here manufactured and the painting there displayed are one and the same."

We hereby do so, and in witness thereof, we attach our signature.

I presume it is superfluous to remind the reader that the name "Boronali" is nothing more than an anagram of "Aliboron"—Neddy the Jackass, of La Fontaine's fables.

Not very long after this exposure, which set all Paris agog, I was at a concert given by the "Société Musicale Indépendante," an organization devoted to public presentation of the works of contemporary composers. Theodor Szanto played some piano pieces alleged to have been written by one Zoltan Kodaly, whose name was entirely unknown to me. The music seemed incomprehensible and tedious. "It bores me stiff," said Chevillard, who was sitting next to me (only he used a picturesque and untranslatable French obscenity). "Farceur!" (humbug), somebody remarked, very loudly. "Raseur!" came a voice from another quarter. Several people yawned ostentatiously and some laughed. The performance was not a success.

After the concert, a number of us walked over to the café to discuss the whole affair. On the whole, we were calm and I cannot imagine why we got so excited when Kodaly's name came up. "Miserable rubbish!"—"Any Conservatoire pupil could do better."—"Why does Szanto play such stuff?"—"Why does the Société allow it to be played?"—and so forth and so on. "Wait a minute," said Florent Schmitt, than who there was no more ardent champion of modern musical idiom. "There is something in this music, I assure you." A storm of jeers greeted his statement. "Of course you would say that."—"Listen to the prophet!"—"Kind of a Schönbergist, so *this* makes you feel at home, n'est ce pas?"—"C'est entendu" (agreed), shouted someone else, "there is something in it, but what? Cela pue singulièrement." (It stinks strangely.)

It seemed to me that I was the only one who knew the answer to it all. "Listen to me, you others," I said. "Apparently none of you have divined the truth. If Szanto were here, I would force him to confess that he wrote this silly stuff himself as a hoax. There is no such person as Kodaly." A momentary silence fell over the group. Then: "What is this?"—"How do you know?"—"After all . . . the reputation of the Société."—I interrupted them. "Have you all forgotten Boronali?" I roared. "Can't you see that it is exactly the same kind of hoax? The name is enough to give away the whole thing. It is once again the tail of the donkey that is responsible for this musical 'masterpiece.' 'Koda,' or 'cauda' is Latin for 'tail,' isn't it? And 'ali' only has to be jointed to 'boron' to complete the name: KODALY-BORON. It is clear as good morning."

Florent Schmitt was the only person who did not laugh. He shook his head gravely, saying: "You are all mistaken. Kodaly is a real person and he lives in Budapest. I assure you he is a sincere musician of great talent."

The party broke up hilariously. At the end, we neither knew nor cared anything about Kodaly or the other composers whose works we had heard. We were all full of beer and hard-boiled eggs, and the whole world of music lay before us. It was not until years later that we realized the value of the distinguished Hungarian composer.

I suppose the foregoing was written with the idea of proving that there was something unsound in French educational methods, which, so often, gave the impression that brilliancy of execution was considered equal if not superior in value to depth of understanding, thereby creating the habit of forming superficial judgments. I am aware that I have proved nothing beyond the fact that my own mind, principally occupied in balancing one opinion against another, very seldom reached any conclusion at all. Hence my continual digressions. How useless it was, after all, to expect people to have the same likes and dislikes. The brilliant mediocrities I knew sometimes agreed and sometimes disagreed with the masters—and why not? The masters seldom agreed with each other. For example: St. Saëns considered César Franck a second-rate musician, but d'Indy did not think so. Fauré disliked the compositions of Brahms and so, for that matter, did many other French composers, but Brahms was nevertheless acknowledged to be a master "worthy to stand beside Widor," who, unquestionably, was a very great musician but whose works, today, appear unlikely to survive.

Perhaps one of the reasons that we all love Paris so much is precisely the difference of opinion that we hear expressed so forcibly on every hand. This undoubtedly adds vivacity and interest to Parisian life.

I was not alone in my feeling that there was too much rigidity in the Conservatoire. Vincent d'Indy, founder of the "Schola Cantorum" and one of the very greatest of French musicians, broke away from the Conservatoire as a young man and, after fruitless efforts, directed by the French government, to reorganize the great national institution, established and directed the "Ecole Supérieure de Musique," proclaiming his aim to produce artists rather than virtuosos.

The great pianist Alfred Cortôt, also a product of the Conservatoire, established the "Ecole Normale de Musique," in association with Jacques Thibaud and several others, all former Conservatoire pupils. Like the "Ecole Supérieure de Musique," this school was intended to progress beyond the academic and conservative methods of the older institution.

Before relinquishing all memories of public gullibility, I must relate one more instance. This, too, originated in a newspaper article. One morning, the first page of the Paris *Figaro* (where editorials were usually to be found) was given over to an article headed by the words: "Consider the Ant." The writer described in amusing and pseudo-scientific language the habits of the insect, laying particular stress on two factors—namely, its gregarious instinct and the extraordinary strength, relative to its size, that it possessed. The conclusion drawn was that since the social life of human beings was so complex, we should take example from the ant and build up our strength in order to withstand the constant strain to which we are subjected. Whence does the strength of the ant proceed? From formic acid, replies science (at least the science quoted by the writer). Then by all means let us absorb formic acid until, like the ant, we become able to carry weights ten times our own, or even more.

Everyone read the article and, apparently, everyone immediately went insane and began to ask for formic acid.

Trade, chemistry, and industry were not slow to reply. The first thing to appear, I believe, was formic acid soap. This was followed by toilet preparations of all sorts, hair tonics, perfumes, powders, and cosmetics, all containing formic acid. The hairdressers did not even have to use the words. After a haircut, shave, or shampoo the barber would merely inquire: "With or without, Monsieur?" The penetrating but not disagreeable odor was everywhere, and all kinds of healing qualities were attributed to the stuff. Formic acid cough drops, formic acid digestive tablets, formic acid pain-killing tablets abounded. It was a stimulant, a germicide, a tonic, and, needless to say, an aphrodisiac. Everyone who wished to retain and develop strength, health, and vitality should use formic acid every day, so ran the gossip. Physicians were implored to prescribe it and to have it introduced into every kind of medicine. Perhaps they did.

The craze lasted for nearly a year and then disappeared completely.

It is far from my intention to suggest that these two instances of popular credulity could have taken place only in France. In our own country we have had innumerable examples of freaks of taste which have come and gone, nobody can say exactly why or how.

Today the prevailing fad is vitamins, yesterday it was appendicitis operations, Paderewski's minuet, or the ouija board. These popular waves have no necessary connection with either true or false values, and in the final analysis it makes no difference whether they are pleasing or the reverse. Some of us submit to them without a struggle, while others, particularly those of the Latin race, make a virtue of necessity and are apt to be most vociferous in proclaiming the glory of the force which momentarily overwhelms them. Most curious is the manner in which waves of taste seem to originate in musical circles, causing involuntary and sometimes embarrassing duplications of programs. It will happen that a soloist or a conductor will select unfamiliar compositions for his program, only to discover that several of his colleagues have done the same thing and have announced the same works. Some people may conclude that this is done purposely, in a spirit of rivalry, but it is far more probable that the coincidence is quite accidental, although both strange and annoying. What are these "waves"?

Seven

MY PLEASANT AND LIFELONG ACQUAINTANCE WITH ISAAC
Albeniz dates from our meeting on the jury at one of the
Conservatoire examinations. This gifted and original musi-
cian, before devoting himself exclusively to composition,
had been a fine concert pianist admired in every capital of
Europe.

His early piano pieces, without revealing great musical
depth, are full of charm, and a pleasure to play because of
the fluent and brilliant character of the passage work, in
which the composer's complete mastery of the keyboard
is never allowed to obscure the musical lines of the composition by the employment of excessively difficult technical
devices.

This, unfortunately, is not the case with many of his
later works. One evening, after I had been dining at his
house, Albeniz produced a manuscript just finished, sat
down to the piano and played me the first two numbers of
the suite which later received the title of "Iberia." I was

delighted with this enchanting music, which I have since played frequently in my concerts. Then he turned to the third number, "Fête-dieu à Seville," with the words: "You know, mon cher, that I am no longer a pianist. This will be easy enough for you, but my technique has left me. I can only give you an idea of the music." He started the piece, and all was well for the first two pages. When he came to the more complex and difficult parts I was literally aghast. He seemed to have forgotten entirely the technical limitations of the piano, and the manuscript was cluttered up with passages that were absolutely unplayable. In his excitement, that was not of the slightest consequence, and he went through the piece howling out the theme—I was going to say, like a madman, but what I mean is: like a composer— and making the wildest leaps with his hands over the keyboard in the effort to give something approaching the impossible technical passages he had written.

The serene and poetic ending of the piece enabled him to get back his breath, and at the close he turned to me with a smile: "Eh bien, mon ami, what do you say?"

I hesitated a moment and then said gloomily, "The music is beautiful, but nobody will ever be able to play it."

The smile faded away and for a moment he looked at me in silence. Then he burst into hearty laughter: "What nonsense are you talking! It will be child's play for you or any pianist who will take *that* much trouble," he said, squinting at the tips of his forefinger and thumb tightly pressed together in the characteristic Latin gesture, "and if the music is good enough, it will be played! Come, let us drink another glass of wine—and please! don't annoy me with these follies."

I wish that he had been right, and I wrong, but unhappily that was not the case. This beautiful music is seldom played

—because it is too difficult. Pianists are not lacking who have sufficient technical ability to overcome the awkward and complex passage work in most of the "Iberia" pieces, but it is very doubtful if the necessary accuracy can be achieved without sacrificing the exquisite and nonchalant freedom of this charming music in which Albeniz is revealed as the most romantic of Spanish composers.

I knew many members of the American colony in Paris, and I also had a number of pupils who came from the United States to study with me. Americans in those days generally thought that a proper musical education was obtainable only in Europe, and the average European was inclined to speak in derogatory terms of America whenever culture was mentioned. "How should those people know anything about art? They have no history!" was the usual way of putting the matter. This attitude was frequently imitated by American citizens who had taken up their residence in various European cities and who thought fit to apologize for what they called the crudeness of their native land. No particular harm was done, but it seemed unfair to disparage the country which continued to supply them with the means of living abroad, and I sometimes had the impression that this seeming absence of patriotic feeling created a kind of barrier between them and the Parisian, who carries Paris with him wherever he goes.

My recitals in Paris were invariably crowded. After one of them, I was surprised and delighted to see Moszkowski appear in the greenroom. We had not met since I went to his home in Berlin.

"What a pleasure to see you in Paris!" I said.

"Is this really Paris?" was his answer. "I have heard so

much English spoken this evening that I thought I must be in Switzerland!"

I never knew anyone with a readier wit. As a young man he had achieved immortality as a humorist through a line he wrote in a lady's album. Hans von Bülow had just signed his name to the following rather pompous pronouncement: "Bach, Beethoven, Brahms! Tous les autres sont des crétins." (All others are idiots.) Moszkowski wrote: "Mendelssohn, Meyerbeer, and your humble servant: Moritz Moszkowski. Tous les autres sont des chrétiens." (Christians)

The witticism is a fine example of delicate humor which inflicts no wounds on anyone. I used to marvel how he could keep poison out of his humor, for it seemed impossible for anyone else to be witty without being malicious. But such was the nature of Moritz Moszkowski. When I last saw my friend, he was on his deathbed, in no pain but terribly weak, and it was plain that the end was not far off. Knowing him to be profoundly philosophical in his attitude toward life, I was painfully distressed and surprised to find him filled with grief and despondency—inconsolable.

"This war," he said despairingly, "is the end of everything!"

I tried to cheer him up.

"Do not be so despondent, dear friend," I said; "after all, the war is over."

He half rose in his bed and clutched my hand.

"The war is over. C'est entendu. Very well. But, mon cher, *peace has broken out!*" (La paix a éclaté.) "And nobody will ever see the end of this 'Peace'!" Was he a true prophet? Who shall say?

This was toward the end of the year 1922, and, contrary to all expectations, our dear friend lingered on, miserably, for over two years. His financial resources were exhausted, and a number of us joined forces in giving a concert for his benefit in New York. The proceeds (nearly $10,000) were remitted to him, but at the beginning of 1925 nothing was left; he was once again in desperate straits. We arranged a second monster benefit, which this time took place at the Metropolitan Opera House. Instead of sending the money, we made arrangements to convert it into an annuity payable through a life insurance company.

He died before the first payment was made, and the insurance company, although in no way legally obligated, assumed charge of the funeral expenses.

I played a great deal in those days and visited many different countries. Although I was in demand as a solo performer, I always thought it more interesting to give concerts with someone else, and whenever possible, I shared the program with a violinist, a cellist, a string quartet, or even a vocalist, provided the singer possessed some musical qualities. (I particularly enjoyed the concerts I gave with the singers Marie Brema, Jeanne Raunay, and Blanche Marchesi.) In addition to this I had numerous engagements to play with orchestra.

I made my début in Vienna at one of the Philharmonic concerts conducted by Hans Richter, who had shown a kindly interest in me since I was a boy. At his request, I played Liszt's E-flat concerto. I did not realize at the time what tremendous importance he attached to Liszt's music, although of course I was aware of his close connection with Wagner, in whose development Liszt had played so great a part. Incidentally, I recall visiting Richter at his home in Vienna and being received by him in a loose dressing gown, so ragged and dirty that I was quite shocked. "I notice your looks, young man," he said. "Learn that this dressing gown was worn by Richard Wagner."

Curiously enough, this incident was exactly paralleled when, some years later, I had occasion to call on that eccentric genius of the keyboard, Vladimir de Pachmann, whom James Huneker liked to call "the great Chopinzee."

Pachmann said, "I wish to show you something very interesting."

He left the room and returned a moment later attired in a dirty old dressing gown, much too tight for his chubby form.

"This dressing gown," he told me, "belonged to Chopin. It makes you cry, n'est ce pas?"

Returning for a moment to Vienna, where I subsequently played quite frequently, I had the pleasure of meeting Theodor Leschetizky, who invited me to supper at his home, following a meeting of his large class of students. I don't know why I should still remember his remark, looking over the group of chattering young women with an expression of mingled humor and philosophy:

"Just think! Some fellow must be found for each one of these girls, and his sole reason for existence will be to nullify their studies and ruin their careers."

The statement was neither particularly witty nor necessarily true, but it stuck in my mind. So, for another reason, I recall a remark of his made after one of my recitals when I played Chopin's C-sharp minor study, Opus 10, No. 4.

"You played it so fast," said Leschetizky, "that it sounded as if it were in D minor!"

Before leaving Hans Richter and his attachment for the music of Liszt, I must relate the following incident. He invited me to play at one of his concerts in Manchester, where he directed the orchestra founded some years before by Charles Hallé.

"What shall I play, Master?" I inquired, thinking that he would propose one of the major concertos. Somewhat to my surprise, he said he wanted me to play Liszt's "Todtentanz" (variations on the "Dies Irae") for piano and orchestra.

"And what else?" I respectfully inquired.

"Nothing else."

The program was composed of three numbers: Beethoven's "Lenore" Overture, the "Todtentanz," and Strauss' "Heldenleben." At supper after the concert Richter said:

"I wanted you to play the 'Todtentanz' so that the public could realize where all these modern composers get their ideas from."

I cherish my memories of meetings with orchestral conductors as much as anything in my long musical career.

When I was a boy violinist, one of my favorite pieces was Svendsen's "Romance," and I used to like the chamber music of Friedrich Gernsheim. What a thrill it was to meet and play with these two men, the one in Copenhagen and the other in Rotterdam! Then, my first appearance with Nikisch in Berlin, the Schumann Concerto and the heart-sinking feeling that no soloist—I least of all—could hope to equal the beauty of sound that he conjured from the orchestra in the opening theme.

Felix Weingartner was a good friend of mine, but I played only once with him. He came to Paris to direct a series of Beethoven concerts. At the closing one the program included, together with the Ninth Symphony, the Choral

Fantasia, in which I played the piano solo part. All I remember of this concert is that it took place on Labor Day, when there was a general strike involving all city transportation, and I had to walk from my home to the Opera House, where the concert was given. The piano was out of order and caused me the greatest distress. I forget just what it was: the pedals fell off, or the strings broke, or the keys stuck, or something. The event, to which I had looked forward, was ruined for me.

For some reason which I never fathomed, I was *persona non grata* with Charles Lamoureux, the conductor of the celebrated Lamoureux Concerts, which were given at the Cirque d'Eté on the Champs Elysées. Finally a mutual friend (I believe it was Monsieur Blondel, director of the Erard piano factory) put on some pressure, and I was invited to play at one of the Sunday concerts. I use the word "invited" advisedly, for no fee was attached to the appearance.

I went to the rehearsal on Saturday, and the conductor, after a curt nod of greeting, started the E-flat Liszt concerto, which I was to play. Following the first orchestral measures which precede the entrance of the solo part, he sustained the last chord, at the same time indicating that I was to start. Since the harmony is different, I was perplexed and waited for him to stop.

"Why don't you come in when I give the sign?" he growled.

"The piano has a different chord," I protested.

"I know what I am doing," he retorted, and we started again.

For the second time he signed to me to start. I could not do it, and I would not do it. He became furious and shouted at me:

"Monsieur, I warn you that if you do not follow me now, I shall not follow you at the concert."

My blood suddenly boiled.

"You will not be given the opportunity to spoil my performance tomorrow," I shrieked at him. "I shall not play with you at all!"

And with that I slammed down the piano lid and stalked out, feeling very angry and very grand. No sooner was I outside than my conscience began to nag me. I stifled it, but little by little the thought took definite shape: What a fool I am! It did not really matter. I have lost an opportunity, and I have made an enemy.

Dear Memoirs, let me take this opportunity to set down the confession that I have been cursed all my life with a quick temper which has led me into sudden outbursts of anger and indignation for causes of very small moment. Although at the time it seems that my violence is not only justifiable but is, in a sense, a duty I owe to humanity, subsequent events invariably show that nothing whatever has been gained, but that, on the contrary, a good deal has been lost through my lack of self-control.

I was delighted beyond measure when the opportunity came one day for me to meet the great violinist Sarasate, one of my boyhood idols, of whom I have previously written. I was introduced to him at the Café Royal where, I learned, he was in the habit of taking his "bock" every evening. I noticed that he had a very beautiful malacca walking stick furnished with a chased handle and, as we sat and talked, I saw that he was letting it slip through his fingers until the motion was arrested by the head—in precisely the way he used to let his violin slip through his fingers, to the consternation of the public, all those years before in London. I told him of this, and he admitted smilingly that he had a collection of canes and that he enjoyed playing with them. I went to his home on the Boulevard Malesherbes, and he showed me there a truly astonishing array of walking sticks he had assembled from various parts of the world, many of these having been gifts from reigning sovereigns who had learned of his foible.

Sarasate had a most original character. One could never be sure if he was witty or—I was going to say "half-witted." But that would be too much. His observations were frequently very keen but seemed sometimes quite childish. He asked me where I was going to play next.

I replied, "In Spain, as it happens, and I shall have the pleasure of playing in your native city of Pamplona."

"Bravo!" he said, "Bravissimo! Spain is a good country for music, and you can give concerts there every day except Sunday, when everyone goes to the bullfight."

"Monday is a very good day," he continued reflectively, "but not Sunday, because of the bullfight."

There was a pause.

"Tuesday is also a good day," he went on, "but not Sunday, because of the bullfight. Wednesday or Thursday, why not? But not Sunday, because of the bullfight."

Another pause. He lighted a cigarette and took a sip of beer.

"Friday, yes, but not Sunday, because of the bullfight. Saturday, excellent! But, my dear friend, do not make the mistake of giving a concert on Sunday, because everyone goes to the bullfight on that day."

On another occasion, I found the great violinist in a philosophical mood.

"Has it ever occurred to you," he began, "to consider the

vast difference between a musical performer and the conductor of an orchestra? For example, I take my violin. I make music. The conductor has a little stick."

Pause.

"Reflect only," he proceeded, "you have your piano. You make music. The conductor has a little stick. The singer has a voice and makes music. The conductor has his little stick."

Sarasate struck a match.

"What would happen," he said very quietly, looking at the end of his cigar, "if you took away the little stick from the conductor? Would anything be left?"

Another of my memories of Sarasate has to do with the first performance of Debussy's opera *Pelléas and Mélisande*, to which I had been looking forward with considerable interest. I knew Maeterlinck's play, and I had read the piano score of the opera, which was already published. The evening came, and I was enthralled by this new music, completely carried away, and beside myself with enthusiasm. I was sitting alone, and after shouting myself hoarse for the final appearance of the artists on the stage, I hurried off to the Café Royal, where I knew I should find some kindred spirits to discuss the great event of this new opera.

It was a warm spring night, and I saw Sarasate sipping his glass of beer on the terrace.

"Where are you going so fast, young friend?" he called to me.

Breathless with excitement, I held up my piano score of *Pelléas and Mélisande*.

"Genius! Marvellous! What an evening!" I gasped out.

"Voyons, let me see," said the great violinist, taking the book from my hands.

He flipped the pages through without looking at them, just as he might have handled a deck of playing cards and then, handing it back, remarked lazily: "You know, I don't care much for the music of these fellows!"

I ran away with my book to the crowd of enthusiasts for whom I was looking and spent the rest of the night with them excitedly discussing the genius of Claude Debussy.

I wish it were possible for me to say that this incident was followed by a reconciliation with Debussy, with whom I had quarreled some years before. This was not to be. It was still some time before we met again.

A mutual friend, who was responsible for an annual series of concerts, each devoted to the work of one composer, came to see me one day in 1908 with a request, purporting to come from Claude Debussy, that I should introduce, at one of these concerts, a little suite he had just written entitled "Children's Corner." I was touched and pleased, and of course I consented. When I had learned the pieces, I wrote to ask him to hear me play them. He gave me an appointment and I went to his house.

Contrary to my hope and expectation, our meeting was quite formal. I played the pieces, and he expressed himself satisfied. One little thing alone broke the stiffness of the occasion. After I played the last piece, "Golliwog's Cake-Walk," he remarked:

"You don't seem to object today to the manner in which I treat Wagner."

I had not the slightest idea what he meant and asked him to explain. He then pointed out the pitiless caricature of the first measures of Tristan and Isolde that he had introduced in the middle of the "Cake-Walk." It had completely escaped me. I laughed heartily and congratulated him on his wit.

The concert came off. The hall was full. To my chagrin, Debussy was not there. I played the suite and went out into

[141]

the courtyard of the old house whose ballroom had been converted into an auditorium. I found the composer walking up and down with a very sour face. He came up to me and said, "Eh bien! How did they take it?"

I was immediately filled with an immense pity for him. I realized that this great man, who had struggled so long to obtain recognition of the new idiom he was bringing to our art, was *nervous*, scared to death at the thought that his reputation might be compromised because he had written something humorous.

I looked him straight in the eye.

"They laughed," I said briefly.

I saw relief pour through him. He burst into a stentorian roar of glee and shook me warmly by the hand.

"Vous savez? Je vous remercie bien!" he said.

It was enough. We were friends. But I never saw him again. Engagements called me to various parts of the world, and he died during the war, in 1917, after which I gave up my residence in Paris.

I gave many concerts with Pablo Casals in England, Holland, Belgium, and Switzerland. I also played frequently with Thibaud, Ysaÿe, Hollmann, Marsick, Gerardy, and others. As I have said before, I always preferred joint concerts to solo recitals and was disappointed when some of my colleagues took a different view.

Fritz Kreisler and I once arranged to give a series of solo recitals in the principal cities of Norway, Sweden, and Denmark, under the direction of a Scandinavian manager. The manager expressed his confidence that if our separate tours proved artistically successful, he could arrange a highly remunerative joint tour for us the following year.

Fritz started first. Following him some weeks later, I went to Christiania, where his tour had begun. The manager told me that the tour had been a grand success and that Fritz had left me a note and a message. The message turned out to be a few small Norwegian coins which represented the net profits of his opening concert. This was "to encourage me"!

However, his concerts had really attracted a great deal of attention and so, subsequently, did mine, and the manager felt sure that a joint tour the following season would prove financially successful.

It was understood that Kreisler and I would provide money for advance publicity and expenses. When the time came it appeared that I had a little money, while Fritz had none. It did not matter; I sent along the funds and the tour was announced. One week before the date of the first concert I was aghast to receive a telegram from a friend of Fritz's in Berlin.

"Kreisler compelled to leave suddenly for America on urgent business regrets inability to join you on Scandinavian tour."

The "urgent business," of which I could not conceive the nature, turned out to be his marriage. I was left in the lurch and hastily communicated with the Norwegian manager. What to do? The answer came, "You can play alone." So I went off, and the public and critics received me quite cordially throughout the tour. No resentment was expressed for the cancellation of the original plan.

Mention of Scandinavia naturally brings to mind one of the most delightful and original composers.

I met Grieg at the home of my dear friend Julius Röntgen in Amsterdam. I had hoped to see him again in Paris, where he had been engaged to conduct one of the Colonne concerts. However, he had developed such hostile feelings toward France on account of the Dreyfus case, which then was preoccupying the entire world, that he had refused at the last moment to visit "a country where such injustice was possible," to quote from the letter he wrote.

Later, I met him and his wife again in London, where he was acclaimed by an enormous audience. He played, with the violinist Johannes Wolff, his Sonata in C minor, and he also accompanied Madame Grieg in two groups of songs, which she sang charmingly with a flutelike voice. Then he played a number of short compositions, and the public was most enthusiastic.

Both the composer and his wife were of diminutive stature, but he had, nevertheless, a leonine head. They were simple and delightful people. I met them once again in Copenhagen and then, some years later when I was in Bergen, I visited their home. Neither of them was there. Nina Grieg was living with friends in Copenhagen, and the body of the composer reposed in a tomb cut into the living rock overlooking the fiord. All that marks the spot, set high above the footpath and now a national shrine, is the name, Edvard Grieg, engraved on the block of stone which seals his resting place.

In the spring of 1911, Casals, Kreisler, and I were engaged as soloists at a special series of concerts designated as the "London Concert Festival."

Each of us was extremely successful. The audiences were large and enthusiastic, and much was said and written in praise of the performances. As a result, we were engaged by an enterprising manager to make a joint tour the following autumn in the principal cities of England as well as in London. When the time came to give out the preliminary announcement of the programs, it transpired that we were at cross-purposes with the manager, who expected each of us to play solos as well as concerted works. We wanted to play trios, and nothing but trios. We were quite obdurate about this; but we had reason on our side too, because a program consisting of two trios, together with solos for piano, violin, and cello respectively, would have lasted altogether too long. Consequently the manager, greatly chagrined and fearing that the public would not attend chamber music concerts in any large numbers, felt that he had but one course to follow—namely, to announce the names of the performers and to say nothing at all about the program.

This was done and, to his surprise and relief, the concerts were completely sold out everywhere. The public seemed quite satisfied, there were no protests, and there was an immense amount of applause.

We shall never know if everyone who came to those concerts fully realized what was taking place and what they were hearing. The program included three trios, and nothing else. At one of the concerts, so crowded that those of the audience who had been given seats on the stage almost touched the piano, I noticed a man with a peculiarly inexpressive countenance sitting on my immediate left. He neither applauded nor gave the least sign of approval throughout the evening; I noticed, however, that his eyes wandered occasionally from Kreisler to Casals and then back to me. The program ended with Mendelssohn's Trio in D minor, where the coda enters with an impassioned lyrical outburst by the cello. My man took his hands from his knees, where they had rested the whole evening. He gently tapped his neighbor on the shoulder, and I heard him whisper hoarsely: "I suppose *that* one will be Casals?"

The so-called "Philharmonic Society" was established about that time in Paris. I say "so-called" because as a rule "philharmonic" is used in connection with a symphony organization, whereas our society was solely for the purpose of chamber music and mixed programs.

The opening concert was given by Ysaÿe and myself. I enjoyed playing with him so much that when he invited me shortly afterward to play at one of the orchestral concerts which he directed in Brussels, I begged him to play a sonata with me.

"Out of the question at a symphony concert," he said, "but since you wish it, we will nevertheless play together. First you will play a concerto, and we will end the program with the great Bach Brandenburg Concerto for piano, violin, and flute."

It was kind of him to do this, and the performance was excellent. But I can never forget how small the flute player looked next to the giant Ysaÿe!

I went from Brussels to Italy. In Florence, the manager asked me just before the concert if I would allow one of the "great ladies" of the city, who was in mourning, to sit in the anteroom during the performance so that she could listen without being seen. I consented at once without inquiring who the lady was.

She was not there when I went on the stage for the first number. As I came out, I saw a woman's figure dressed in flowing draperies rise from the armchair which had been placed in a shaded corner of the anteroom for her. She approached me, hands upraised, with the words: "Homme heureux!" (Happy man!) I recognized Eleonora Duse and bowed low before her.

"I am deeply honored, Madame," I said. "You remarked?"

"Homme heureux!" she repeated gravely. "You are alone on the stage all the time, while we others. . . ." She shook her head sadly.

I was greatly impressed.

"You mean, Madame," I said, "that the presence of your colleagues on the stage is disturbing to you?"

"Unless I feel certain that they are sharing with me the emotion required by the play, it is torture!" she replied.

We exchanged a few more words in the same sense, and then I had to return to the piano. She left before the end of the concert, and I never saw her again.

Those few words long remained in my mind, however. They raised once again a question which has always troubled me—the question of the relation between emotion and intellect in art. Does the artist experience the emotion that he expects the audience to feel?

Sarah Bernhardt and Coquelin Cadet had both said to me that an artist must never be carried away by emotion. He must dominate it, study it, dissect it, and learn to reproduce its manifestations and direct these toward his public. Otherwise (with a shrug of the shoulders) what he does cannot be called art at all.

Duse seemed to take a precisely contrary view. Apparently, however, both methods have always existed and both may be successful. I once read a dialogue of Plato's in which Socrates jeers at the tragedian who asserts that no matter how often he plays the same part, he actually feels that he passes through the dramatic situation each time. "It must be hard to have to die so often," retorts the philosopher.

My own experience is that whenever I have felt certain that I was producing a particular effect upon an audience, I was myself cool and unmoved. But that proves nothing and, anyhow, it is terribly hard for an artist to escape from emotion. I am quite sure that the feeling of being especially "well disposed" or "in good form" has not, in my case, necessarily corresponded to the verdict of the public; and I am equally sure that my listeners have not always agreed with me when I felt that everything was going wrong.

Here is an example of the last-named state of affairs.

I had announced a recital in San Francisco with a new program. It was a fine Sunday afternoon; I felt very well and was looking forward with pleasure to the concert. I began to play and was disconcerted to find that one of the keys stuck. After the first number I looked around for my tuner and then remembered with consternation that he had left for Los Angeles, where I was to play the next day. It was out of the question to get anyone else, the day being Sunday.

I gritted my teeth and decided I must go through with the concert. For the rest of the program I had but one thought—to lift up the key after I had depressed it, in order to prepare for the next stroke. All my pleasure was gone. I was in misery and wished I were dead. At long last the concert was over and I retired disconsolately to the artists' room, after playing the usual encores. I found an old friend there, one of the few people on whom I could rely to tell me the truth about my playing and in whose judgment I had implicit confidence.

"Well!" he said. "Whatever came over you today?"

I started to explain, but he interrupted me.

"I want to tell you," he remarked impressively, "that I have never heard you play with the ease and freedom that you displayed today. From beginning to end you were completely absorbed in the music, and your performance was an inspired one."

[148]

I did not return to Italy for a good many years. I was then engaged for a series of recitals. Italy had changed considerably under the Fascist regime.

The manager of the San Carlo theater in Naples, where I was to play, came to my recital at the St. Cecilia Academy in Rome. I remarked that I expected criticism of my program, which would probably be unsuitable for such a large auditorium as the celebrated Neapolitan opera house.

"Precisely," he said. "The program is much too short. We have to fill the entire evening from nine to twelve, just like an opera."

I was aghast. How could a piano recital replace an opera? But he went on to explain that this was an altogether exceptional event. The Duce had just taken over the portfolio of Minister of Fine Arts, and the initial concert of the San Carlo series must be commensurate with the importance of the occasion. I yielded and gave him the longest program I ever made in my life.

On my arrival in Naples, I observed streamers with my name across the streets, announcing the first concert of a series sponsored by the University of Fine Arts.

"All very well," I grumbled to myself, "but there are certainly not four thousand people in Naples who will come to the San Carlo to listen to a piano recital."

I was mistaken. The hall was full. I have related elsewhere that the Queen of Portugal sat in a box with the Queen of Italy. It was obviously an official occasion. And what is more, the audience applauded vociferously.

The concert lasted until midnight, and I went to supper at a large restaurant with my manager and a few friends. Afterward, with the cigarettes and coffee, I began to ask some questions.

"There must be a catch somewhere," I said. "Why in the

name of heaven did all those people come to the concert? Piano recitals in Naples are infrequent because the public prefers opera. What can they find in piano music to make them applaud as they did?"

"Ha ha! Yes sir!" said the manager very loudly. "A splendid evening it was indeed. Everyone very happy!"

Something warned me to say no more. An hour later, the café was almost empty, and the manager touched me on the arm.

"Don't you realize," he almost hissed at me, "that there are many people in Naples who are not Fascists and who do not like Mussolini? *They* it was who crowded the opera house and applauded the loudest, so that they should not be suspected of subversive activities."

Eight

THE WRITER OF THESE SCATTERED REMINISCENCES MAKES NO apology for his encyclopedic ignorance in the art of writing a book. This must long since have been apparent to the most indulgent reader, and the sad condition cannot be remedied. It is one thing to have memories and another thing to mold these memories into orderly sequence and form. Mr. George Frideric Handel, when reproached with appropriating themes written by others, retorted that he was in reality rendering a service to an ignorant fool who did not know how to make a proper use of his tune. I wish that he or somebody else were here to tell me how to escape from the predicament in which the final words of the foregoing chapter have left me. My story led up to the year 1920, and now I have to move back the hands of the clock no less than twenty years. An artist in words would know how to do this with ease and elegance, just as a composer, following the development section of a sonata which leads him far into the future, uses skillful modulations in order to return to his first theme, which already belongs to the past.

Schubert, that angel who came in where fools were afraid to tread, shortened academic processes of modulation as much as he lengthened—some say to excess—other academic processes of composition. A single miraculous chord would have sufficed for him to bridge a gap of twenty years. Perhaps not even one chord would have been necessary. Here we are in the key of C major, he tells us. In the course of time we move through various adventures in various places, finding ourselves ultimately in the key of F-sharp major, from whence, sooner or later, we must return home to see what has happened in the meantime. Do we have to go the long way, modulating through all the related keys? Not necessarily. We might fly home by the nonstop route. Why not?

Step on my magic carpet, says Schubert, and you will be carried back instantaneously—F-sharp major and C major are suddenly shown to be next door to each other, a fact which nobody had previously suspected. Twenty years apart? Nonsense. Sheer illusion. Time does not move, and life, like a musical composition, is a complete whole, within which the imagination and the intelligence of the performer are free to come and go. This—in part—is what Schubert's music seems to tell me.

Dare I attempt to follow in the footsteps of the divine Franz, disregarding what we mistakenly call the flight of time? I have no alternative but to try. Gentle reader, deign to set foot in this humble buggy, my poor substitute for the magic carpet. I have nothing better to offer you, and we shall reach our destination if you will kindly excuse the bumps while I turn the hands of the clock.

We are now at the turn of the century, A.D. 1900, and I have just received an invitation to go to America and play with the Boston Symphony Orchestra. In the meantime, everyone is concerned with the great "exposition univer-selle" which has opened with enormous éclat in May. A few strange conveyances, called automobiles, are seen in the streets and parks, and Santos Dumont has just circled the Eiffel Tower in a dirigible balloon. Visions of "heavier-than-air" aviation are still regarded as fantastic and irresponsible dreams. Paris is covered with flamboyant signs urging the purchase of bonds to finance the Great Show. "Be Patriotic!—Show Civic Pride!—Bring New Prestige and New Prosperity to Paris! Buy Exposition Bonds—You Cannot Lose! Bonds Will Be Redeemed with Interest! Every Purchaser Will Have the Benefit of Free Admission to the Exposition Grounds!"

This last announcement appealed to me. I bought a few bonds and obtained a few free admission coupons. Of course the bonds were never redeemed. The Exposition was a glorious success, I am told. Strange to say, I have forgotten everything about it with but four exceptions. The old Palais d'Industrie on the Champs Elysées was torn down, giving place to two beautiful and ornate buildings used permanently for exhibition purposes. There was a new bridge across the Seine. A rolling sidewalk, covering practically the entire circumference of the Exposition grounds, was constructed —a noisy marvel. And finally: the Only Girl in the World, with whom I walked about practically every day during the summer.

Everything else in the Exposition is forgotten.

Alas! I have completely forgotten the Only Girl in the World too.

I accepted the invitation to go the United States at once, without question or hesitation, in the same spirit with which, some years before, I had agreed to go to Russia. I was ambitious and adventurous and would have said "yes" to anything that indicated the possibility of advancement in my career. It was not until long afterward that I realized the frantic wager I had risked with destiny, for nothing was offered me beyond the one engagement with the Boston orchestra, and, although I did not know it then, my whole future was to depend on the artistic result of this single occasion.

However, my mind was occupied with matters of more immediate importance. It was necessary for me to establish relations at once with a piano manufacturer and with a concert manager in America, for, after all, it was not impossible that I might succeed in obtaining more engagements. I knew only one American piano: the Steinway. Following my inquiries, I was crestfallen to learn that the great firm was not interested in my forthcoming visit. It was not until later that I had the privilege of meeting the president, Frederic Steinway, from whom I received many marks of friendship. In the meantime, my friend Mr. Sebastian Schlesinger, a Boston musical amateur living in Paris, to whose recommendation my Boston invitation was largely due, introduced me to Marc Blumenberg, the founder of the *Musical Courier* and a man of great influence in musical affairs. Through him it was arranged for me to play on the Mason and Hamlin piano and for a New York manager to take charge of my business. The Mason and Hamlin firm agreed to pay the expenses of recitals in Boston and New York following my début and to try to obtain engagements for me in other places. Blumenberg expressed confidence in my future, and I agreed, in the event of success, to pay for advertisements in the *Musical Courier*—an entirely new idea to me, since it was considered undignified

in Europe for professional people to advertise like trades-
men. However, I was quite willing to admit that Americans
might know better. As I had met a great many cultured
Americans in Paris, I believed implicitly in their statement
that the Boston Symphony was the greatest orchestra and
the Boston audience the most sophisticated and critical in
the world.

Mr. Gericke, the conductor, had written to ask me what I
wanted to play, and I gave the matter of my début a great
deal of thought. It seemed unwise to risk comparison with
the greatest by playing one of the works constantly heard
such as Beethoven, Liszt, or Schumann concertos, so I suggested the D minor by Brahms with the sole idea that this
great work was probably played less frequently. Mr. Gericke
said that would do very well. It was not until I got to Boston
that I learned that this particular Brahms concerto had
never been played before at the symphony concerts; that the
public did not particularly care for Brahms' music, although
Mr. Gericke played it frequently; and that the principal
music critic Philip Hale (who was undoubtedly a most distinguished scholar) disliked it so much that it seemed a
foregone conclusion that the presentation of a Brahms composition would be severely criticized.

Mr. Hale had no use for the Brahms concerto, but generously admitted that I had given care to playing it; some
of the other critics were kinder, and my success, on the whole,
was a good success. But I have always thought that my
seeming act of defiance was the reason why the Boston public
from that day took me to its heart, while on the other hand
New York, secretly resentful of Boston highbrow ideas,
would have none of me for nearly two years as a result of
the episode.

Before I left Paris, Marc Blumenberg had told me that

he was looking for a man to be the general European representative of the *Musical Courier*. I introduced him to my friend Chester, who, it seemed to me, possessed the necessary qualifications. The result was that Chester and I shared a cabin on the "Kaiser Wilhelm der Grosse" and sailed for New York in November. The trip was terribly stormy, and I almost died of seasickness. I was quite sure that if I survived I should never be able to return to Europe, and this made me very sad. One day a wave burst into the cabin, soaking all our clothes, and I was greatly concerned for the manuscript of Fritz Delius' symphony which, as related elsewhere, I had promised to submit to the conductor of the Boston Symphony. Fortunately no damage was done to the music.

I was met at the dock by hospitable friends who immediately took me off to stay at their home. Chester completed his arrangements with the *Musical Courier* and returned to Europe a few weeks later. As European representative of the magazine, he was able to render important services to all the artists he knew, including myself, and some years afterward he became my concert manager. During the two weeks of my first stay in New York I met a number of musicians, some of whom I had already known in Paris, and I thought, quite mistakenly as it subsequently transpired, that if I had the good fortune to succeed at my Boston début, these acquaintances would be useful to me. But it was only in Boston that I was given the feeling of being admitted to the musical life of the community. Even before my first concert, I had met and had been cordially welcomed not only by Wilhelm Gericke and his then concertmaster Franz Kneisel but by such eminent musicians as Chadwick, Foote, Loeffler, Parker, Whiting, Converse, and my good friend Wallace Goodrich, just back from his studies in Paris. Henry

Mason, then artistic director of the Mason and Hamlin firm founded by his father, introduced me at the St. Botolph Club, and I thought that I had never met such an aggregation of artistic and interesting people as in this delightful place, although I was familiar with the Savage Club in London, the only institution of the kind to which it had some resemblance.

Following my début with the orchestra, I gave several recitals in Boston with constantly growing success, and various appearances were arranged for me elsewhere. The fees seemed enormous to me, and I knew that they were larger, on the average, than those paid to the most celebrated performers in Europe. It took me some time to realize that, if the fees seemed high, the expenses were still higher in comparison with Europe. I was stunned when it first became clear to me that the purchasing power of a dollar was little more than that of a franc in Paris. It seemed impossible to adjust myself to such a changed scale of values, and I met the new situation as best I could—that is to say, very badly indeed. I found, at the end of my three-month tour, during which I played some thirty concerts, that after paying my traveling and hotel expenses, my manager's commissions, my advertising bills, and various incidentals (which were far too large and extravagant) hardly any money was left when I got back to Paris. I determined to do better next time.

The friends who entertained me during my first American visit lived in New York on Lexington Avenue near 34th Street. This was considered a convenient and semifashionable neighborhood. The street and the house reminded me of London, inasmuch as both were completely lacking in character or beauty, and I was surprised that anyone would want to live on a streetcar line. The noise of the underground cable which drew the cars along seemed terrific to me, and it went on day and night; however, I became accustomed to it. The family consisted of the two parents, an uncle, three sons, and one daughter, all grown up. The rooms were spacious and comfortable, lighted by gas (electricity had not come yet) and warmed by hot air from a furnace in the cellar. There were two bathrooms for the family; none for the two maids and the cook, whose rooms were on the top floor.

In addition to these servants, there was a man who came in every morning to clean the shoes, attend to the furnace, and set the garbage out to be carried away. There was a great deal of work to be done. As in European homes, the bedrooms were provided with washstands, but there was no running water except in the bathrooms. Each morning, the male members of the family found a can of hot water for shaving outside their respective bedrooms. Open fires were lighted in the living rooms every day, and sometimes in the larger bedrooms as well.

With exception of the hot-air furnace (a method of heating which I had never seen before), I was reminded constantly of London, and the atmosphere was that of the home of a prosperous middle-class family in that city. I had expected something else, but what, I did not know. Certainly family life in France and in Germany seemed quite different, and this was not due to language, for I felt at home in both of these countries. Very possibly, the similarity I felt between English and American ways of living was due to nothing more than prevailing customs of eating at certain hours, together with the kind of food which was served at meals. In any event, it did not take me long to dis-

Nicholas Muray

Harold Bauer

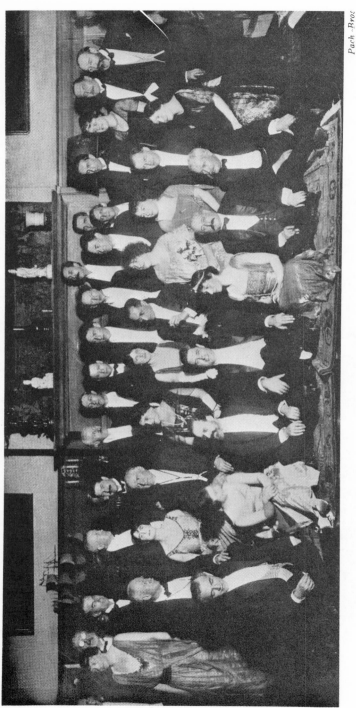

Pach Bros.

MUSICIANS AT MOSZKOWSKI BENEFIT, 1922

Back row: Mrs. Ernest Hutcheson, Ernest Urchs, Howard Brockway, (?), Artur Schnabel, Alexander Lambert, Ernest Hutcheson, Efrem Zimbalist, Josef Lhevinne, Ossip Gabrilowitsch, Ernest Schelling, Harold Bauer, Willem van Hoog-straten, Leo Ornstein, Alfredo Casella, (?), (?), Georges Barrere. Middle row: Richard Aldrich, Germaine Schnitzer, Walter Damrosch, Marcella Sembrich, Alma Gluck, Artur Bodanzky, Elly Ney, Mrs. Josef Lhevinne, Wilhelm Back-haus, (?), Sigismond Stojowski, John McCormack, Ruth Deyo, Rubin Goldmark, Louis Svecenski.

cover that the resemblances were more apparent than real, and that life in the United States possessed many features as novel as they were surprising to me.

More than anything else, the impression of a driving and irresistible energy seemed to set this country apart from every other. I am well aware that a statement of this kind must appear the baldest of truisms; but I shall try to qualify it from the standpoint of my own personal reaction to the force in question.

It was clear that something was pushing and urging me onward in a manner which defied comparison with all previous experience. I observed that others were similarly urged and pushed about. I did not like this at all, especially when I found that it interfered seriously with the plans and principles I had formulated with respect to my public career.

My European background had always fostered the idea that a concert was a great event—a special occasion. One prepared for it with assiduity and care, and when the moment arrived, one went through the flame of this adventure with feelings which partook of pride, humility, desperation, ecstasy, terror, and sometimes a dizzy sense of power over the audience. It was an experience like no other on earth.

After the concert was over, one relaxed, one ate and drank, one talked, and above all, one rested. There was no thought of the morrow, no question of a repetition of the same adventure. When the next concert came, it was something entirely new. Each performance was an end in itself, disconnected with the future, and this discontinuity seemed a logical and satisfying element in the career of a traveling virtuoso.

Unlike the actor, whose talents and opportunities are circumscribed by such externals as language, stage properties, and so forth, the field of the musician is practically un-limited. He is constantly called upon to meet audiences of strongly marked national characteristics in countries which are not his own, and he must set forth every effort to project the music in terms which are appropriate to his immediate surroundings but which, at the same time, con-vey the sense of the universal and unchangeable qualities of that music. I am not referring here to those performers who, without making any particular effort to adjust them-selves to local conditions, are universally acclaimed because of their possession of unusually brilliant powers of execu-tion. Still less do I take into account those who, because of the accident of birth, are regarded as solely competent to interpret the works of the great composers of their own nationality. There are few theories more offensively non-sensical than the dictum which proclaims that one must be German to understand Bach and Beethoven, French to un-derstand Debussy, Viennese to understand Schubert, and Polish to understand Chopin. An artist's equipment con-sists of imagination, observation, and application. The com-bination of these qualities is known as talent—and talent admits of no artificial limitation.

It stands to reason that economic considerations could never be completely relegated to the background, what-ever efforts one might make to observe principles of artistic freedom and independence. Money was indispensable, and its scarcity caused a painful and unescapable preoccupation. But in spite of this, I could not bring myself to accept any conception of an artist's mission other than that of a dis-penser of something beautiful which could be neither bought nor sold. It seemed to me that the very nature of art forbade commercial dealings in it. Financial rewards to even the greatest artist were similar, in the last analysis, to pennies dropped in the hat of the street organ-grinder—an expression of appreciation for what was given away for nothing. I had a vague idea that it was preferable in some ways to be a beggar rather than a hireling in the domain of art. And as to the final outcome—how to live if pennies did not drop into the hat—I was satisfied to leave that in the lap of the gods. Although there was nothing in my family history to justify the belief that Providence would in some fashion provide for the needs of old age, youthful optimism seemed to insist that if one worked conscientiously for a certain number of years, it would be possible to retire and live on one's savings in the manner of my favorite heroes of fiction—Robinson Crusoe, Lemuel Gulliver, and Sinbad the Sailor.

All these nebulous notions were quickly dispelled in America. I soon learned the nature of the force that seemed to drive everyone forward, incessantly and irresistibly. It was given various names, but the best title for it was Ambition. With numberless examples before it of the rise from poverty to power and wealth, the whole country had yielded itself up to a ceaseless race for supremacy in one form or another. Every boy was instructed that there was nothing in the world to prevent him from becoming President of the United States provided he possessed the necessary talent and energy, and every girl was given to understand that there was no limit to the power she could exercise with proper cultivation of her feminine qualities; in a word, everyone was possessed by the desire for achievement; and it seemed sometimes as if the grand principles of freedom and equality were capable of being distorted to mean that all men were given equal opportunity to dominate their fellow creatures, the two main requirements to this end being tireless energy and unremitting work.

[161]

I can honestly say that I had no idea what work could really mean until I came to the United States. This statement refers not to manual labor but to the occupations of the business and professional man, which seemed absolutely unending. None of my friends and acquaintances ever seemed to enjoy any leisure or rest, and when they indulged in games or sports it was with the same terrific energy that they employed in their business affairs. They were continuously pursued by visions of progress, expansion, increase of capacity, and increase of power resulting therefrom.

The thought that a business should pass from father to son, unchanged through several generations, as in Europe, was never for one moment entertained. It must become bigger and better, and the son must be specially trained to enable him to assume larger responsibilities and wield greater power than his father ever dreamed of.

Sometimes the financial operations involved in building up a business became stretched beyond the limit of credit, and bankruptcy resulted. It was surprising to find that this did not appear to carry the moral stigma which attached to business failure in Europe. The impression was created that bankruptcy, in America, was generally regarded as little more than a stroke of hard luck, and it seemed, as a rule, that the bankrupt, having settled with his creditors upon the proportion of his debts that he could pay, experienced no difficulty in obtaining new credit and resuming his business immediately afterward. It was understood that sheer determination and hard work would make up for everything and was certain to succeed at the end.

The following incident illustrates sufficiently the frame of mind which at that time seemed to me characteristic of the whole country.

One day I received a letter from a young man who begged for an interview on the grounds that I was the one person who could answer a simple question upon which his entire future depended. I was impressed by the intense earnestness displayed in the letter and gave him an appointment.

"My question," he said very rapidly, "is a simple one. Answer it, and you will help me to shape my life. Which is the more difficult: the art of composition or the art of playing the piano?"

I was staggered, but successfully evaded giving a direct reply by asking him for an example of his ability in both fields. It transpired that he could play nothing but his own compositions, so that simplified the matter to some extent, and he then sat down to the piano and performed a little piece in a manner which immediately revealed the fact that he possessed not the slightest spark of musical talent. He was quite insistent on having my judgment, so I told him as gently as I could that I saw no evidence of artistic ability and must therefore suggest that he follow some other pursuit, leaving music as a hobby.

He replied very coolly that he had not asked my opinion of the degree of his talent and that he was well aware that he had a great deal to learn. What he wanted to know was merely whether it was more difficult to achieve greatness in performance than in composition, or vice versa, "because," he continued, "I shall naturally choose the line of least resistance, and" (gritting his teeth) "I am determined to succeed."

Determination is a fine thing, of course, but I felt bound to tell him that I feared it would not work in his case.

For half an hour we talked back and forth on his preposterous theme. Finally he left me, a deeply injured and disappointed boy, with the conviction that I had refused, for some inexplicable reason, to give him a plain answer to a simple question.

It may well be asked why my interpretation of American conditions in 1900 should be considered worthy of being chronicled and why these conditions should have affected my career.

The answer is that I found it hard to adopt the rapid tempo which prevailed here, and I doubted my ability to adjust my temperament to the constant urge for more energy and more movement. It was new to me to think of the end of a program in connection with the departure of a train which was to carry me through the night, in order to arrive in time for the orchestral rehearsal the following morning in another city. I shrank from the thought that the manager, in order to obtain engagements for me, used precisely the same methods as would be employed by a tradesman in selling goods. Above all, I was bewildered and concerned by the seeming necessity of describing and advertising a performer as the greatest living . . . whatever he or she might be. My manager showed me the proof of a circular he was preparing to send round containing extracts from laudatory press notices and proclaiming me the "greatest living pianist," in accordance with the invariable custom. I could not bear it, and appealed to my friend, Henry Mason, who, from the more conservative angle of Boston's Beacon Street, gave thought to the problem of combining blatant advertising with decent tact, and evolved the term "master pianist," which seemed less absurd and bombastic, so it was adopted and I was described as "master pianist" for many years until William J. Henderson, known as the dean of New York music critics, suddenly decided that I must be called the dean of pianists. But that title never caught on. I was amused, one day, to find on the program of a concert I had given in England, as a little boy, that I was designated as "Master" Harold Bauer. One of the meanings of this word, according to Dean Swift, was a "term applied to a boy of more or less social standing, too young to be called Mister." So I started as Master, then I became Mister, then Master again, and now I shall be only too happy if my simple name survives.

Although my success in Boston counted rather against me than in my favor in New York, I gave two recitals in New York that first season, and was politely received, without, however, selling enough tickets to cover expenses. I also played with the Kneisel quartet in Boston, New York, and several other cities. On the whole, this first American tour, while it interested and delighted me enormously, was, I believe, one of the least impressive visits ever made to the United States by an artist who had acquired some status in Europe. I think I left the name of a young pianist who had shown competence in the three fields of concert recitals, chamber music, and playing with orchestra, and who could be relied upon for a decent average performance.

On my return to Europe, I discovered that my prestige had been materially increased through the American tour. This was different from the experience of most artists, who rarely went to the United States until their reputation in Europe had reached its zenith. The fortunate result for me, however, was that I was in great demand in various European countries through the whole of 1901–1902.

In the autumn of the latter year, I undertook another American tour. This time, my manager was, I think, as surprised as I was by the number of demands for my appearance that came from various parts of the country. I believe I played with nearly all the orchestras which then existed in the United States. I recall with special pleasure my performances that season with Victor Herbert in Pittsburgh, and with Theodore Thomas in Chicago. In New York I played with the Boston Symphony Orchestra, conducted by Gericke, and also at one of a series of symphony concerts given by Hermann Hans Wetzler, a great musician whose talents never received adequate recognition in this country.

My reputation had not, as yet, attracted the attention of the other New York orchestral organizations, and my manager insisted that there was no alternative but for me to continue giving piano recitals at a loss, until public recognition should finally come. I yielded unwillingly to his judgment. It annoyed me extremely to have to lose my earnings in this manner, for my New York recitals never covered their cost.

One afternoon, I walked up to Mendelssohn Hall, where I was to give a recital, feeling particularly ill-used and resentful. I had just come back from a successful little trip, and I had a pocketful of money; "and now," I reflected bitterly, "I shall lose it all in paying the expenses of today's recital. Why am I such a fool?" I saw a lot of people streaming into the hall. "Yes," my thoughts continued with concentrated fury, "this is indeed the last stroke. He picks up people in the street, gives them all the tickets and chases them into the hall. I wonder that he does not offer them a bribe to come to my concerts!"

For two pins I would have walked away; however, controlling my chagrin and disgust, I strolled into the hall. My manager was standing at the box office, and it seemed to me that he was looking rather pale. He seized me by the arm and whispered in my ear: "We're selling standing room now!" I thought this was a very bad joke, and I immediately boiled over with rage. "Leave me alone," I snarled at him, and I shoved him rudely aside with my elbow in his mid-riff, stalking on to the greenroom.

The hall was filled to the last seat, and when I started to play I thought of nothing but the music. It was only after the concert was over that I discovered that it was not merely a bad joke. The public had really paid for the tickets, and New York had finally recognized me. My manager forgave my assault upon him, and we went off together to celebrate the occasion.

This New York "victory" should have established me at once, according to generally accepted principles, in the class of artists who commanded both popularity and high fees, but there were several reasons why I never reached that kind of position. In the first place, I wanted to play anywhere, and everywhere regardless of the fee, if the conditions were such as to please me. Secondly, I did *not* want to play in any place where the conditions did *not* please me. Thirdly, I was quite averse to playing music which did not seem first-class, or to temper my programs to what a local manager considered necessary to attract an audience.

In the beginning I was often asked to play simple music by popular composers, "because," it was said, "our public will not understand the kind of music that is played in New York." What a change came about a few years later! People in small towns who had previously begged for a "light" program were positively insulted if there was the least evidence on the part of the performer that a New York program had been toned down to meet the supposed taste of a less sophisticated audience.

Finally, as I came to know the country better, I felt it incumbent upon me to do all I could toward the development of musical culture in remote towns and colleges where there was no opportunity to hear concerts, and this was feasible only if my fee were set sufficiently low to meet the financial resources of such places. After some preliminary experiments, I decided to adopt this principle definitely, and I requested my manager to carry it into effect. He protested energetically that such a course would be highly detrimental, not only to my interests but to his as well, inasmuch as it would brand me as a "low-priced artist" and prevent him from demanding the higher fees which he considered due my standing. However, I was obdurate, for it seemed more important, if a choice had to be made, to make some contribution toward cultural progress than to be a high-priced public entertainer, and he unwillingly gave in. I must admit that his objections were well-founded and his prognostication entirely correct—not that it matters in the least. I have never regretted the decision made at that time, for it brought me a gratifying sense of participation in the cultural development of this country.

The rapidity with which this growth of culture proceeded was indeed truly astonishing. I am sure that nothing like it has ever been known, and I am inclined to attribute its beginnings to that characteristically American feminine social organization known as the "bee." I have personally witnessed the evolution of the sewing bee, the spelling bee, and similar social gatherings into women's clubs of the greatest cultural importance to the community, and it is the merest truism to state that musical life in the United States could not possibly have attained its present status without the activity of these women's organizations.

Since my tour that year (1902) was quite extensive, I had ample opportunity to observe the progress of musical taste in various parts of the country. I missed the constantly changing surroundings, the differences of language, national customs, and methods of life that gave to a concert tour through European countries so much interest. In comparison, a great sameness pervaded the American atmosphere, redeemed only by sometimes startling manifestations of that national energy to which I have referred and which reminded me of the feats of the jinns summoned by Aladdin's magic lamp. "Let there be a new concert auditorium, a symphony orchestra, a public library," proclaimed the Women's Club, and, lo and behold! there it was, apparently only a few days later.

I did not always take a bedroom with an adjoining private bath, for that involved extra expense, but when I did, I thought it a wonderful luxury. There was no such comfort in Europe. Train travel was also a new experience in comfort, especially at night in the Pullman sleeping cars, but I could never accustom myself to the terrific overheating which was customary in both hotels and railroad cars, even when I gave up the curious European habit of dressing warmly in winter, and it was a long while before I learned all the contortions that were necessary in order to undress in a lower berth.

My recollection of the American practice of overheating in winter reminds me of the amusement with which I read, only a year or so ago, the report of a stockholders' meeting at a well-known English manufactory of woolen underclothing. The president, in a speech deploring the decline in public demand for the product, explained that the bad business must be attributed to the perverted habits of Americans, who had successfully introduced the idea of central heating into the British Isles, thereby inducing people to wear lighter underclothing in winter.

In European hotels, I used to put my shoes outside the bedroom door to be cleaned. I am convinced that I was regarded as a lunatic when, in my ignorance, I tried to continue the practice here. I soon discovered that shoe cleaning required the services of a specialist.

I made new discoveries every day. It was without pleasure that I ascertained that Mr. Hannibal Chollop (who required two foot clear in a circular direction and undertook to keep within that circle) had apparently left an unlimited number of descendants, each one of whom had a brass spittoon (called in higher society a cuspidor) placed at his disposal in every public or semipublic place. In Pullman cars and the better class of hotel, they were kept brightly polished and clean, but in the second-class coaches and the more ordinary hotels, they were objects of horror. Today, these articles are no longer seen. They have gone to join the glass finger bowls containing perfumed water with rose leaves sprinkled on it and holding a small drinking cup, which in France were placed on the table at the end of every well-served dinner. With characteristic French directness they were called "rince-bouche," and their purpose was to enable the ladies and gentlemen who had just dined to wash out their mouths and expel the ensuing result into the bowl. Sometimes (but not necessarily) the details of the operation were screened behind the napkin held elegantly before the face.

I believe this custom prevailed throughout Europe at all formal dinner parties; however, I do not recall seeing the finger bowls used in that manner outside of France. Perhaps there was less difference in national customs than I had been led to believe. Finger bowls are seen occasionally here, but the cuspidor has evolved into a monstrous cylinder filled with sand, that is placed on each floor of a great hotel at the elevator doors. They say it is there for cigarette butts, but I know better.

Why the sand?

Before leaving this subject, I must relate my experience in a small city in New England where I was engaged to give a recital. The wife of the mayor, who was president of the local Women's Music Club, invited me to stay at her home for the night, and accompanied her invitation with an insistent request to be informed whether I liked to eat oysters. I accepted the invitation and replied that I did like oysters. The two charming old people met me at the train and took me to their home. Dinner was ready, and the oysters were on the table—hundreds of them, it seemed to my dazed vision, in slimy heaps piled on soup plates. "So glad you like them," said the dear old lady. "Jonathan and I always think it is so much unnecessary trouble to take them out of their shells, so we get them in cans."

I have no means of knowing whether my reader will heave at the thought of eating oysters in this manner, as I did at that moment. However, noblesse oblige, I said mentally, and I managed to choke down a few, plentifully besprinkled with horrible homemade pepper sauce. I pleaded inability to eat more because of the concert. My kind hostess brought coffee. "Do you smoke?" she said. On my answer in the affirmative, she cackled, "I thought you might. My Jonathan there doesn't either smoke or chew." With that she hurried out of the room and returned, bearing in her arms an enormous ornamental cuspidor, standing about two feet high, which she set at my feet. I thanked her politely and assured her that I did not need it. "It's no trouble at all, young man," she replied, "and it may just as well stand there." A few moments later, her husband, the mayor, asked me to go and look at his new cabinet organ in the adjoining room. The old lady toddled after me carrying the cuspidor while I continued to smoke my cigarette.

We then proceeded to the church where the concert was

given. Everyone enjoyed the performance, and I promised to return the following season. There was a party with ice cream and cake at the mayor's home afterwards, and when the last guest had left, my kind hostess showed me to my bedroom upstairs, bearing the large cuspidor with her in spite of my remonstrances. "It's no trouble at all," she repeated. "You never can tell if you might not need it."

I did go there again the following year, but I wrote in advance that my doctor had forbidden me, temporarily, to eat oysters. The cuspidor was still waiting for me, and Jonathan neither chewed nor smoked.

$\mathcal{N}$*ine*

ALTHOUGH I HAVE NEVER BECOME RECONCILED TO THE IDEA of eating uncooked oysters otherwise than *alive*, that is to say at the moment the shell is opened, I did, in the course of time, learn to appreciate certain features of the American menu which, at first, seemed like curious lapses or perversions of taste.

The frequent absence of bread at meals was a sore trial to anyone coming from France, and the hot biscuits which took its place seemed a poor and indigestible substitute. While it was true that an occasional glass of wine was served at dinner, the usual pitcher of ice water gave a cheerless atmosphere to the meal, and the drinking of coffee or milk with meat and vegetable dishes was nothing less than a gastronomic crime in my opinion.

I could hardly believe my eyes when I first encountered the "fruit salad" of America, an incongruous mixture soaked with mayonnaise sauce, and I thought the taste was horrible. "Why don't they add onions, strawberry jam, and anchovy paste while they are about it?" I wondered.

Other mixtures seemed equally indiscriminate and perverse; the cocktail a vicious substitute for the apéritif and ruinous to the taste for wine; waffles with sausage and syrup the aberration of a lunatic; and cheese with pie a combination to which only a starving person would resort. As a rule I did not enjoy the food I had while traveling, and the cooking in most hotels and restaurants was almost incredibly bad. Then, too, it seemed to me that in spite of the many new conveniences and luxuries available in the United States, some of the services we had always taken for granted in Europe were not to be found, or, if obtainable at all, were prohibitive in cost.

For example, I had, in Europe, already reached that stage of bourgeois prosperity which permitted me, each time I went out of the house, to choose among three alternatives: shall I walk? shall I take an omnibus? shall I take a cab? And the last-named procedure involved no special hesitation on the grounds of expense. But here! Even if I had been able to hail a cab on the streets as I could in every European city, I should have regarded the expense as quite unjustifiable, except on special occasions. Elegant hansom cabs were seen on Fifth Avenue only, and it cost a dollar to travel merely a few blocks. Cabs to drive to the railroad station were summoned by telephone except at large hotels, where a few were always stationed. In Boston and other large cities, where the winter brought heavy snowfalls, cabs and other vehicles were mounted in that season on runners in the fashion of sleighs.

There were only two railroads having terminal stations in the city of New York—namely, the New York Central and the New York, New Haven and Hartford lines. These converged at the Grand Central Station, then newly constructed in 42nd Street. For all other lines, it was necessary to cross the Hudson River, and although this trip was made as convenient as possible through the use of large and luxurious ferryboats, I found it very tedious, both leaving and returning.

The new Grand Central Station built in 1913 caused many building changes in its vicinity, and Mendelssohn Hall, situated also on 42nd Street, was torn down. Most of the large businesses were then in process of moving northward, and Steinway Hall on 14th Street, once the most important auditorium in the city, had been given up. Steinway & Sons moved to 57th Street some years later, and Carnegie Hall, opened by the youthful Walter Damrosch in 1891, was no longer too far uptown to attract the public.

The Aeolian Company, which had achieved rapid fame and untold wealth through the invention of the pianola, moved uptown to 42nd Street and constructed an enormous building which housed not only their own products and extensive offices, but contained one of the most beautiful auditoriums then in existence.

The capacity of this hall was about twelve hundred, and it became, for many years, the home of the New York Symphony Orchestra, founded by Walter Damrosch, as well as the most fashionable auditorium for all organizations and individual artists who did not expect to fill the larger spaces of Carnegie Hall. Apart from my frequent public appearances there, I spent many, many hours in the offices, editing and correcting the paper rolls on which my performances had been mechanically recorded for the pianola, later electrified and re-named the Duo-Art.

I made, from first to last, some two hundred records, taking infinite pains in the editing that was essential to their completion.

The final result was always somewhat discouraging in

spite of all this trouble, for the reason that the dynamics, set to produce certain effects on the piano which was being used for such editorial purposes, varied when the record was played on another piano. This was due to minute differences in quality of tone and in resistance within the action, and there was no way of overcoming the difficulty. I learned two important principles in piano technique through the mechanical limitations of the pianola. One was the fact that tonal variety (i.e., difference in quality of piano tone) is obtainable solely through control and combination of the percussive sounds which result from the tapping of the finger on the key, the tapping of the key on its base, and the tapping of the hammer on the string. Since the mechanical player uses but one of these three factors—namely, the tapping of the hammer against the string—it follows that the human hand, which has all three percussive noises at its command, can vary sound quality in a manner which is totally denied to the machine.

I am aware that some scientists, as well as some distinguished pianists, refuse to recognize the value of these sounds in the production of piano tone; nevertheless, I have successfully proved to many of my colleagues that when they convey expressive variety of tone to their performance, they are invariably making use of these noises, although generally quite subconsciously.

The second thing I learned from the mechanical player was that it was best, in accentuating a single tone contained within a chord, to allow this tone to precede the other tones by a fraction of a second, instead of insisting that all tones be played simultaneously. This had to be done in correcting the paper rolls of the mechanical record. The illusion of simultaneity was perfect, and it sounded better that way, so I introduced this method into my technical practice.

The most ambitious of the Aeolian Company's plans was to prepare records of piano concertos for performance with symphony orchestras under the leadership of their regular conductor. I believe I was the first to make such a record. It was the St. Saëns Concerto in G minor. Following its completion, it was performed at a special concert given at the Academy of Music in Philadelphia by the Philadelphia Symphony Orchestra under the direction of Leopold Stokowski. The hall, containing invited guests only, was completely filled, and I was placed "on view" in one of the prominent boxes.

Although quite familiar with the practice, already adopted, of giving public performances of recorded music, I still recall with a shudder the strange feeling I experienced when, the lid of the piano having been raised and the orchestra and Stokowski having taken their places, the manager came forward and said that Mr. Harold Bauer would now play the St. Saëns Concerto in G minor. "You will see Mr. Bauer sitting in that box," he continued, motioning toward me.

For one moment it seemed like a nightmare. But the performance was a sensational success, and it was subsequently repeated by Walter Damrosch in New York, by Alfred Hertz in San Francisco, and by a number of other organizations in various countries where the Aeolian Company had their representatives.

Stokowski and Damrosch both told me that they had never been so nervous in accompanying any soloist. In making the record, all the shorter time intervals between piano and orchestra had been allowed for by blank spaces in the revolving paper roll, but for the longer intervals it seemed safer to arrange for the roll to be automatically stopped and started again by an electric button on the conductor's desk. If the conductor kept strict time, there was no special difficulty, but the habit of yielding to performers who required rhythmical freedom, together with an unconquerable feeling of uncertainty regarding the machine, seems to have made it sometimes impossible for the conductor to follow the performance with the necessary mechanical precision.

These performances took place at a time when the power and prestige of the Aeolian Company was at its zenith. Some of us thought that participation in mechanical performances was almost suicidal, and we deplored the action of those of our colleagues who consented to make concert tours in which they played duets with the mechanical piano player. We listened with mingled skepticism and hope to the promoters of the machine who assured us that familiarity with music through mechanically recorded performances would ultimately create audiences larger than had ever been imagined.

It seems strange today to reflect upon the tremendous energy that was expended in the manufacture and sale of all those machines and paper rolls. It is strange to recall the number of public performances given throughout the civilized world with the sole object of publicizing this peculiar industry. And it is strange to think that nothing survives of all that work.

And yet . . . am I justified in saying that *nothing* survives?

We know today that the prognostications of a glorious new age of music which were held out by promoters of the machine were not merely shadowy baits to induce us to accept substantial financial rewards. We know now that the voice of the tempter was the voice of the prophet, and we know that the art of mechanical reproduction of musical performance has increased the taste for music, the desire for musical education, and the attendance at concerts to an extent that could not have been dreamed of thirty years ago. But in spite of this, the thought of mechanization still holds something alarming. And new inventions are constantly appearing.

It seems only a short while ago that I received a wireless message from my manager, in mid-ocean, as I was returning from a concert tour in Europe. I learned that I had been engaged to play, immediately on arrival in New York, at a radio concert which was to link up, for the first time, performances coming from various points throughout the United States, and broadcast these performances in the form of a complete program from the Waldorf-Astoria Hotel, then situated on 34th Street, where the Empire State Building now stands.

The sea was stormy, and the boat was delayed over twenty-four hours, with the result that I was snatched off at Quarantine by special orders and rushed to the Waldorf-Astoria, arriving only a few moments before the concert started. Walter Damrosch conducted the orchestra; I played the first movement of the Schumann concerto and the first movement of the Moonlight Sonata. Of the other performers, located at various points through the country, I can remember only Ernestine Schumann-Heink, who sang in Chicago, and Will Rogers, who spoke from San Francisco. The concert was not long, but the occasion was impressive, for everyone realized that the feat of broadcasting in this manner had never been accomplished before, and that it was an historical event.

A few years later, I was engaged to take part in the first demonstration ever staged of moving pictures combined with sound. This was arranged by Warner Brothers at the theater on Broadway which bore their name. There were a number of performers on this, another occasion of historic interest. I played part of the Kreutzer Sonata with Efrem Zimbalist.

It is a grand thing to bring great art within the reach of all the people, but an uneasy suspicion creeps in that popularization is dangerously close to vulgarization. The French language, incidentally, does not differentiate between the meanings of these two words, and this possibly indicates practical, if somewhat cynical, recognition of the fact that the two things are very likely to merge together.

I am delighted when the elevator boy tells me that he has enjoyed my recital the previous evening; I am horrified when he proceeds to whistle the melody of a Beethoven sonata in jazz rhythm and, when I hear the strains of Isolde's Liebestod coming from the radio in a busy grocery store, I ask myself (just as any old fogey might ask himself) what we are coming to, and whether the magic of music may not be in jeopardy through casting it into unsuitable surroundings.

My good friend, Monsieur Blondel, head of the great French piano firm, Erard, was accustomed to say that the invasion of the machine into fields distinguished by fine handiwork was an unmixed evil, destructive to our civilization. He was totally opposed to modern devices applied to the manufacture of pianos. I frequently heard him deplore the introduction of the typewriter, which, he said, represented the beginning of the end, inasmuch as it would inevitably lead to the total disappearance of one of the most beautiful of all arts—the art of calligraphy—and further, because it substituted an impersonal mechanism for the refinement always needed in human intercourse, as well in business as in private relations, which could only be maintained through personal contact, personal speech, and personal letter writing.

I remember this because I was always an admirer of fine handwriting, and I disliked the thought that it might become a thing of the past. I rarely see good handwriting nowadays, but I have never known an artist whose handwriting was not marked by character and a sense for beauty. Isadora Duncan told me that she considered the decay of the art of handwriting to be due not only to the use of the typewriter but to a steady decline in the art of the dance, in which, she said, modern custom had so curtailed and restricted the natural grace which should flow out of the fingertips that hands seemed to have become superfluous. She did a great deal to restore what she regarded as forgotten ideals of beauty through pose and gesture, and her handwriting was unquestionably characteristic and elegant.

I have in my possession an autograph letter of Beethoven's, in which, writing to a Viennese piano maker, he said that the new piano was *too good*, inasmuch as its modern improvements deprived the performer of the sense that he was creating his own tone. I often think of this, wondering whether or not today's mechanisms may be in process of destroying something strictly personal and vital in each one of us.

It was not alone in music that one had the feeling of passing from a "hand-made to measure" to a "ready-made by machine" state of existence. I had great difficulty in getting any article of clothing which would fit me. In Europe I had been accustomed to having all my suits, shirts, hats, and shoes made for me, because ready-made things came only in shapes and sizes that I could not wear. Here the same condition confronted me. The great difference was the cost of custom-made articles, three or four times the price of similar articles in Europe, and even then almost unobtainable. For example, I don't think I ever saw a hatmaker in America, and very seldom a bootmaker. Everything came from the factory.

My difficulty did not arise from being overparticular or hard to please. On the contrary, I did not dress in the way that a person having pretensions to gentility is supposed to dress. I wore detachable shirt fronts (dickeys) and detachable cuffs. I wore ties made up to hook over the collar button, and I wore gaiters (spats) over high button shoes (which, without the spats, were considered dressy). My winter overcoat had a removable woolen lining and a removable fur collar, so that it served for very cold as well as moderate seasons. Worst of all, my coat suits, although tailored to measure, were provided with cotton twill linings, calling forth an ingenuous remark from one of my English friends: "By Jove!" he said, "I never knew that coats could be lined with anything but silk."

I must not forget that all men of social standing superior to that of the laborer were slaves to that ridiculous abomination, the tall silk hat—any other kind of head covering, excepting for strictly informal use, being considered plebeian and lacking in dignity.

The long silk nap of these hats had to be kept smooth and shiny, and the only correct way to do this was to have it ironed at the hat store. A less expensive method was to smooth it over oneself, with a specially prepared greasy substance. This is what I did, and in so doing I was unhappily conscious of the fact that I set myself outside the pale of propriety. I also used to varnish my horribly hot and uncomfortable patent-leather high button shoes with a preparation called "Vernis Guiche." It gave a clean and glittering result, but of course it was not the right thing to do. In a word, my many violations of social etiquette, if they had been summed up and made known, would undoubtedly have closed all doors to me in polite circles. Such things, as London might have said, were "just not done, dontcherknow!"

But though heedless of social conventions (mainly from reasons of economy), I was absolutely compelled to conform to these to the extent of having a silk hat made to fit my head. A ready-made one either would have come below my ears or would have toppled off. There was no "give" to it, as in today's soft felt hat.

I am convinced that it was the spirit of American democracy which finally insisted that a poor man must be able to dress just as well, within his means, as his wealthy neighbor or employer. Factory methods were improved, more shapes and sizes came into the market, and before very long, I, together with most other men whose measurements did not conform to existing limited patterns, was able to wear ready-made articles of clothing with comfort. From that moment, certain things were doomed to extinction, although even now they have not totally disappeared. But the silk hat, the starched shirt and collar, the button shoes, the swallow-tailed and so-called Prince Albert coats —in fact, any kind of clothing which restricts liberty of movement—must all go the way of everything that savors of dictatorship in a world of free men.

The custom which prevailed in certain quarters, of calling some people ladies and gentlemen who, in other countries, would have been considered members of a lower class, was rather perplexing. I had heard so much about the abolition of class distinctions in the United States that I was most eager to adapt myself to the customs of the country, but I never could feel quite sure, when people spoke of a char-woman as a "lady" and a shoeblack or a bartender as a "professor," whether they were serious or facetious.

I was never offended or embarrassed when I was referred to as "this man," whereas the plumber, the carpenter and the candlestick maker were the "gentlemen," but I regretted the frequent blunders I made in trying to conform to social conditions which were new to me. These blunders generally took the form of shaking hands warmly with butlers and chauffeurs, and I cannot say if it was a help or an added confusion for me to remember that table waiters in Germany, the most class-conscious of all countries, had but recently been promoted in the social scale. One no longer called for the "Kellner," but for the "Oberkellner," and sometimes even for "Herr Ober."

In any case, it was not hard to bear in mind that the word "servant" must never be used in the United States, for it had been definitely replaced by the appellation "help." So, little by little, as I became familiar with these features of American life, a proper sense of social equilibrium was established.

It was tremendously impressive to witness the advances that were being made at that time in public education. Never had such schools been built for the people, and I was amazed to note the growing importance attached to art in these institutions. The music instruction was very elementary and the teachers were not particularly competent; however, the pupils enjoyed the bands, orchestras, and singing groups immensely and it was confidently asserted that the music stimulated their imagination and made them brighter all-round students. This was the beginning of a regular system of teaching music in the public schools of America which I believe to be superior to anything of the kind in other countries.

It is impossible, in fact, to overestimate the value of this musical education, elementary and incomplete though it was, when one considers the drab monotony of the average small town in the United States. Music has opened the door in these places to a sense of beauty; and this, in the final analysis, develops an astonishing kind of civic pride which in turn creates the firm conviction that the home city, whatever its present limitations, is destined to be "just as good" as the greatest metropolis. Truly, this is the spirit of decentralization at its best. It may be one of the reasons why the capital of any one of the United States is not invariably the largest or the most important city in that state, and, from a more restricted point of view, it is certainly the reason why it was possible for me and other musical pioneers of my time to give concerts in remote towns which displayed a desire for cultural activities without a parallel in similarly situated towns in other countries.

For example, it was a commonplace among musical performers who had great traveling experience to refer to university towns in Europe as "bad for concerts." Yet, for some reason which I have never fathomed, the attendance at concerts in university towns in the United States has always been very large. Possibly the fact that many universities and colleges were coeducational may have something to do with it. The boys and girls liked to go to a show together, and there were always impressions to be exchanged after a piano recital.

College girls always looked very pretty to me, and I greatly enjoyed getting letters from them. Sometimes they wrote poems to me. I recall the first line of one of these: "Come, child of the inhumans"—which was certainly a most enticing invitation. I forget the rest of the poem.

Whatever the cause underlying the interest taken in concerts by college students, it is certain that the seeds of discrimination and taste were sown among these unsophisticated youngsters, and the result, taken as a whole, was surprisingly good. American audiences showed greater receptivity toward contemporary music than Europeans did. I have referred elsewhere to the fact that I played the compositions of Debussy in the United States at a time when French audiences spoke with complete disdain of the composer.

My remarks must not be taken as implying, however, that American audiences were altogether superior to audiences in other countries, for such is not the case. There was a great deal of crudity here, an inevitable consequence of the kind of publicity adopted for musical performances, which suggested that a concert was a "show" like any other form of public entertainment. Josef Hofmann told me of an intoxicated man who was ejected from one of his recitals for making a disturbance. "I haven't touched a drop," he protested indignantly; but on being asked why he had been so noisy at a piano recital, he was silent for a moment, then said: "I take it all back. I must certainly have been as drunk as an owl to go to a piano concert."

Nor was there lacking the feeling that a piano recital, in certain conditions, might be a positively harmful thing. One evening in a small Western town I was mildly annoyed by the sound of banging drums, tambourines, and loud singing just outside the hotel dining room. When I went out on my way to the concert hall, a stalwart Salvation Army lassie threw herself into my path. "Don't do it, dear brother!" she entreated me earnestly. "Don't lead these poor people into sin and misery with the arts of Satan. Bring them to the Lord with us."

She had made up her mind that it was a sin to give a public concert, and there was nothing I could do about it. I asked her to pray for me, then I broke away and went about my guilty occupation.

The Mason & Hamlin Company, whose magnificent pianos I used for nearly thirty years, always sent an experienced tuner with me on my tours. We always traveled together and became close friends. I am sure that I stood nearer the heart of Pop Bacon than anyone or anything else except his pianos, which were like children to him. He felt himself responsible for my comfort and health, and he spared no pains to render me small services at every moment. He also liked to advise me occasionally as to my relations with other people, and he was greatly concerned by my habit of making occasional satirical remarks. "You ought to be careful, Mr. Bauer," he used to growl at me amiably but apprehensively. "These people don't understand sarcasm and they don't like it. You can't tell what may happen. Supposing some big husky chap were to haul off and land you one, where would you be? You aren't in any kind of physical training and I'm sure I don't know . . ." and so his voice would trail off rather miserably.

We arrived one day at a western mining town, very wealthy and very crude. My concert was announced in the Opera House, and streamers with my name were stretched across the main street. The house was filled to the last seat; and before I came on the stage, the noise of banging down the seats, together with the cries of the ushers selling peanuts, chewing gum, and candy, was deafening. Roars of applause greeted my entrance. I had my first, startling experience of shrill whistling as an expression of enthusiasm.

I had previously thought that whistling signified disapproval. I sat down to play. The audience continued to be noisy, but I imagined that they might become quiet as the music progressed. They did not. I wondered what to do, getting more and more uncomfortable. I finished the first piece. Again roars of applause. I walked off the stage, returning to bow my acknowledgments. Some latecomers banged down the seats and called to the usher to bring peanuts. After a short pause I went on again and started (I think) the Moonlight Sonata. In the middle of the first movement I heard the cry "Chewing gum, candy, peanuts!" and the ushers banged down the seats for some more latecomers.

I stopped playing. I rose from my seat and advanced to the footlights, trembling with fury. Roars of applause. I made a speech. "Ladies and gentlemen," I said, "I must humbly beg your forgiveness for having neglected to make better arrangements for your convenience this evening. Through some quite unaccountable lapse, I quite forgot my duty to see that you were not disturbed in listening to the music. I should, of course, have personally turned down all the seats quietly, and I should personally have dispensed those refreshments which are needed, outside, instead of inside the auditorium. If you will bear with me a few moments, I will see that the ushers are comfortably accommodated so that the concert may proceed without further interruption."

Roars of applause. I walked off, boiling. Pop Bacon was in the wings, sadly shaking his head. "You shouldn't have been so sarcastic, Mr. Bauer," he growled morosely. "They don't like it, and they don't understand it. Some fellow will haul off and land you one. . . ." I went on the stage again, played the rest of the program and finished the concert. The enthusiasm was tremendous. It was a triumph. Finally the public began to leave and some of the lights were extinguished. Pop Bacon smiled feebly and uneasily. As I stood in the wings, wiping my perspiring head, a cheerful voice was heard from the other side: "This way, gents," and a group of solemn-faced, determined-looking men appeared, walking toward me. "My Lord, there they are!" gasped Pop Bacon, and promptly retired upstage. I stood my ground awaiting the group. The spokesman made a dignified gesture and said: "Mr. Bauer, sir, we have come to express our appreciation of your magnanimity this evening. We do not consider, sir, that it was up to you to instruct the ushers to keep silence. We think it was up to the theater management to do so. We thank you, sir, for your generous gesture, but we cannot permit you to assume the blame. No indeed, sir. And we certainly hope to see you again in ——." (Wild horses would not drag the name of the place from my lips.)

We shook hands all round, very warmly, and I went home to bed. "You were quite right, Pop," I told him.

Poor old Pop Bacon! If ever a man died in the performance of his duty, it was he. The following year, while preparing my piano for a concert in a western city, he collapsed from a heart attack. They brought him back to the hotel and laid him on the bed. I was sent for and took his hand. "The piano will be all right this evening," he whispered, and never spoke again.

Ten

I WAS OVERJOYED WHEN MY MANAGER TOLD ME THAT I WAS
to make a tour on the Pacific Coast, for I greatly desired to
see California and all the country west of the Rocky Mountains. Since there were very few good "concert towns" between Chicago and San Francisco (that being the most direct
route to the Far West), it was decided that I should go by
the longer, southern way, where I had some engagements,
and return via the northern railroads after visiting British
Columbia.

I started the trip in St. Louis, where my old friend, Max
Zach, formerly violist in the Boston Symphony Orchestra,
was conductor of the St. Louis Symphony Orchestra, and
I gave my first performance of the B-flat concerto by Brahms
under his direction, to my great satisfaction. I have always
felt the need of merging the solo part with the orchestra in
the two Brahms concertos; this cannot always be done because of traditional insistence on giving prominence to the

Harold Bauer, from the bust by Brenda Putnam

Oggia

Harold Bauer

virtuoso, but Zach fell in with my ideas, and the result was good.

From St. Louis I went to Oklahoma City, where I had the interesting experience of seeing a great city in process of actual birth. The principal street showed, on one side, a very large and up-to-date hotel, several churches, and a number of splendid stores and office buildings. On the opposite side of the same street, many people were living in primitive conditions, housed in small wooden shacks and tents. I think there were Indians among the number, but of this I am not sure.

The Women's Club of Oklahoma City had engaged me for a recital, and I found a refined and intelligent audience. It was very impressive to see how culture was not only keeping pace with the building up of the city, but was actually outstripping it.

My schedule then called for recitals in Dallas, Fort Worth, and Galveston. Nothing of moment occurred in the first-named cities, but in Galveston I received a telegram from my manager which upset me considerably. It brought the message that the manager in California insisted upon my arrival two days earlier than the date originally planned, and threatened cancellation of the tour if I failed to do so. There was no material obstacle to this, for I had no engagements between Galveston and San Francisco, but the situation was complicated for another reason.

Some weeks earlier, the Mason & Hamlin Company (whose pianos I had used from the beginning) had gone into receivership, financially exhausted through the manufacture and exploitation of a magnificent instrument constructed regardless of cost. Pending the reorganization of the company (which to me was a foregone conclusion, and so, in fact, it proved to be) I had undertaken the responsibility and expense of transportation of the pianos used at my concerts. This led me into more than one slight predicament.

At that particular moment, there were no concert grand pianos in San Francisco, although one had been shipped there from the East. Since nobody could foresee whether this piano would be there in time, it was imperative for me to take the piano used in Galveston with me on the long trip. The time being strictly limited, I had no alternative but to engage a special train in order to leave Galveston immediately after my recital and make connection with the transcontinental express at Houston, some sixty miles north.

This arrangement was consequently made. With my piano tuner, who accompanied me everywhere, I watched the packing and loading of this piano, following my concert, on the special train which left Galveston, I think, shortly after midnight. Then came the transfer at Houston at about four o'clock in the morning, and this also had to be supervised. As I prepared to go to bed the Pullman conductor remarked, in genial appreciation: "You couldn't have taken more trouble if it had been your mother's corpse, could you?"

On arriving at Oakland, California, I was tremendously impressed by the palatial ferryboat to San Francisco, the wonderful view of the bay, and the nearing of the tower at the city ferry station. I immediately fell in love with the place in a manner I had not experienced since my arrival in Paris as a very young man, years before. And, as in Paris, everything about San Francisco enchanted me. I liked the atmosphere, the hills, the unexpected line of the streets and the smells. I thought the St. Francis the finest hotel I had ever seen, the reception clerks the most friendly in the world, and the food the best in the country.

The concert manager was my good friend at once and,

with him, I found the man who was the leading spirit in musical culture there: Oscar Weil, a splendid musician, a cosmopolitan of wide interests, a scholar and a gentleman. I never knew anyone who was better able to combine the task of awakening artistic appreciation with that of intellectual and technical training. His influence was a real godsend to San Francisco, and I doubt if any student interested in music failed to derive benefit from it.

I gave two recitals in San Francisco and made many friends. Among these I must mention a man of great charm and unusual character named Sir Henry Heyman. It was rare to meet anyone bearing an English title in the United States, particularly an American, as this man was, so I inquired how it had been conferred upon him. It appeared that he had gone to the Hawaiian Islands during the time of the English overlordship of the group (then known as the Sandwich Islands) and had played at a concert there in the presence of the reigning, sovereign King Kalakoa, who, in pursuance of the powers vested in him by England, had conferred the title in question. I believe that it was a unique case. Sir Henry was an extremely hospitable and generous friend; he took me in charge, introduced me at the celebrated Bohemian Club, and presented me to many most interesting people: painters, writers, scientists, architects, actors, and, in particular, several people who were engaged in an art to which I had never paid any special attention: the art of bookmaking and typography. All of them were members of the Bohemian Club, and I had never in my life met such an aggregation of people active in artistic pursuits. I notice that the above list makes no mention of musicians, but I shall leave it unchanged. Good musicians there were in plenty, but for the moment I forgot them because all those other artists interested me so much.

My success at the two recitals was sufficient to justify giving a third one. I also played in Oakland and several neighboring cities, after which I went to Los Angeles. The impression I received there was of a totally different kind. There were plenty of pretty streets with nice houses and trees. There was also frequent evidence of considerable wealth. But, on the whole, Los Angeles in those days was a sprawling provincial town, lacking in artistic distinction and apparently built without regard for any shape or plan. I enjoyed the climate, and I prowled about the streets with constant and ever increasing curiosity, for there were many things that were entirely new to me.

Judging from newspaper advertisements and the innumerable placards and posters attached and scattered everywhere, more attention was paid to methods of spiritual development and salvation in this city of the angels than in any other place on earth. One could not help being saved. If redemption were not forthcoming at the hands of this or that "revivalist," one needed only to go next door or across the street to obtain more fervid intercession. The names of the various religious sects were legion, and their leaders were of both sexes and all ages. In one large temple there was a little girl evangelist; in another, a little boy evangelist. There was the large Rubens-like lady evangelist whose opulent form obviously gave a foretaste of Heaven to many; there was the Buddha-like Oriental, with an impassive smile and an Oxford accent; there was the thin, haggard fanatic who had just stepped down from one of Greco's canvases; and in addition to all of these there were quite a number of ladies and gentlemen in ordinary attire who, without extravagant gesture or raising of the voice, pointed out quietly and reasonably that they possessed the secret of the only way to sal-

[194]

vation—a secret which they were willing to share with their fellow-creatures.

Aside from all these merchants of religion, the city literally swarmed with fortune tellers, crystal gazers, mediums, and fakirs of all sorts who, I believe, were liberally supported by every class of society, for I rarely met anyone in Los Angeles who failed to admit that at some time—"just for fun"—he or she had consulted a fortune teller. Some people, I know, were accustomed to do this quite regularly.

One afternoon, noticing a group of people gazing intently into the window of a large saloon, I went to investigate. There were two cages, one containing a fairly large bear, and the other a wildcat. A printed card gave the information that these two animals would fight each other at a public exhibition a few days later. Those who were examining them and comparing their respective points were, at the same time, discussing the bets they intended to place at the forthcoming battle.

Continuing my walk, I saw displayed in another window a rattlesnake and a mongoose (specially imported from India) which were also to be pitted against each other. Cock-fights and so-called "dog courses" (which I found meant dog fights) were likewise liberally advertised. I do not recall seeing any announcements of human contests, such as boxing or wrestling, but I do remember, after the first shock of sickened disgust, that the question crept irresistibly into my mind: how can one explain why organized fighting between human beings is considered noble, while organized fighting between animals should be regarded as degrading?

The answer is, I suppose, that "sport" does not mean the same thing in different countries. But it is curious to reflect how far the definition may be stretched. To some, "sport" implies a kind of equality, if only at the outset of the struggle, between the parties engaged in it; rules must be observed and cheating is forbidden. To others, sport means gaining the advantage by any and every means— "no holds barred," as they say in wrestling circles—and the palm is awarded to the one who has best succeeded in unfairly tricking his adversary. Consider the words of Schubert's "Die Forelle"!

Speaking for myself, the only enjoyment I ever experienced from sport (games, of course, excluded) was that common to all nasty little boys—namely, the catching of flies and other insects in order to ascertain their ability to adjust themselves to their environment after their wings and legs were pulled off. With regard to contests between human beings, I have never changed the opinion formed the first time I witnessed an exhibition of fencing, wherein the factors of attack, self-defense, skill, and endurance seemed to me to be trained to the highest conceivable point. The superiority of this over any other kind of physical contest is so great that it stands absolutely alone as an art which combines the supreme struggle with the refinements of civilized life.

My comments on the brutality of these animal fights were received with an airy wave of dismissal. "We pay no attention to these little things," said my Los Angeles friends. "They are due to low Mexicans and cheap adventurers who come here from the East to make their fortunes. You will see how promptly they will disappear when L.A. becomes one of the greatest cities in the world."

I gave three recitals in Los Angeles, which were warmly received, and I visited a number of smaller towns in the vicinity, including, of course, the lovely and sleepy old city of San Diego. The city I liked most was Pasadena. There seemed to be a spirit of civic pride in that place which I had rarely seen equaled, and I had the impression that the inhabitants were all determined that it should develop into a center of beauty and culture. I was taken to a hotel of a kind I had never previously imagined: an incredible glorification and magnification of the American boardinghouse, where every conceivable luxury of accommodation in lodgings, meals, private entertainments, garden surroundings, and so forth, was furnished for one price, which covered the whole expense. No wonder they called it the "American plan." There was nothing like it in any other country.

My former pupil in Paris, Miss Alice Coleman, had become the guiding musical spirit of Pasadena, and had instituted an admirable series of concerts, given each year, in the interest of chamber music. She was then Mrs. Ernest Batchelder, and at her home I met a large number of people distinguished in various fields, among them the great scientist, Robert Millikan. Through the kindness of this gentleman, I was invited to spend a night with the group of astronomers assembled at the top of Mount Wilson, where the largest telescope in the world had recently been installed.

The day after my recital, Ernest Batchelder and I set out on the trip, the most memorable in my experience. The drive up the mountain was very steep; the narrow road cut into the side was on the edge of what seemed to me a frightful precipice growing more terrifying every moment, and my heart was in my mouth. Finally, after an interminable time, we arrived. Night had already fallen. The temperature in the city had been hot, but here there were several feet of snow on the ground. We drove into a large garage, and I got out and began to collect my scattered wits. "Where is the big telescope?" I inquired. "You are in it," came the answer. And, sure enough, what I had taken for a garage proved to be the enclosure of the telescope with its characteristic turning roof. From that moment, every question I put elicited a reply which was exactly the opposite of what I expected. No sooner was I reconciled to the idea that a telescope was not necessarily enclosed in a tube, than the shattering reply to my question: "Where do you look through it?" came with the simple words: "You don't look through this kind of telescope." When I saw that the lower end, obviously the outer side of the reflecting mirror, was carefully covered with tarpaulins, I remarked, knowingly, that one couldn't be too careful with these reflecting compounds; the slightest scratch being sufficient, of course, to distort the image. "But," my informant stated, "the glass alone would distort the image, so the reflecting compound, if employed at all, is on its surface and not back of its surface." I gibbered: "Then why the glass at all?" My companion was engaged with the complicated mechanism that controlled the motion of the mighty engine, and did not reply for a moment. Finally: "Eh?" he said. "I suppose it is because we can't get anything else quite as smooth and flat. Sealing wax would be just as good, but it is too brittle. Now we can go upstairs."

I climbed up a steel ladder about fifty feet high and came out on an open platform with a railing round it. My companion pointed out that a small frame in the steel structure had been placed immediately opposite a mirror which reflected the image received by the main object glass below. He explained that this secondary reflection was intended primarily for photographic work, not for the human eye—which, I learned, is incapable of receiving light rays which may have taken many thousands of years to reach the earth. "But," he said, "you shall, nevertheless, have a glimpse of one of the most spectacular objects in the sky, the great nebula in Orion. Hold on tightly to that railing."

Not knowing in the least what was coming, I obeyed him. There was a faint whirring sound as he touched a button, and the earth seemed to fall away from me. I became a mere point in space, and saw everything around me moving in all directions at once. The shutter in the roof opened, and the entire dome began to revolve. The angle of the telescope was altered to find the required direction, and the platform on which I stood was raised or lowered (I forget which) to correspond to the changed position. I think I should have fainted from dizziness in another moment, but the various motions ceased immediately the proper position was attained.

I was next instructed to hold a small magnifying glass in front of my eye, and to peer through it at an almost invisible slit in the shutter which closed the small frame previously described. The view of the terrific conflagration presented by the Orion nebula which lay before me almost caused me to recoil in fright. The flames and clouds of smoke being motionless, however, I realized that the fire was quite a long way off, and I was able to contemplate the stupendous spectacle calmly, if with awe.

My guide then altered the direction of the telescope and invited me to look again. I saw a few stars and, in the center of the field, a black and empty space. "We have to discover what is there," he informed me. "The path of a star in the vicinity seems to indicate the influence of another star which, so far, is invisible, but photography will tell us something about it, provided it is giving out any light at all." He proceeded to tell me that the camera had been trained on this black space for several hours during the past few nights, and that they expected (for some reason which I do not know) to obtain a result now. With that he adjusted the camera, and I was taken away to visit other telescopes and to inspect the laboratory where the astronomical calculations and researches were being carried on.

The entire night passed in this fascinating way. Just before dawn the camera was brought down to the laboratory and the negative was closely inspected. "There it is," said one of the eminent astronomers, pointing to a faint white dot revealed in the development. I looked at it with complete unconcern and asked: "What comes next?" "With this white dot as a basis," said the astronomer impressively, "we can determine the mass, the weight, and the temperature of a star which will forever be invisible to the human eye. We can also discover of what materials it is composed, and possibly this may lead to new scientific discoveries on our earth." I thought for a while, and then said, with some hesitation, that the likelihood of achieving anything important seemed remote, whereas the work involved was lengthy and tremendously costly, when all factors were taken into consideration. "What is the use of it all?" I asked rather uncomfortably and desperately, hoping that he would be able to furnish me with a satisfactory answer. He was. "Mr. Bauer," he remarked pleasantly, "I'm sure I shall be able to reply properly to that question, if you will kindly tell me what is the use of Beethoven's Sonata Appassionata."

My next destination was Phoenix, Arizona. The father of one of my Paris pupils owned and operated a music store in this thriving town, just rising from the sandy desert. I was cordially welcomed into the family, and, thanks to their kindness, I spent four pleasant and interesting days there. I had no previous conception of what could be accomplished by irrigation in bringing fertility to the desert, and the sight of oranges and grapefruit growing plentifully in the sand, which gave no evidence of containing any soil, was fascinating and almost incredible.

My recital, given at the Opera House, was a great success. I met there a gentleman who was director of a school situated at the Indian reservation about five miles out of the city, and he asked me to go there to examine the educational work he was doing for the Indian children in elementary art and music.

This was a pleasant and instructive visit. The older Indians, some of whom could not speak English, were dignified and very courteous; the children, on the other hand, were full of animation and curiosity to see the white man who, they had been told, had given a concert all by himself in the big city. The director showed me their pictures and their clay modelings, in which the attempt to combine Indian patterns with those of European origin, which they were learning, was interesting, but, I should say, only fairly successful. Next, the director gave me a demonstration of their musical training in a band performance. About fifty children took part in this, playing on all the instruments available in the school. It is no reflection on the ability and patience of their instructors to report that the result was both ludicrous and horrible. But it did not matter; they were all keenly interested in absorbing the white man's culture, and they had a wonderful time.

Crowding around me, the children begged me to play for them. Since the only piano there was a small, wornout upright, lacking a number of strings and hammers and shockingly out of tune, I was unable to do myself justice, and their disappointment could not be concealed, for what I did on that old box was neither more nor less than what they were accustomed to hear daily at their lessons.

I had a bright idea. After consultation with the director, and telephoning to the city, I announced to the children that I was going to give a special concert on my big piano at the Opera House in the big city, for Indians alone, and that I was happy to invite them and their parents to attend it the following evening. This announcement was greeted with the wildest enthusiasm, and I think I remember that something like a war dance ensued.

With the help of my friends, arrangements for the concert were rapidly completed. I sent out three or four special streetcars to bring in the audience from the reservation (which was very near the terminal of the streetcar line).

I have always regretted that I did not have a photograph made of that audience. It was unique, for many of the older people, wishing to honor me, had donned their tribal costumes. But their faces I can never forget. The youngsters, full of eager curiosity, and their elders, impassive, dignified, and courteous, made a truly impressive picture. Although the concert was not announced as a public performance, the theater was besieged by city residents who wished to hear me again, and these white people were admitted to a separate part of the auditorium.

Neither the older Indians nor the children applauded very much, but I occasionally heard little whoops or restrained yells from the younger members. I did not realize the full measure of their appreciation until, about a month later, I received a copy of the school paper, in which a number of the children had recorded their impressions, which, I am happy to say, were altogether favorable. I was particularly pleased by the expression, repeated in several letters to the paper, that "the box did sing"; but the gem of these reports was that written by a little girl who thought that "it was lovely to see the way Mr. Bauer hit his working piano, and we all hoped he did not hurt his beautiful hands." The term "working piano," I realized, was drawn from my criticism of the old instrument at the reservation, which "did not work."

After leaving Phoenix I returned to San Francisco, where I met Fritz Kreisler. I cannot recall whether we played together in that city, but I do remember that we played separate recitals, and that we left together immediately afterward for Portland and Seattle, where we were engaged to give joint concerts.

A large reception was given in our honor after the concert in Portland, and at about midnight Fritz and I, yielding to insistent requests, consented to make a little music. I do not know whence the idea came, but in a spirit of hilarity I borrowed Fritz's violin, he sat at the piano, and we played part of Beethoven's Kreutzer Sonata in this way. (The work had figured on our program earlier in the evening.) Nobody ever knew how it happened that the report of this impromptu performance was circulated all over the country. Even in Europe, years later, I was asked to tell about the concert I gave in America wherein Kreisler had played the piano, and I the violin.

I have always suspected that the enthusiasm of our listeners at that reception, when they imagined they were listening to a public concert instead of an improvised joke, was due to the potent and delicious whisky punch which was freely imbibed on that occasion. My violin playing was, at that time, on its last legs, so to speak, and although I regret having lost the ability to play on that instrument, I do not believe that I could have kept it up under any circumstances. There is no reason why a violinist should not play the piano, for that involves no particular strain. But a pianist cannot play the violin. If this statement seems paradoxical, I beg the reader to make the most of it. Let it suffice to say that a violinist has to adopt a distorted and twisted position of the body, which cannot be maintained without constant practice.

Fritz and I proceeded to Seattle, which was then in the throes of one of the colossal real-estate booms for which the United States has achieved unenviable notoriety. Speculators had decided not only that the city was destined to become one of the largest in the entire country, but that it was bound, in addition, to develop into one of the world's greatest seaports.

Perhaps they were not far wrong in their predictions, but in the meanwhile the wildest gambling on these issues was taking place, and the result, in all probability, was that far more money was lost than gained in the process.

Kreisler and I were immediately pounced upon by some of these speculators, to whom we doubtless seemed likely game for their traps and tempting snares. The bait extended to us was the grossest kind of flattery. Seattle was infinitely honored by the visit of such artists. These great artists would doubtless wish to leave, for the benefit of future generations, a record of their visit and, by the merest coincidence, the present situation provided an opportunity, unique in history, to perpetuate the memory of a musical event which, etc., etc. Here were two parcels of real estate going for a mere song. What more simple than to call one of them the Bauer corner, and the other the Kreisler corner? The day before yesterday these lots were valued at $100 each. Yesterday they sold for $1,000 each; tomorrow they will be worth $100,000 each. Why not accept Seattle's homage and have one's name inscribed in perpetuity on the annals of this growing metropolis?

The proposition, considered from the standpoint of an investment alone, would represent a handsome fortune and a life income to the fortunate purchaser of the lots. But this, of course, was purely incidental.

"Not interested? Well, I never supposed you would be. Real estate, after all, requires supervision, and, of course, you don't want to be bothered. Now, here is something very special—just the thing for you. Paderewski is in it."

The new proposition involved the purchase of a tree—yes, one tree. The plans for development of the city naturally included a park system; there was a grove of sequoia trees threatened with extermination at the hands of the lumber dealer, and an enlightened group of citizens proposed to preserve them by raising a special fund. The purchaser of each tree was entitled to attach a brass plaque, engraved with his name, to the trunk, thus leaving a record which might be expected to endure a thousand years or more, according to the age of the tree when purchased.

We were invited to inspect the tree that Paderewski had acquired in this grove. It was alleged to be about two thousand years old, and a commemorative tablet bearing his name and a date had been attached to it. One sensed the implication, in the admiring comments made by the two gentlemanly real-estate operators who were accompanying us, that since this great artist had participated financially in the plan for conservation of these mighty trees, we could certainly do no less than follow his example.

The grove was a wonderful sight, and I wandered a few steps away from our party, when I was accosted by a middle-aged man, dressed in workman's clothes. "Don't let them fool you, brother," he said hoarsely, "Paderoosky never bought none of these here redwoods. They *give* him one and put his name on it because he got stuck with a lot of land that he never wanted. Now, if you arsk *me*, there's only one thing a man should put his money in out here, and that's mud flats."

"This fellow is worse than any of them," I thought to myself. "The hoary old villain thinks I can be taken in by a scheme based on a word I never heard." So I asked him politely what he meant by "mud flats."

"See here," he started impatiently to explain, "the city's going to be a big seaport, ain't it? It's got to have plenty of waterfront to build docks and storehouses and roads and railroad sidings, ain't it? Has it *got* plenty of waterfront? No, it ain't. Well, whatcher going to do about it? You got to *make* yer waterfront, ain't it? How yer going to do it? Well, yer take the top of that hill that the city's creeping up on, and yer wash it down into the water, and there's yer mud flats, ain't it?"

I understood what he said and what he meant, and of all the monstrous rubbish that had ever been advanced to swindle and delude the public, that plan seemed to me the most fantastic. I learned afterward that many people were advocating it.

"There is certainly no limit to the gullibility of human beings," I reflected philosophically. "Many people have been persuaded to buy the Brooklyn Bridge, and, doubtless, many more will be led into buying nonexistent land which is to come into being by turning a water hose on a hill."

My philosophy was completely at fault. The scheme, wild and extravagant as it appeared to me, was actually realized and turned out to be the most practical and profitable of all the plans that had been devised to make Seattle one of the great seaports of the world.

I cannot remember whether Fritz and I invested any money there or not. I was much more timid than he in matters of speculation, and it is possible that he yielded and I resisted.

Our paths separated temporarily after the Seattle concert, and there followed a rather uneventful trip to Vancouver and thence eastward, with a stop in Cleveland, where I was engaged to play with the orchestra.

It was on another visit to Cleveland, years later, when I was playing with the orchestra under the direction of Nicolai Sokoloff, that I was shown the plans of a new auditorium, which had been offered as a permanent home for the symphony orchestra by a wealthy art patron, Mr. Severance, and I went, the next day, to see what had already been accomplished in its construction.

Mr. Severance explained, at length, the various modern devices and improvements which were to be introduced in the building, and laid special stress on the complex system of indirect lighting, with all conceivable shades of color and degrees of intensity, controlled from a single switchboard. "When this is installed," he said, "the operator will sit at the switch table and play on it as if he were a pianist." I thought this over for a few moments, and suddenly I had a vision. I seized Sokoloff's arm and shouted at him. "Scriabin!" was all I said. He looked at me in amazement, and then he too saw the vision. "But, of course!" he cried, "and we will do it together at the opening concert next year!" Mr. Severance, to whom this was so much Greek, doubtless, thought that both Sokoloff and I had suddenly gone insane. In explanation I must, as usual, digress, without apologies to the reader.

The composer Scriabin was a good friend of mine and had frequently visited me in Paris, where we spent many hours discussing his musical and esoteric theories. I could not always follow him through his mystical speculations, but I was keenly interested in his conviction that many fields of art offered virgin territory for exploration and were capable of yielding aesthetic sensations of an entirely new kind. He claimed that the effect of music heard in the dark was quite different from its effect when heard in strong light; this fact, he insisted, had always been recognized by composers who wrote for the theater. Continuing, he asserted that organ music, written for performance in the surroundings of a church, where the prevailing illumination was that of daylight colored by its passage through stained-glass windows, could not possibly be properly appreciated in white light. "Unconsciously," he said, "the listener is affected by his submersion in the ambient light. And why should this not be so? Differences of color mean differences in vibration frequencies, and nothing can prevent the body from responding sympathetically to these varying frequencies, precisely as it responds to changes of temperature."

He spoke of the need for establishing scales, corresponding to musical scales, in colors, in perfumes, and in tastes. In this, he followed the ideas expressed by Huysmans in his remarkable book A *rebours*, and he deplored the coarseness of our musical scale, which forbade the use of those sounds which must necessarily lie concealed between the leading tone and the octave. A considerable part of his music reveals a passionate searching for such tones and harmonies: "What is this elusive thing which is hidden in the modulation of dominant to tonic?" he seems to implore.

One of Scriabin's greatest compositions is the tone poem "Prometheus" for piano and orchestra, in which the idea of the Fire-Giver is set forth through the use of colored light, in combination with the music. The score includes a part for a keyboard instrument, designed to control the illumination of the entire auditorium. This part is written in ordinary notation, and is based upon a scale established by the composer, wherein colors are substituted for tones. The effect desired was to intensify sensations of color received more or less subconsciously, through an all-pervading illumination from indirect sources, fluctuating like the curves of a melody in accordance with the composer's indications.

Since no mechanism for the control and diffusion of colored light existed at that time, Scriabin never witnessed a performance of "Prometheus" in the manner in which he had conceived it. He authorized it to be played with the use of a lantern projector, which threw color patterns on a white screen, in view of the audience. The effect of this was disturbing, and after a few unsuccessful experiments the color instrument was discarded.

What I saw at Severance Hall in Cleveland convinced me, and Sokoloff as well, that the time had come, at last, to present "Prometheus" in the manner intended by the composer. It was settled, before we parted, that I was to play the important and difficult piano part at the opening concert of the following season, which would correspond to the dedication of the new hall and the first demonstration of the elaborate color switchboard.

The end of this little story is somewhat curious. The following year, shortly before the date set for the opening of the new hall in Cleveland, I received a letter from Sokoloff, informing me that the completed switchboard which controlled the thousands of colored lights in the auditorium had proved so complicated that it was impossible to find anyone to perform the part as written by Scriabin, and therefore we would be compelled to play it without the lighting.

It was a great disappointment to me. As far as I know, the complete realization of Scriabin's plan has not yet taken place, although it may be assumed that the obstacles which formerly existed are now cleared away, for the lighting system of Severance Hall is no longer the unique thing it was, but is to be found in most of the larger moving-picture theatres.

$\mathcal{E}leven$

THE SEASON 1912–1913 WAS GIVEN OVER ENTIRELY TO EUROPE.
I had outlined a plan for making a tour around the world,
and I hoped to realize this the following year. I had already
received offers from Australia, Japan, and the Dutch East
Indies, and it remained to link these various points together.
I wished, also, to include some of the larger cities of China
and India, and there was every prospect that all arrangements would be carried out exactly as I desired. But I never
made that tour. The war intervened in 1914, as will later
be seen, and the same opportunities never occurred again.

I played quite frequently in Germany during that season.
Concert-giving in that country seemed to me different from
anywhere else. There was a certain air of festivity about
it, and yet, it appeared, in many respects, to be quite a commonplace activity of everyday life. The opera and the symphony concerts in most German cities had a certain glamour
imparted to them through their connection with the royal
or ducal courts, by which they were supported, but although

this involved the appearance of a good many elaborate military uniforms at the performances, the aspect of the audience in general was bourgeois, if not plebeian. Applause, though never perfunctory, was rarely demonstrative. The audience did not applaud unless it was satisfied. A great deal of food and drink was always consumed during the intermission at opera performances, the food being occasionally brought from home. Music was obviously a part of daily nourishment and as essential as beer, but concerts did not always satisfy the demands of fine and discriminating taste, mainly for the reason, I think, that the quality of tone which seemed to prevail most frequently among singers and instrumentalists was somewhat unrefined and coarse.

I played with the symphony orchestra at the Dresden Opera House, where I had an example of the methods adopted by the Royal Intendant. A magnificent carriage and pair, with uniformed driver and footman, was put at my disposal for the rehearsal and concert; refreshment was provided in the artists' room, and the following day the specially appointed messenger from the royal cashier's office at the royal opera, called ceremoniously at my hotel and royally counted out my fee in gold pieces onto the table, taking a receipt in exchange. This custom prevailed in most of the cities where opera and symphony concerts were under the immediate protection of the reigning sovereign.

Sergei Koussevitzky, the celebrated contrabassist and a good friend of mine, came to the two recitals I gave in Berlin. He told me that he was conducting a series of symphony concerts in St. Petersburg and Moscow, and invited me to play with his orchestra there the following season. I did not know at the time that he had recently made an extraordinary tour along the entire length of the Volga, taking with him an entire symphony orchestra on a specially chartered steamer, and conducting concerts on the way at most of the important cities situated on that river. Neither did I know, to be precise, that he possessed any talent or ambition as a conductor. He had been acclaimed as a great virtuoso on the contrabass in many countries, and had made a successful concert tour in the United States. I doubt if any person then living would have predicted for him the career as one of the greatest geniuses of the baton which he has since achieved.

I went, in due course, to Russia, and I met a number of distinguished musicians at Koussevitzky's home in Moscow. The man who interested me most was Rachmaninoff. During dinner we spoke of music in France, and Rachmaninoff, who had recently played his second concerto there with immense success, expressed his surprise at the prevailing catholicism in French musical taste. "They like everything," he said, "even their own moderns." I asked him if he played Debussy's piano pieces, and he said no, he did not care for that music. Koussevitzky, after dinner, asked me to play some Debussy, which I did. Rachmaninoff sat silent for a few moments, and then suddenly started up and began haranguing Koussevitzky. "Speak French or German," said the latter. Rachmaninoff turned to me and attempted to explain exactly why Debussy's music displeased him, but he was too excited and lapsed into his native tongue again, so I never found out.

Josef Hofmann was, at that time, Russia's pianistic idol. Each year he gave a long series of concerts in the principal cities to large and enthusiastic audiences. I went to one of his recitals in Moscow at the magnificent "Hall of the Nobility," where all important concerts were given, and we spent part of the following day very pleasantly together.

The two concerts for which Koussevitzky had engaged me were followed by a few recitals in Russia, and I then proceeded to Helsingfors for an orchestral concert. From there I crossed to Stockholm for a rapid trip through the Scandinavian cities, and then continued southward to Holland. That was one of my busiest seasons; I visited more countries that year than ever before.

Arrangements for my long world tour were completed, and in the late summer of 1913 I left for America once more. That, again, was a long and busy season, relatively uneventful, since I went to few new places, and it was not until the month of April that I found myself in San Francisco, preparing for the trip to Australia.

Since there was plenty of time before the date on which my concerts were supposed to start in Sydney, arrangements had been made for me to break the journey at Hawaii, and to play in Honolulu. This proved a most delightful interlude and was one of the rare occasions when I was able to combine the attitude of a tourist with my professional activities. When the Sydney-bound steamer called at Honolulu some two weeks later, I was at the dock to meet it. As it tied up to the wharf, I heard my name being called in a manner which I can only describe as a shrill screech. I looked up, and there stood Mischa Elman on the top deck, grinning at me. "Harold!" he yelled again, and his voice was full of malicious, triumphant glee. "Put your head down, so that I can see your bald spot again. There it is! Hooray!"

Everybody knows that Mischa lost most of his hair when he was a young boy. He was, or pretended to be, envious of me, because I had a great deal of hair and kept it until quite late in life. It was nice to know that he, too, was bound for Australia, and we had plenty of fun together on the long voyage.

Kipling himself could never convey in writing, nor did I ever imagine, a Cockney accent as broad as that which greeted me on my arrival in Sydney. At first I thought people must be talking that way in jest, but I have no doubt that after a few days I was just as colonial in my speech as any of them.

Beyond the fact that I had agreed to give an indefinite number of concerts in Australia within a certain limited period, I had no very clear idea of the manner in which a tour was usually arranged in that country, and I was somewhat dismayed to learn that I was expected to keep on giving recitals at intervals of two days in Sydney as long as the public continued to buy tickets, and that after that I was to go to Melbourne to repeat the same process.

This meant, of course, a great deal more preparation and practice than I had ever before contemplated. My repertoire was extensive, but I had never thought of doing anything like that. However, there I was, and I had to conform to prevailing custom. The concerts were announced in pairs: after the second concert, two more were announced, and so it went on. I had to prepare eight different programs, and this represented daily hard work, which I did not enjoy. I had very little time for recreation and amusement, and I insisted on a few days of vacation before proceeding to Melbourne.

After I had repeated the same eight programs in Melbourne, my manager brought me back to Sydney for six additional recitals; these were followed by six additional recitals in Melbourne. I never worked so hard in all my life, and if I am to be absolutely honest, I must say that I do not understand why the public kept on coming to my concerts. I gave, in all, twenty-eight concerts within six weeks in the two cities, playing fourteen programs, which, although the repetition of some numbers was insisted upon by the public, were all different from one another.

I then proceeded to Adelaide, South Australia, where I was to give a shorter series of recitals before going on to New Zealand, my next objective. I was immediately conscious, on my arrival in that city, of a more staid and conservative atmosphere than that which I had encountered in Sydney and Melbourne. It did not take me long to discover that of the three principal cities of Australia, Adelaide laid claim to being the most dignified and aristocratic.

I registered at the hotel. The clerk, extending a welcoming hand after reading my name, said: "Glad to see you back, Mr. Bauer." I replied that he must take me for someone else, seeing that I had never been in Adelaide before. "Oh, but surely, Mr. Bauer, I cannot be mistaken. Nobody could forget you!" I lapsed into irony. "The mistake is mine," I said, "I was here before, about a hundred thousand years ago, in a previous state of existence." The clerk smiled politely, and, slightly raising his eyebrows, replied: "I thought so, Mr. Bauer. Well, sir, you won't find Adelaide much changed."

The morning after my second recital, the manager telephoned me: "Have you seen the newspaper?" "No," I replied. "I am still asleep." "Well," he continued, "we must cancel your remaining concerts. War has been declared between England and Germany."

Just like that. My concerts were nothing, of course, but the thought that a few—a very few—human beings, a couple of kings, a statesman or two, and some small groups known as parliaments, had the power to jerk civilization to a sudden stop in this way, came as an overwhelming blow, crushing, appalling, devastating. And the thought immediately following, that humanity as a whole, far from repudiating this action with horror and disgust, would be certain to invest it with honor and glory, was just as tragic and . . . just as futile.

A practical plan had to be determined upon. "Can I go to New Zealand?" The answer, "Communications between Australia and New Zealand have been suspended, owing to the presence of German warships in the vicinity," might have been foreseen. There were no passenger ships of any neutral country available. If a Japanese steamer had been there at the time, it would have suited me perfectly. But for the moment I had to face the obvious fact that my world tour was now out of the question, and the only thing to do was to get back to the United States. Was there an American steamer? Yes, there was, and it would leave next week. Quick! Quick! The telephone! The telegraph! Everyone will want to escape from Australia on that boat! A cabin at any price!

I obtained one of the last remaining rooms and immediately cabled my manager in New York informing him of the changed plans, and asking him to fill my time, if possible, in the United States when I returned. Mischa Elman, in the same predicament as I, was also on the steamer, and we had as fellow-passengers all the members of an international scientific congress, which had assembled at Sydney for purposes of discussion and research.

We sailed for San Francisco on the date designated, and, although everyone on board was greatly perturbed by the dreadful conflict which had broken out, the anxiety and tedium of the long voyage was considerably lightened through the generosity of the eminent scientists, who gave us lectures and demonstrations almost every evening. I became very friendly with one of these gentlemen, who was a celebrated ethnologist. He spoke with enthusiasm of the investigations he had made in New Zealand, explaining to me that the Polynesian civilization was one of the oldest known to history. Learning that I intended to leave the steamer in Honolulu for some more concerts, he told me that the natives of Hawaii were a part of the group which included the Maoris of New Zealand, and said that they had probably preserved the same musical practices as all the other members of the race, in particular the insistence upon the observance of absolute pitch in their tribal songs. He had personally inspected a large resonant stone giving forth a definite musical tone, which, he said, was a standard consulted periodically by specially appointed persons who came from remote points, for the purpose of adjusting the instruments of their own group to this central standard. He indicated a simple method whereby I might test this faculty of absolute pitch among the Hawaiian aborigines, and it was not long before I was able to follow his suggestion.

Leaving the steamer at Honolulu, I gave two more recitals in that delightful town. Toward the end of my stay I was enabled to meet a group of native Hawaiians who lived in a little settlement at the far end of the island and who, apparently, were completely untouched by the white civilization which surrounded them. Since they spoke no English, an interpreter accompanied them, and I was thus able to make myself understood. They played and sang to me some of their ancient songs, and I took careful note of the melody. The rhythm, occasionally very complex, eluded me. I may as well say, at this point, that my sense of pitch (which seems to have no connection with musical talent) is absolute. After they had performed for about half an hour, I asked them to repeat one of the songs, purposely singing it at a different pitch from that which they had used. They looked blank, and said they did not know that song. I insisted that they had sung it and repeated it again and again, each time starting on a different note. The interpreter told me that they disclaimed having ever heard it, and that they knew no white man's music. Finally I sang it at the pitch they had used. Their faces brightened: Yes, that is our song; and they sang it to me again.

Pitch, to these people, is the music itself, and I feel sometimes that we have lost something very precious in allowing ourselves to become indifferent to it. Some of the great composers have sensed it more keenly than others. I believe that Beethoven was particularly sensitive to pitch and, to give but one example, I know that the Moonlight Sonata sounds altogether wrong to me when played at the pitch of A444, to which many pianos are tuned nowadays, and it needs to be transposed to the key of C minor in order to give a sensation of authenticity to my ear.

Upon my arrival in San Francisco I was glad to find a telegram from my manager, informing me that he had arranged for a series of concerts with the Boston Symphony Orchestra, and that my entire season would be well filled. Nothing could have given me greater pleasure than to learn that I was to make a tour with this great orchestra, of which Karl Muck was, at that time, the distinguished conductor.

The season turned out to be a busy one, and I played many more recitals than usual. I was keenly conscious of a great deal of agitation in certain parts of the country; the German element dreading the possibility of the United States being drawn into the war, and the so-called "hundred-percenters" proclaiming, in spite of the official insistence upon American neutrality, that the United States should, immediately, proceed to "lick the stuffing out of Germany." It was a sad and anxious time for lovers of peace.

The summer of 1915 found a number of European musicians, who, in peacetime, would have been at their homes, stranded in this country. The question was where to go during the vacation months. It was Frank and Walter Damrosch who, both having summer homes in Maine, described the beauties of this state in such glowing terms that every one of us wanted to go there. And so we did, some to Seal Harbor, where Frank Damrosch lived, and the others to Bar Harbor or Northeast Harbor, where Walter Damrosch and Harold Randolph had their homes. The Seal Harborites included Kreisler, Karl Muck, Salzedo, Friedberg, Olga Samaroff, Stokowski, Gabrilowitsch and myself. Josef Hofmann, Francis Rogers, and Arthur Whiting were in Northeast Harbor, Ernest Schelling in Bar Harbor, and Franz Kneisel in Blue Hill, only a few miles away. There were a good many other musicians in the neighborhood as well.

Groups of this kind are frequently found in European summer resorts, although they do not last very long, the vacation period being shorter. Here such a gathering was unique, and furthermore we were dealing with a very long vacation period, lasting from May until October. It was entirely due to the exceptional conditions caused by the war that this meeting between a number of artists from many different countries came about. We all worked enormously, for we had to think of the responsibilities of next season, and we played and enjoyed ourselves enormously as well. Very frequently we made ourselves thoroughly ridiculous, but I am not going to describe our antics, for they have been vividly set forth in two books by Clara Gabrilowitsch and Olga Samaroff respectively. I will only say that the climax of our serious fellowship was reached at a magnificent party given by Walter Damrosch at his home in Bar Harbor, when every musician in America seemed to be present, and the climax of our absurdities was reached, I think, at a hair-cutting ceremony instigated by Leopold Stokowski, who had decided that the time had come for all musicians to cultivate a new growth by clipping their hair close to the skull. I have a snapshot showing the way in which this had to be done. Josef Hofmann threw me down, Gabrilowitsch sat on me, and Stokowski ran the lawn mower over my head.

Carlos Salzedo once brought Nijinsky to visit me in Seal Harbor, and I remember this for a rather curious reason. I had sent him a message that I would like to see him dance Moussorgsky's "Pictures at an Exhibition." He replied that he did not know the piece, so I played it for him. He showed great interest in the music and said afterward that it would make a splendid ballet. I asked him some questions as to the detail of the various parts of the suite, and he looked at me with a puzzled expression. "You do not imagine that I am going to attempt to impersonate all these different characters by dancing them, do you?" he said. I replied that that had unquestionably been my idea. "But not at all!" he cried. "That would never work. I shall be the person who walks through the exhibition and examines the pictures." I looked at him admiringly. "Marvelous!" I said. "What an imagination! I never would have thought of that!" Nijinsky never created the ballet, but in 1944 a ballet based on that music was staged by his sister, Bronislava Nijinska.

Gabrilowitsch and I were seriously exercised, at this time, over the question of management. The man who had directed my affairs since I first came to America had contracted with Ossip, believing that I should not be available that season. The cancellation of my world tour changed the situation completely. The manager wanted to keep me as well as Ossip, and the question had to be decided whether the same manager could work successfully for both of us.

Unlike the usual custom in Europe, it was not considered practical in America for the same person to manage two artists in the same field during the same season. In the present instance, our manager advanced the rather curious argument that if he worked for both of us, he could keep us apart.

"It is true that he could arrange for us to be in different parts of the country," remarked Ossip, "so that the struggle for the same dates, such as other managers might indulge in, would be avoided." "Yes," I mused, "and he could also bring us together if we all wanted it. How about giving a few two-piano recitals? It would be a novelty and it might fill in time occasionally, with profit and pleasure. What do you say?" Ossip said "Done!" and there was nothing more to discuss.

The following day we signed our agreements with the manager, and notified him that we would be willing to play together whenever suitable opportunities occurred. In this casual and informal fashion a close and friendly collaboration was established, which ended only with Gabrilowitsch's untimely death in 1936. We gave many, many concerts together, and, since the repertory of works for two pianos was very scant at that time, I added considerably to it by making two-piano arrangements of classical works originally composed for four hands at one piano. These arrangements were received with cordiality by the public, and our concerts were in great demand.

Returning from a trip in 1917, I found Pablo Casals in New York. He was in the midst of a successful tour, and we were engaged to give a number of concerts together in various cities. A few weeks later Fritz Kreisler joined us in two performances of Beethoven's Triple Concerto for piano, violin, and cello, given at one of Walter Damrosch's symphony concerts at Carnegie Hall. The success of these two performances was immense, and I have never ceased to wonder why. It is hard to find a good word for this composition, certainly one of the very weakest of the master's works, although written during the glorious period which produced such immortal masterpieces as the Rasoumovsky quartets, "Fidelio," the G major piano concerto and the Appassionata Sonata. But the Triple Concerto is tedious and undistinguished. The thematic material is commonplace, the passage writing for the three instruments is both clumsy and difficult, and the work, taken as a whole, is neither pleasing nor effective. Yet the performance was immensely successful, as above related, and this remains a puzzle. I can find but one explanation and that an unlikely one: namely, that we were applauded for the conscientious and laborious efforts each one of us had made, singly and in joint rehearsals, to do the best we could in a most unrewarding task. I repeat that this is an unlikely explanation, because it implies that the listeners were aware of the difficulties of the work, and this could not be the case, considering that the Triple Concerto is practically unknown to concert goers.

It seems strange that the most experienced public performer, accustomed all his life to the study and the calculation of effects which he expects to produce upon his audience, should find himself occasionally on such uncertain ground. He knows, naturally, that he is taking chances when he submits what he believes to be a masterpiece to the verdict of the public, but it is harder to understand what the public can find to applaud in a composition which the performer himself regards as of inferior quality, and introduces solely for special reasons. A musician's career contains many surprises, and this is one of them. I am not referring here to the matter of classification, in which, it seems to me, we are fundamentally all in agreement; for example, if I am asked to acknowledge that Liszt's Second Rhapsody is the greatest piece of music ever composed, my tendency is to acquiesce, with the mental reservation, "and so is the harvest moon the largest object in the sky."

I returned to Europe that spring for a number of engagements, including an appearance with the London Philharmonic Society, on which occasion I was to be presented with the Gold Medal of that venerable organization. I looked forward to this event with mixed feelings. The medal, struck originally in honor of this English musical society's relations with Beethoven, had been awarded to none but the world's greatest artists, and that but rarely. I was proud and yet awestruck at the thought of being included in that glorious company, but what occasioned me the most acute distress and anxiety was the thought that I should have to make a speech at the supper following the concert, when the presentation was to take place.

I had never before spoken publicly at any formal event, and I was sick in advance with nervousness. My performance of the G major Beethoven concerto was quite adequate, I believe, but my mind, every now and then, received a thought which pierced like a dagger: "Now comes the end of the first movement; then come the second and third movements, then the end of the concert, then the banquet and then . . ." And a little later: "Now comes the end of the Concerto, then comes the applause and the bowing and hand-shaking, then comes the end of the concert, the banquet and then . . ." So it went on, and I felt more and more like a criminal being led to execution. I had scribbled down a few words on a piece of paper which I clutched convulsively in my pocket. When the moment came and I was actually on my feet at the banquet, I drew out that paper, which was so crushed and blotted by the nervous perspiration of my hand that I could not read a word. The formal presentation of the medal was made, and I stammered and stuttered some kind of acknowledgment. Everything I had thought of saying was utterly forgotten. I was in a condition of the blackest misery, and I think the one thing that kept me from collapse was the smiling, affectionate faces of two dear young girls, Irene Scharrer and Myra Hess, who seemed a thousand miles away at the end of the long guest table.

The concert season terminated shortly after this event, and I had arranged to spend the summer in Switzerland, where a large class of pupils from various countries was to meet me. During all these years, the thought of teaching attracted me more and more. I had formulated certain principles of study, and I welcomed the opportunity of discussing them and trying to apply them with a group of intelligent students and teachers.

I had no thought of concealing the fact that I was not equipped to teach according to generally accepted methods. Since I had never had any academic training, I was unable to pass along rules and principles derived from other teachers, with whom I had but one link—namely, personal experience of the subject matter. Inevitably, I found myself in conflict with certain consecrated principles, alleged to be fundamental. I did not like to practice technique dissociated from music. I did not like the idea of studying even scales, because I could find no justification for even scales in expressive compositions. For me, study represented the patient effort to analyze and to obtain musical effects and to continue working at them in exactly the way they were ultimately intended to sound, until fluency was acquired.

It speaks a great deal for the generosity and tolerance of the friends I had made among the great teachers of the day, that they did not resent what they must have looked upon as an anarchistic influence in their midst. But they were genuinely interested in the fact that although I had never had any technical training and did not practice piano exercises of any kind, my playing, without being especially brilliant, was just as accurate, just as powerful, and just as well controlled as that of the average good performer who had undergone years of muscular training in technical exercises. I think they probably felt that as long as I had acquired a certain fluency without special training, it should be evident that I could go a great deal further if I did study exercises. Very likely they were right, and I dare say it is to this that I owe the honor of a dedication from my eminent friend, Moszkowski, of a set of studies for the left hand, and of a similar dedication from my equally eminent friend, Isidor Philipp, of a set of studies for the black keys.

The house I rented that summer on Lake Geneva was ideal for purposes of study and teaching, and I never had a more interesting and enjoyable season. Many of my students were exceptionally talented and have since made important careers. Some of them, on the other hand, were quite incompetent. I had no means of examining them in advance, and some curious things resulted.

There was the nice little Chinese girl who played a Chopin etude quite fluently, but did not know what key it was in, because she had "never studied theory." My first impulse to smile at a statement which sounded comical gave way to feelings of indignation against the teacher responsible for such ignorance. The disquieting thought arose, nevertheless, that our musical education might be in danger of attaching undue importance to academic details, for what, after all, is tonality? Music can get along very well without it. Besides, East is East and West is West. In England, people eat eggs and bacon for breakfast, and in the United States, they eat bacon and eggs.

Then there was the young man from Texas, who was entirely self-taught, and played the organ at the local church' in his small town. He came all the way to Switzerland to study with me because, it appeared, some traveling salesman had once told him that I was the best pianist. He brought with him several bound volumes of piano music of every possible description, classical and popular, and he played a Bach invention, a transcription from *Trovatore*, and a Sousa march with equal gusto, and with a display of native musical talent which, under the circumstances, was quite surprising. He demurred when I asked him to play Chopin's Waltz in B minor, saying that he had not finished studying it. But he finally consented and played it through from beginning to end on the white keys alone, with a result more easily imagined than described. In reply to my question why he had consistently avoided the black keys, he reminded me, apparently somewhat hurt, that he had not finished work on the piece. "The books told me not to put in the expression before I knew all the notes," he said, "and I always thought the black keys were part of the expression. Isn't that right?" he inquired anxiously.

I repeat that this boy possessed natural musical ability, and I am glad to say that the story has a happy ending. He followed all my classes diligently and intelligently, and when he had acquired a certain skill and understanding, he returned to Texas. His position improved immediately, and when I heard from him some years later, he was busy, successful, and prosperous in the musical career he had carved out for himself.

I must not omit to mention the busy piano teacher from an important western city, whose visit to my home in Vevey was so hurried that it passed off more quickly than I can tell about it. "My vacation, Mr. Bauer, is just about over, and I sail for home next week," she stated. "I always combine business with pleasure during my holidays, and I have studied technique with Godowsky and interpretation with Busoni. Somebody told me that you are the greatest authority on the use of the pedal, and I have never studied that. Don't you think, if I hired you for a daily lesson, that I could learn all about the pedal between now and next Monday?"

I told her no, it couldn't be done, and off she went, in the same frantic hurry that had brought her to me.

There were many artists and musicians living in that part of Switzerland, and I had frequent visits from some of them. Josef Hofmann had a home in the mountains just above Vevey, and so did Mr. Edward de Coppet, the founder and patron of the Flonzaley Quartet, with whose members I had so many delightful meetings. The musician I saw most frequently at that time was Emmanuel Moór, whose career was quite extraordinary, if not unique in musical history. He was a prolific composer, a painter and an inventor gifted with a remarkable mechanical intuition that almost amounted to genius. His music possessed a certain histrionic and expressive quality which, to many of us, and at that particular period, was irresistible; we all wanted to play it, and to get everyone else to play it too. I believe that those who were most persistent in that respect were four in number: Mengelberg, Ysaÿe, Casals, and myself. Casals was the most faithful of all the Moór enthusiasts, and continued to play his music long after it had ceased to enthrall the others. However, Ysaÿe played his violin concerto, Casals played his cello concerto, and I played his piano concerto. He composed a triple concerto for piano, violin, and cello in the hope, I am sure, that we three would perform it.

I played the piano concerto with the Boston Symphony Orchestra while Karl Muck was the conductor, and the public received it very warmly. Muck did not care for the work, but felt compelled to admit its power and effectiveness. "Es klingt," (it sounds) he said to me, screwing up his face in that Mephistophelian manner for which he was famous. That was all he said. There was no adjective.

I have a vivid recollection of this Boston performance, for the reason that Paderewski was present and, saying he did not wish to be seen in the hall, came to the artists' room. He had probably forgotten that the stage, back of the orchestra, is completely shut off, and music cannot possibly be heard there; so, when I started the concerto, he stepped into the orchestra section very quietly and stood there, concealed, as he thought, by the risers as well as by a double bass which was in front of him. But his hair gave him away, and he was immediately the cynosure of all eyes. I thought it rather unfair.

$\mathcal{T}welve$

THE EFFECT OF THE WAR WHICH STARTED IN 1914 WAS NOT limited to death, destruction, and ruin. It is probably not too much to say that the life of every individual in the civilized world was changed to some extent by it. Families were disrupted, homes were given up, friendships of many years' standing were shattered, and thousands of people went to live in new countries, renouncing their former allegiance and adopting new nationalities. Throughout those frightful years there was no folly and no injustice too great to be perpetrated in every country in the holy names of hatred and nationalism. Reputable citizens associated themselves openly with the blind passions of the mob, and it was tragic to observe the moral degradation which was the inevitable consequence. In our country, a number of weak-minded individuals were led to believe that the cause of democracy and freedom could be served by burning German books and suppressing German music. Musicians were sometimes threatened with violence because their programs included classical compositions of Teutonic origin, and in some cities censorship of concert programs was exercised by the police. It was all very distressing and very stupid. I should hesitate to give to any one of the daily absurdities the palm of utter imbecility, but I think the remark of a lady who protested against a performance of Schumann's "Two Grenadiers" is hard to beat. "It isn't that it's *German* music," she said, "but there's altogether too much about the Kaiser in it."

Just before leaving Australia, I had been asked to give a recital for the benefit of the "Australian" Red Cross. It was stipulated that, in the event of my compliance, I should play only what was called "Allied" music, that I should not use the Bechstein piano which had figured in all my concerts, and that the spelling of my name should be modified in order to make it look British.

Before giving a definite answer, I inquired if it might not be as well to follow the example of other countries in using the term "Red Cross" alone without the qualifying addition of any country, so as to indicate its international character.

My suggestion was received with a kind of incredulous indignation. "You would hardly expect us to take care of the *enemy* wounded, would you?"

The hardest task for a person who believes in tolerance is to treat intolerance with tolerance. I have never succeeded in learning that valuable lesson. My feelings were too strong for me; I could not help myself, and I declined to give the concert.

I think I was justified in expressing my conviction that my name, if changed, would not be recognized by many and consequently would have no drawing power. But I failed to realize that the ladies who invited me had correctly gauged the feelings of the populace who in many cases were venting their patriotic fury on fellow-citizens whose sole offense was the possession of names of German origin. Neither did I imagine that a royal example of the propriety of name-changing in wartime would be forthcoming from England, where the previously honored name of Battenberg was altered to Mountbatten.

And I have felt sorry ever since that I did not give that recital in Sydney for the Australian Red Cross, no matter what restrictions and conditions were attached to it. Intolerance is probably inseparable from the patriotic call to arms, as witness the ingenuous remark of the farm laborer when put into uniform: "It ain't no use," he said, "I cain't fight 'cause I ain't mad."

There is more talk and more preaching against intolerance now than ever before in history, and I sometimes wonder if that means that it is also more prevalent. I know that if I were a statesman, I would consider it good policy to denounce intolerance at every opportunity, in order to stimulate and release it in its fullest fury at the requisite moment. Avoid anticlimax, says the musician. *Crescendo, diminuendo, crescendo, piano subito, crescendo* again, repeating the process as often as you like, but keep back the *fortissimo* for the grand explosion.

A distinguished German diplomat once said to me: "Our soldiers learn that one must always honor one's enemy. If the enemy proves himself unworthy of being honored, the consequences are frightful, for chivalry has been killed."

I looked at him with admiring horror. "So that's *one* way of doing it," I thought privately.

It was early in 1917, I think, that an old acquaintance, the celebrated English actor Beerbohm Tree, came on a sort of "good will" dramatic tour to the United States. He spoke in terms of bitter disillusionment of the effect of the war on the British theater. "For fifty years," he told me, "I gave my life to educating the public to a notion of the value of the drama. This bloody war comes along and knocks everything into a cocked hat. The theater is dead in England. It is exactly the same with music."

I think his statement was correct. During the war, the aesthetic taste of the British public was satisfied with vaudeville and low comedy. Attendance at plays and concerts had fallen to the lowest ebb. But it proved nothing beyond the fact that people preferred to obtain the more refined forms of relaxation and entertainment by reading books and visiting museums and picture galleries.

In every country, during the years of privation and rationing imposed by the war, people had to make their choice between what was essential to them and what they could dispense with. "Give me my books and my pictures," said the Englishman. "Take everything, my food and my clothing," said the Frenchman, "but leave me my theater!" I am told that in Russia as well as in Germany, both musical and dramatic performances continued on a scale as nearly normal as possible, while in Italy every possible sacrifice was made in order that the opera could go on in the numerous cities of that country.

And what of America, the country which naturally interested me most, since I was living here? I believe I am correct in saying that it was the entirely unexpected which took place. The United States, notwithstanding the tireless efforts of its resident musicians and the generosity of its wealthy patrons of art, had never given signs of being what is called "a musical nation." But no sooner did it become apparent that the war economy required reduction or elimination of things not regarded as essential, than the whole country seemed to rise up and proclaim in unmistakable terms that music could not possibly be dispensed with.

Rationing of sugar, shortage of all kinds of luxuries, prohibition of liquor—all those things could be borne, but we must have music, everyone felt. Never mind if we have to cut out German music for the present. We all know that such a state of things cannot endure, but we will not give up our concerts.

The result was that concert giving and concert going swung up to an all-time high level, from which it has never since receded. Music, considered from the viewpoint of business no less than that of culture, has become one of the major activities of the United States. Aside from concerts, operas, musical comedies, conservatories, private studios, and individual practicing, the radio takes care that it shall be on tap from morning until night and from night until morning. For those "fit for treason, stratagem, and spoils" music today is a nerve-racking and ceaseless torture, as hard to escape from as the noise of the airplane or the buzzing of the ubiquitous housefly.

My old friends in Paris, the three Chaigneau sisters, had organized a relief agency for distressed musicians in France during the war and asked my help in raising funds in America, which of course I was only too happy to give. Concerts were given, collections were made, photographs were sold, and with the generous co-operation of my colleagues I was able to send over a good deal of money. I received from Debussy a number of his autograph portraits for sale, and I prevailed upon several prominent musicians to charge a fee for signing programs when requested by autograph hunters. I forget what the average amount of this fee was; but as for myself, I thought that twenty-five cents was about as much as I could get in view of the fact that most of those who used to storm the artists' room after the concerts were youngsters who could not reasonably be expected to have much cash.

At one of our joint concerts, Gabrilowitsch was thoroughly disgusted with the smallness of the amount (about twenty-five dollars) which we had collected in this way. "It ought to have been a thousand!" he vociferated. "Perfectly ridiculous. Just think of the labor of writing one's name over and over again for a quarter—and for a good cause too," he added hastily. "Let us charge a dollar in future."

I demurred. "These children don't have a dollar to spend, much less two dollars if they want both signatures," I said. "I don't believe we should sell a single one at that price. Besides, it's easy enough to scratch off signatures—for a good cause," I added hastily.

"All very well for you to talk," he retorted. "You have a short name. Look how long it takes to write *my* name. I will compromise with you, however. Fifty cents."

"No," I replied.

"Very well," said Ossip. "You can stick to your miserable quarter and I will sell longer and better signatures for half a dollar."

The result was that I made twice as much money as he did. But of course I worked twice as hard!

Our little society, "L'Aide affectueuse aux musiciens," was later merged with the large organization known as "Musicians' Emergency Aid" established in New York under the presidency of Walter Damrosch. After the war, I was immensely gratified to learn that a number of the most distinguished musicians of France had joined in a request to the French government for official recognition of what they were generous enough to describe as valuable services rendered by me to French musicians and French music. The result was that I was awarded the Cross of the Legion of Honor (which, by the way, is not a cross at all, but a star).

The recipients of decorations are naturally flattered by the honor conferred, which they are prone to measure in terms of what they believe to be its rarity. Many Frenchmen have expressed the feeling that the original prestige of French decorations has deteriorated through indiscriminate liberality in awarding them. I once saw this feeling illustrated in a pitiless satire performed at a Montmartre "café-concert." The celebrated detective, Chère Loque Ollmesse (find Sherlock Holmes if you can!) is investigating a crime. One individual is suspected, but how to find him?

"You tell me he has brown hair and brown eyes, is middle-aged, carries an umbrella, and wears pointed shoes. Is there nothing else, no personal characteristic by which he may be recognized?"

"Nothing whatever, Monsieur the detective."

A long silence, during which Chère Loque Ollmesse clutches his brow and reflects gloomily. Finally, raising his head, he inquires:

"Is he decorated?"

"No," comes the unhesitating reply.

"Aha!" shouts the great detective triumphantly. *"Not decorated*, eh? Then we shall very soon lay our hand on him."

On the other hand, I have met French people who take the view that a decoration is practically the equivalent of a canonization. It is assumed that the recipient is not only honored and beatified thereby, but that he is expected in return to render lifelong service, the nature of which anyone is entitled to define. Here is an example of that attitude: Maurice Ravel dedicated what I shall always regard as his finest piano composition, "Ondine," to me. I played it in Paris when it was first published, and I have played it since then, repeatedly, in every part of the world where I have given concerts. Never have I played any piece of music more frequently than *my* "Ondine." At my first Paris concert after the war, "Ondine" did not happen to figure on the program. I noticed in the following issue of a French musical journal a very long and, apparently, a most complimentary article about me. The writer spoke of the many years of my residence in Paris and of my close association with French musical life during that period; he mentioned my successes and praised everything I had ever done in great detail. Then, as a final climax to the article, came a dramatic *volte-face*.

"Yes, Mister Bauer, you have been acclaimed for years as a true artist and as a loyal comrade to your fellow musicians. Paris has covered you with honors. What do you do in return for these honors? What, ladies and gentlemen, does this distinguished foreigner do? He gives a recital and ignores, in the most conspicuous manner possible, the royal gift which was made to him by one of our country's greatest composers: Maurice Ravel."

It was a fine climax to the article, and it made me just as unhappy as it was intended to. The "most unkindest cut of all" was that referring to me as a "foreigner." However, there was no sense in arguing the matter, and I played "Ondine" at the next recital.

At this point I must stop to rebuke the pen which, as usual, has carried me beyond the period I was writing about. It is necessary to go back to the year 1918.

Toward the close of the summer of that year there was a general conviction that the defeat of Germany could not be delayed longer than a few weeks. We were all in Seal Harbor, and we realized that it was improbable, after the end of the war, that Fate would ever bring us together again in the same place and for as long a period. I had conceived a certain plan which I hoped would interest my colleagues. After I had talked it over with Frank Damrosch, the latter invited Stokowski, Kreisler, Hofmann, and Gabrilowitsch to discuss it with me at his house. It took me quite a long time to formulate for their consideration a scheme which until that moment had been somewhat vague and visionary, but they listened to me with patience. The longer I talked the more interested they grew, until at the end, following exhaustive discussion, we were all pledged to create and support a musical organization of an entirely new kind.

We agreed that it would be appropriate for all musicians to join in a gesture of comradeship and international solidarity as soon as possible after the war was over. We believed that a series of concerts given in a spirit of disinterested fraternity by groups of artists of various nationalities would express our feeling suitably, and we thought that such a gesture might indicate faith in the restoration of normal human relations and in the eternal survival and supremacy of art. We hoped that people might discover in this united action a sincere effort to soften the bitterness of ruin and destruction left by the war, and an attempt to heal some of the grievous wounds inflicted upon civilization and culture, among which none, in our opinion, seemed more harmful than those proceeding from intolerance and national arrogance. It was to be clearly understood that these concerts should contain no element capable of leading to personal display; that the performers should receive no remuneration whatever, and that the proceeds should be donated to purposes of musical interest in any part of the world, such purposes to be determined by vote of the members of the society, the name of which, it was decided, should be the Beethoven Association. Those present at this initial meeting then decided that since the idea originated with me, I must be the president and do all the work. I accepted and immediately asked Frank Damrosch to help me by assuming the duties of treasurer. He consented, and a few weeks later I had the good fortune to enlist the coöperation of Oscar G. Sonneck as secretary of the society, a post he retained until his death.

The end of the war found us all prepared for an early start, and I was chagrined to learn from my manager that it was totally impossible to arrange for the proposed series of concerts during that season, since all suitable dates had been booked at the Aeolian Hall, the sole auditorium suitable for our purpose. There was no remedy for this, and we had to wait. The season passed off as usual, and I obtained a number of new adherents to my plan. A preliminary announcement was given out containing the list of distinguished artists who promised to take part in the series, and this was given considerable prominence by the press.

On November 4, 1919, the first concert of the Beethoven Association was given by a group consisting of Jacques Thibaud, Willem Willeke, John McCormack, and myself. As I had fully anticipated, McCormack rebelled furiously against the requirement that he should sing compositions by Beethoven, but the Association was obdurate. He finally gave in when I reminded him that as the most successful singer of the day, it was clearly his duty to prove to other vocalists that Beethoven's songs could be sung not only beautifully but effectively as well. I am sure he studied his two numbers with special care. He sang magnificently, but the strain was apparently terrific, for he mopped his brow as he came off the stage and sank into a chair ejaculating "God damn Beethoven!" with the most heartfelt fervor.

This initial concert was a tremendous success. The remaining concerts of the series were sold out, and for fifteen or sixteen seasons following every available seat in the auditorium was subscribed for.

The members voted unanimously at the close of the first season to devote the profits of the concerts to publication of Thayer's monumental biography of Beethoven, a work which until then had been available only in the German translation and was now newly edited by Henry Krehbiel. Space forbids mention of more than a few of the beneficiaries of the Beethoven Association during the years which followed. Grants were made to the Library of Congress, the Festspielhaus in Salzburg, the London Philharmonic Society, the Paris Conservatoire, the Schumann Museum in Zwickau, the Beethoven Museum in Bonn, and many other institutions, a total of over $100,000 being thus distributed.

The association was dissolved in 1938, leaving to the New York Public Library the important collection of books written upon Beethoven, which had been assembled by Oscar Sonneck, and all its remaining assets. This, together with the Sonneck Memorial Fund set up in the Library of Congress, constitutes something of a permanent record of an organization which, although relatively short-lived, accomplished a certain number of things of definite value, besides affording a great deal of enjoyment to all concerned in its activities.

Several years after the work of the Beethoven Association had become known in Europe, I was asked by some of my colleagues in London to try to establish a similar organization there. We held a preliminary meeting, and it was decided to start, not with a series of concerts, but with a single event at which the purpose of this new society should be

[240]

made clear. The concert was prepared, suitable announcements were made, the tickets were sold, and the concert, at which a number of prominent musicians took part, was a tremendous success. Afterward, at supper, we made speeches, and as a first step we elected a treasurer, or rather a custodian to take charge of the money which had been made. We were all very enthusiastic, and it seemed that a new Beethoven Association had been born.

But nothing ever happened afterward. Either the spirit was lacking to continue a new enterprise of that nature, or else there was nobody to take the lead at that time in order to complete the work of regular organization. But there were also doubtless some people who had no faith in its principles. About two years later I was discussing the matter with one of London's most distinguished musicians, whose name I prefer not to mention here, since I do not know whether what he said should be regarded as the voice of England or not. But here were his views:

"My dear chap," he said, "you can't possibly expect English people to act like Americans. A thing like your Beethoven Association could never succeed over here."

"And why not?" I inquired.

"Well, if you *must* know," he drawled, "it is because we aren't as bloody mercenary as you all seem to be over there."

I was speechless with indignant surprise.

"Why, what the devil do you mean by that?" I cried. "Nobody gets a single penny from it. All the money goes—"

"Precisely," he interrupted. "*Where* does the money go? You say that its destination is determined by vote of the members. When? Before or afterward? Do they know what they are working for when they agree to donate their services gratuitously? Of course they don't. Can you tell them? Of course you can't. You don't know yourself. All you can say is that these concerts will produce money. And since money is the center and the focus of all activities in America, it follows that all the artists who go there will easily be led to believe that any enterprise which produces money is, for that reason alone, a perfectly magnificent thing. That is what I call the mercenary spirit. In England, we are not accustomed to think in that way. If a busy artist gives his services at a concert, he expects to be told in advance what precise object will be benefited. He will not be satisfied with the mere idea of raising money. That is American. We Europeans want the things that money can bring us, but we find out very often that the best things are those which cannot be bought. Americans simply do not understand this kind of mentality."

Our subsequent arguments were entirely futile. When an Englishman once develops a sense of his superiority, his skin is tougher than that of an elephant. I lost my temper several times, and he merely smiled calmly at me. There were a hundred things to say which might have bowled him over if I had only thought of them, but at the end he was just as convinced as at the beginning that the Beethoven Association had been successful in New York only because of its appeal to the mercenary spirit of the American people, which sometimes communicated itself like a disease to the idealistic, unselfish Europeans who visited our shores.

The nearest approach to the spirit of the Beethoven Association that was made in London was the "Music Circle," a small organization established by my sister, Gertrud Hopkins. Members of this group contributed a sum sufficient to cover the rental of the large studio in St. John's Wood where the weekly gatherings were held and simple refreshments were served at midnight, following a musical program. Many of the greatest artists of the day took part in these informal performances, which gave great pleasure to players and listeners alike. Nobody was paid, and no money was collected for any purpose whatever.

One of the most interesting of all the gatherings at the Music Circle was the evening when Felix Weingartner came to conduct the "Siegfried Idyll" with the principal players of the London Symphony Orchestra. At the close of the evening one of these musicians shook my sister warmly by the hand, saying that he had never spent a more delightful evening. "For ten years," he said, "I have played under Weingartner, but this is the first time I have met him socially and spoken with him." Weingartner left the party with our friend Chester and remarked that Mrs. Hopkins must be a very rich woman to engage all those musicians for an evening's entertainment. "Engage the musicians!" laughed Chester. "That is a good joke. No musician has ever been paid to play at the Music Circle. They do it for their pleasure. That is what *you* did, isn't it?" Weingartner could not get over it. He was utterly amazed. "Perhaps it is different for me," he said rather hesitatingly. "Still, of course . . . they are musicians too . . . but no!" he continued decisively. "It could not be done in any other country in the world. I never heard of such a thing. It would not be possible."

"This," my distinguished English friend would have said, "is clearly *not* mercenary."

But I can readily imagine some distinguished American friend attending one of the gatherings at the "Music Circle" and remarking that Britishers are certainly the most impractical lot of people, by gosh. Look at all that power going to waste! Why don't they *do* something with it?

[243]

I served for several years on a committee of musicians appointed by the Carnegie Corporation for the purpose of investigating applications for money grants and reporting thereon to the Executive Board for action. The funds available for distribution were large, though naturally not unlimited, the spirit governing the selection of beneficiaries was in every respect impartial and liberal, and an immense amount of good was accomplished in the cause of musical education.

Occasionally some slight difficulties arose when, owing to exceptionally numerous applications, the question of spreading the available funds over all of these had to be considered. At such times, the tendency of the committee was to favor those objects whose worth had already been proved rather than to recommend the financing of new projects. This course was not altogether satisfactory to the administration, which naturally desired to extend its benefactions over as large a field as possible, and it was finally deemed advisable to merge the special Musical Committee into a larger one charged with making recommendations for cultural purposes of every kind.

During those years, my work had brought me into frequent contact with the heads of colleges and universities, and particularly with the music departments of these institutions. One result of this, when the Carnegie Corporation established an office for the business affairs of the Association of American Colleges, was that a good many applications came in for my services in a somewhat new field of activity.

Educators were seriously concerned over the lack of what was termed "integration" in the work of their students. It was disconcerting to discover that a considerable number, after several years at college, had apparently learned nothing more than certain facts and principles which were capable of practical application in the business or profession they expected to enter. There was little to show that they had followed the courses prescribed for a well-rounded education, for evidences of ability for independent and constructive work were meager and, as a general rule, they had forgotten most of the things they had studied.

Mr. Henry Ford had recently created something of a commotion by declaring that he was not disposed to engage college graduates for any one of a thousand different jobs that had to be done by the Ford Motor Company, because, he said, roundly and rather derisively, they were always incompetent.

It was no use pretending, as many people did, that this was not a challenge, for it was just precisely that. University education had been placed on trial, and the heads of the various colleges were going to do something about it. After close examination and analysis of the situation, it was found that little or no stress had been placed upon the desirability of correlating any one study with another. Knowledge was dispensed from separate compartments kept as distinct from each other as if their contents were in danger of contamination if they should ever mix.

I was, unhappily, only too familiar with this state of affairs, for I had observed its effects in the highly specialized field of music education for many years. Pupils were taught to pass examinations in the various branches of music study and were left to themselves to discover that it was necessary to combine all these different elements in order to become musicians. Many of them, indeed, never attempted to do so. It is one thing to be a pianist, they imagined, and another thing entirely to understand music, or, in other words, to learn how to apply their successful paper studies of "theory" to the interpretation of a composition.

The secretary of the Association of American Colleges conceived the idea of directing the attention of students toward the desirability of integration in study by displaying the example of some individual who had made his mark in one special field without losing interest in other subjects, which, in fact, had contributed to his own development. This gentleman asked me if I would be willing to visit a number of colleges and universities in this manner. The tentative "modus operandi," subject to revision, was for me to confer first with the president and members of the academic faculty and to decide with them which classes I should visit. It was understood that my attendance at these classes should assume the character of an interested and inquisitive student anxious to discover connections between all branches of learning, and that I should ask any questions and make any remarks on this point that my imagination or my experience might dictate. It was also understood that I should talk to the students and even take over the class at any time considered appropriate by the teacher. Finally, following these various activities and meetings, I was to wind up my visit with a piano recital on the campus.

This proposition, containing so many features that were entirely novel for a concert pianist, required serious consideration; however, I had more than one reason for accepting it and it did not take me very long to decide.

For some time past, I had been uneasily conscious of the fact that public concert giving had ceased to bring me any pleasure. It was becoming a tedious and distasteful job. I was quite aware that my feeling was due, at least in part, to a decline of physical energy inseparable from advancing age, but I knew there were other causes as well. The main trouble lay in the preparation of programs or, in other words, the need for practicing on the piano, which I had never enjoyed and which I found more and more tiresome.

My repertoire was as large as that of any pianist of my time, and I had certainly given more varied programs than most of my colleagues. In the realm of classical music, there were few compositions of any importance which I had not played, and I had been privileged to introduce many new works of permanent artistic value to the public. Incidentally, I have probably spent as many hours as any other musician in the preparation and performance of compositions which I considered good but which were not favorably received and were consequently consigned later on to oblivion—merited or unmerited, who shall say?

Considering this wealth of material from which to choose, it may seem strange that the preparation of a recital program should become more and more of a wearisome task as time went on. But in truth, I was not entirely free to choose the works I should have enjoyed playing. What I had done as a young man was one thing; what I was called upon to do as a mature artist with a background of half a century of public appearances was something else. Like other performers of similar standing, I was generally expected to exhibit my personal interpretation of a limited number of classical works which served as the basis of musical education among the average teachers and students, and as a result there were constant and urgent requests for such well-known pieces as the "Pashionarter" and the "Puppillians," to mention but two.*

* I will not insult the intelligence of my readers by offering a translation of these titles.

I rebelled, but, after all, I was the servant of the public, and it was not for me, who had spent a lifetime in the furtherance of musical culture, to question the very reasonable request of an interested group to hear performances of masterpieces by one considered an authority. Still, it was nothing less than an excruciating bore for me to have to practice pieces I had been playing for fifty years and yet would not perform in public without a careful review, renewed on each occasion, of their technical passages.

With all these thoughts revolving in my mind, it seemed that the proposition of the Association of American Colleges might bring fresh interests into my life. Decidedly, the long journeys and the nervous strain of important public concerts were becoming too much for me, aside from the feelings described above, and although I could find nothing in my previous experience to indicate special fitness for the task in question, I was willing to try, if only because of the confidence shown in me by those responsible for the scheme.

In consequence, I visited twelve universities the first season and, as the plan proved successful beyond all expectation, more than twice that number the year following. In all, the project was introduced to about a hundred colleges and universities over a period of six years, each visit lasting two to three days, and this in addition to regular public concerts, which I continued to give, although in greatly reduced number.

In every one of the institutions I visited, the members of the faculty received me in a courteous and friendly spirit which greatly facilitated my efforts to carry out the program arranged. I cannot attempt to evaluate the work I did, for there was nothing to show immediate results, if any, but it was a most stimulating and agreeable experience for me. I believe that this initial step on the part of the Association of American Colleges has since developed into a regular feature of their educational system.

I do not for one moment suggest that the idea of correlation in study is a new one, or that I was doing something which had never been done before. Every good teacher is accustomed to draw parallels and show analogies in various branches of learning so as to stimulate the imagination and fix certain facts and principles in the minds of his students. The only thing different in my case was that I was a specialist, a public performer, and a person totally lacking in academic training or tradition, and everyone concerned was curious to see how I should tackle the problem. I might add that with this curiosity there was a large measure of friendly tolerance and indulgence. Since I had no system whatever and no idea when an opportunity might occur to point out relationships between one thing and another, the result was something quite unexpected, even to myself.

For example, I took a group of engineering students to the auditorium to explain the mechanics of the piano to them, with the assistance of my tuner. One of the boys, replying to my question, told me that he was specializing in metallurgy. I asked him if he played the piano too, and he said he had never touched the instrument. Here was my opportunity. "What a pity!" I said. "I need a good metallurgist in my piano factory, where we are constantly experimenting with various alloys in the casting of iron frames. Every man in the factory understands the final purpose of his work, and most of them play the piano well enough to appreciate the relation of all its parts. If you were in my place, would you engage as head of a department someone who was unable to use the instrument he was helping to make?"

I thought I had made a point there, and it pleased me to

see the boys nudge each other and grin understandingly. I went on to tell them about many scientists who had distinguished themselves in art and many artists who had distinguished themselves in science, laying stress upon the example left by several celebrated Russian composers. The thought I wished to convey was that nothing in education was more important than development of the imagination, without which life would be one horrid grind of monotonous routine. Being an artist, I naturally believed art to be the most powerful fertilizing agent in this process of development, so I generally employed some kind of artistic illustration to emphasize my meaning. However, I did not care in the least what means were used, either by me or by my listeners, to stimulate their imagination toward the unification of their studies and to bring the understanding that wisdom begins when intuition and intelligence fall into step with each other. I was not there to teach them facts, and if what I told them was incorrect, it seemed to me just as important for them to use their minds to discover the mistake as to check my statements by comparison with a textbook.

Browsing one day in a university library, I found an ancient book which gave me an idea, and I asked permission to attend a class in jurisprudence.

"Who was Hugo de Groot?" I inquired, raising my hand.

A dozen voices were immediately raised with the perfectly proper reply that he was known, under the name of Grotius, as the father of international law.

"Perhaps he was something more than that," I said. "His seventeenth-century contemporaries referred to him as a man of divine genius. He was not only a jurist, but a philosopher, a statesman, a historian, a theologian, a linguist, and one of the greatest classical scholars of his time. He wrote books on all these subjects, and his style was considered a model of elegance and impeccable taste. Finally, he was a poet. Here is a volume of lyrics," I continued, brandishing the book I had borrowed from the library, "which contains not only French translations from the great Latin and Greek poets but a number of original sonnets in the Dutch language as well. Considering what an all-round great man he was, we ought not to be surprised that out of his many accomplishments he left a work on international law which even today is recognized as epoch-making. It would have been far more surprising if he had been nothing more than a specialist in one particular field. Perhaps Grotius is the kind of man to be taken as an example to follow."

One day, as I was speaking at a Roman Catholic women's college on the relation between music and religion, I suggested that the major triad, being built of insuppressible overtones on a fundamental, might be said to typify the conception of three in one and one in three and had been appropriated for that reason by the Christian Church as a symbolization of the Holy Trinity.

This statement was apparently considered irreverent by the head of the music department, who asked me rather sternly what my authority was. I replied cheerfully that I had no authority whatever, that what I said was pure surmise and that I did not know if there was the slightest factual basis for it. I might have added that I was not the only one to hazard this conjecture and that many people had gone considerably further in the investigation of Church mysteries which are so frequently traceable to magic practices in use long before the Christian era.

Percy Grainger, who has made exhaustive studies in this field, agrees with me regarding the analogy between the triad and the Trinity and points out that since early Church music was based on ternary rhythm, written in three parts and sung by three officiants, it would seem only natural that the major triad should be included in a set of symbolic practices which related the conception of the Trinity to everything else in the ritual.

I have laid myself open to criticism by dealing with educational matters in the manner I have described, and many will blame me for making statements and advancing theories which have not received academic corroboration. But once again, it did not seem to me to matter very much what was said as long as the main thing I had in mind was accomplished, namely, the awakening of the imaginative faculty in order to show the possibility of linking all matters of human experience together and the consequent desirability of integrating all subjects of study.

Before leaving the Association of American Colleges, I must relate an incident which caused me every one of three feelings—amusement, perplexity, and regretful embarrassment.

About ten days prior to the date fixed for my visit to a western college, I received a telegram from the faculty professor in charge of the arrangements inquiring if I would consent to act as adjudicator at the Bealy contest to be held on the day of my arrival.

"And just what," I asked the "chargé d'affaires" on arriving, "is the Bealy contest?"

He looked at me and seemed rather puzzled.

"What do you mean?" he said.

I repeated my question, and he said, "There must be some mistake. You promised us to officiate at the beauty contest, which is just about ready to begin."

My jaw fell open with amazement. I reached in my pocket and produced the telegram. There it stood:

"Will you consent to act as adjudicator at the Bealy contest." He began to laugh, but I did not laugh. I thought rapidly of the Carnegie Corporation, of the Association of American Colleges, and of all kinds of undesirable and stupid publicity, and it seemed to me that it wouldn't do at all. He manifested great concern, for, as he said, all the girls had had their hair-do and were waiting for me in their bathing suits. It was customary, he added, to invite a distinguished visitor to the college to officiate at this yearly contest; my name had already been published, and what was to be done? To this day, I cannot think why, the more he pressed me, the more stubbornly I refused. Later on I realized how absurd it was for me to imagine that the dignity of the Carnegie Corporation, of the Association of American Colleges, or of my own obstinate self could possibly be compromised by yielding to the (equally absurd) request, but this idea had taken hold of me and would not let go. Finally I became a little nervous from so much insistence and said that if they wanted a distinguished visitor to judge the contest, why not ask my traveling companion, the piano tuner? To my astonishment, this suggestion, meant to be slightly ironical, was immediately accepted, and the contest was carried out to the satisfaction of all concerned.

I expected that arrangements had been made, as customary in every other place, for me to visit a number of academic classes as well as the music department, but it transpired that the entire college, professors and students alike, had taken a day off "in honor of my visit," I was told, and most of them had gone picnicking with bags and baskets filled with young trees which were to be planted in accordance with the college's plans for reforestation. The music department was closed for the day, and I heard nothing from anyone connected with it. In short, there was nothing whatever for me to do, so I went to the movies, wrote some letters, and went to bed.

The next day I was taken to a few classes, but it seemed impossible for me to establish contact with the music department. I gave my recital that evening in the college auditorium, and as I walked out on the stage a group of young men and women in black caps and gowns stood up to greet me. "This," I reflected, "must certainly be the long-lost music department"—and so it was. I expected that they would all come to speak to me after the concert, but nothing happened. In the morning, just as I was preparing to leave, I had a visit from the head of the music department, who explained that the whole of this strange arrangement had been made out of consideration for me, and that all concerned had sacrificed their desire to see me at their classes in order that I might have the rest I doubtless needed and be in my best form at the recital.

I fear I did not respond to this statement with the gratitude I was expected to evince. I still ask myself sometimes what was the meaning of it all. It was one of the most curious of my many experiences, and, as I have said, it aroused feelings of both amusement and perplexity, leaving me with the baffling thought of having failed, rather stupidly and quite incomprehensibly.

Chirteen

IT IS A WELL-KNOWN FACT THAT CERTAIN MUSICAL COMPOSI-
tions seem to be pursued by bad luck in the same way as
plays, books, pictures, and so forth frequently fail to survive,
for no traceable cause.

Maurice Ravel, at the height of his career, wrote a piano
concerto which was played a number of times by the French
pianist Marguerite Long (to whom the work is dedicated)
in the course of an important tour through the European
capitals undertaken by the composer, who conducted the
various great symphony orchestras in programs of his own
compositions.

The success of the concerto was brilliant, and the publisher immediately received applications for the rights of
first performance in the United States. At that time there
was keen competition for that privilege between the Boston
Symphony and the Philadelphia Orchestra because of the
reputation that both Koussevitzky and Stokowski had acquired in producing new works, and the natural eagerness
of these gentlemen to maintain this reputation.

The publisher finally decided that the only acceptable arrangement was to have simultaneous "first performances" by the two orchestras on the same date. It is not impossible —and let this be said in the friendliest spirit—that the failure to engage a pianist of important standing to perform the Ravel concerto in each of the two cities may have been due to a desire on the part of the respective conductors to appropriate the entire credit for the production. Be that as it may, the solo part was confided, in Boston as well as in Philadelphia, to the young artists who were the official pianists of the respective orchestras; musicians and players of high accomplishment, but as concert performers quite unknown to the public. For this reason, no prominence was given to their personality, and the impression was gained that the new work was intended to be regarded mainly as an orchestral composition in which the piano had a place of secondary importance.

This was particularly unfortunate in view of the fact that the composer, in a preliminary description of the piece when it was first produced in France, had especially defined it as essentially a virtuoso piano concerto of light and brilliant caliber in which no attempt had been made to explore great musical depths. As a matter of fact, there was something more. Ravel was sincerely interested in the rhythmical patterns evoked by American jazz, and the concerto, like several of his other later works, marks a distinct effort to incorporate the more significant features of jazz music into a composition of classical structure.

But nobody paid any attention to these things. At these first performances, the conductors were praised for producing a new work by a much-admired composer, the two solo performers were figuratively patted on the head in acknowledgment of their participation, and the music critics attacked the piece for not containing a certain kind of substance which the composer had expressly disclaimed any intention of employing. In short, a work of great charm and brilliancy, written in a manner possible only to a great master, was ruined—at least for the time being.

I liked the concerto from the beginning, and at the first opportunity I offered to play it at the New York Philharmonic, where Bruno Walter was conducting. When he saw the score, he found it so simple that he thought one rehearsal would suffice. I assured him that he was mistaken and that the piece belied its first aspect, being on the contrary quite tricky and difficult for some of the orchestral instruments. He then offered me two rehearsals, the first one to take place one week before the concert. Following this initial reading, Walter said humorously that he found that we had both been mistaken, I in my request for two rehearsals, and he in his suggestion that one would be enough, for he had now to beg me for four rehearsals. The concerto was consequently prepared with the greatest care, and the two performances which followed were accurate and brilliant. But, once again, although the public reception was enthusiastic, the critics fell foul of the composition, reproaching the composer once again for having failed to do something which he had specifically declared it his intention not to do.

My friend Olin Downes did not like the concerto, and said so in the most unmistakable terms. I hate to think that his criticism, published in the *New York Times*, was taken so seriously to heart by the conductors of two major orchestras as to lead to the request for me to play a concerto other than the Ravel, which had been previously accepted by them. But the fact remained that after the New York performance

I was not asked to play the piece in any other city, and there remained only one orchestra, the National Symphony of Washington, where the Ravel concerto was maintained on the schedule. But the bad luck which attended the piece was not yet at an end.

One week before the Washington concert was to take place, Hans Kindler wrote me that his harpist had the measles.

"That's too bad," I can hear someone remark perfunctorily. "But what has it to do with a performance of the Ravel concerto? Everyone has the measles at some time or other, and there are harpists who do not have the measles." That, precisely, was the attitude taken by the officials of the Musicians' Union to whom Kindler applied for permission to engage a harpist from New York for the concert. The request was denied on the grounds that there was another harpist available in Washington, and although it was urged that the difficult part in the Ravel concerto could only be played by an accomplished performer (which, in Kindler's judgment, the proposed Washington substitute was not), nothing could be done and the conductor felt reluctantly compelled to ask me to play another concerto, which I did.

There was some talk of the Ravel concerto in other places, but I have never played it anywhere since, and it has not, so far, become a popular success.

I do not consider this little story particularly instructive or amusing. It has been recorded here because the incident, slight in itself, meant a great deal to me. It took place at a time in my life when I was beginning to look backward and take stock of the things I had done and left undone, and in some curious way the failure of Ravel's concerto seemed to be bound up with every disappointment I had ever suffered. Should I have felt it more keenly if I had been the composer? I wonder!

In any case, this sour little tale is going to have a sour little chapter all to itself.

Fourteen

I HAVE REFERRED ELSEWHERE TO MY YOUTHFUL DOUBTS AS
to the value of music criticism in the form of daily published reviews of concerts. With advancing age these feelings grew stronger, and I finally came to look upon such
criticism as not alone totally superfluous, but actually ob-
noxious and inimical to the very purpose it was supposed to
serve, namely, that of informing and educating public taste.
This seemed the more unfortunate because of the undoubted
ability and scholarship of those men (many of them my
personal friends) who had adopted the profession of journal-
ist, entrusted with the task of pointing out the qualities and
the defects of composers and performers.

The reputation acquired by writers of this kind leads
people to distrust their own judgment and, consequently,
to abstain from the expression of a personal opinion which
might expose their ignorance. A tragic result of this is that
they soon lose the power to form any opinion at all, since
every function is liable to atrophy if left unused, and the

[260]

more accomplished the critic, the greater will be the harm done in this way, out of sheer deference to what is presumed to be superior understanding and knowledge.

The fragments of conversation which follow here, in illustration of the foregoing, are solemnly declared to be wholly imaginary. Any resemblance to words actually overheard at any time or in any place is, therefore, to be regarded as purely coincidental. Nevertheless . . .

1. A. "How did you like the concert last night?"

B. "I don't know; I haven't read the paper yet."

2. A. "Did you notice that So-and-so's voice was thin in the middle register?"

B. "Is that so? I thought she was fat all through. But if the critic says that, I must certainly watch out for it the next time she sings."

3. A. "It seems that Toscanini's performance of the symphony was a revelation. I see here that he is the greatest of all conductors."

B. "Oh! I'm so glad to know that. I always wanted to hear a revelation. I had thought of going to Koussevitzky's concert tomorrow, but now it doesn't seem worth while. The best is good enough for me."

It is more in sorrow than in anger that I chronicle the fact that the presence on earth of the professional music critic is an unqualified nuisance. What a pity it is that his talents and energies should not be employed in a manner capable of rendering better service to the cause of art! And how thankful we should be when a scholar of great eminence such as Alfred Einstein, is relieved—incidentally, through sheer force of circumstances—from the dreadful and futile business of writing reviews which formerly absorbed so much of his time, without (in my sense) accomplishing anything. The invaluable books this distinguished author has since given us might otherwise never have been written.

When all is said and done, the average human being likes to discover for himself what he enjoys and what he does not enjoy, without being told by someone else. The mission of music is to please the ear and to provide entertainment, and critics, no less than composers and performers, must be guided, sooner or later, by this simple principle, no matter how grandiose and high-flown their theories may be. The development of culture is brought about by examples, not by precepts which merely bring confusion without changing in the least the normal rate of progress.

One of my greatest objections to music criticism is the use, for sordid and commercial purposes, of words and phrases culled from a favorable review. If I am praised by a critic, my manager will quote his words in a circular, confident that this will help him to obtain engagements for me. The preparation of such a circular involves time, skill, and patience. I well remember the pains I took to collect my "good criticisms" in all the countries and cities I visited, the care I gave to editing the circular prepared by the manager, and I recall with a blush my inner smirkings of satisfied vanity when I contemplated the final result.

Sometimes I thought the French system was the best. It certainly gave the least trouble, since it involved no clipping and no editing. In return for a certain payment, the newspapers would print a review written by the artist himself, or by his manager. Since so much per line was charged, obviously none but the most glowing words of praise were used. I remember deciding with my manager that the words "Une salle en délire" (which may be rendered "an audience delirious with enthusiasm") formed one of the most economical and effective lines we could possibly find for our reviews of my Paris recitals, and this phrase was consequently employed several times.

It is to be distinctly understood that this method of advertising involved nothing unusual, and certainly no bribery of critics. Gallic cynicism and perspicacity had simply undertaken to exploit the innate propensity of human beings to believe anything set down in print, and consequently one of the newspaper columns was openly for sale. What did it matter who wrote the review and whether it was paid for or not? There it stood, in the *Figaro*, and that was enough. Besides, the regular critics (mostly great musicians such as St. Saëns, Fauré, Debussy, *et al.*,) wrote about me in terms which were not so vastly different, after all, whenever I appeared at one of the great symphony concerts.

My experience with the music critics in London was interesting when I first returned, after an absence of ten years, to play in my native country. I had known most of these men since I was a boy. I had changed, but they had not. They wrote about me with the greatest cordiality, expressing admiration for my performance. But the effect of their praise was entirely lost, because they felt it necessary to refer each time to the fact that my audiences remained very small. I called on them all and begged them, for heaven's sake, if they wished to be kind to me, to refrain from mentioning this circumstance. They were kind, and in subsequent reviews it was not mentioned. Later on the public came.

The subject of music criticism naturally brings forward the question of authoritative interpretation. What is it that gives the character of authenticity to a performance?

The answer to this is by no means easy to find. I have tried for many years to discover it. Does it lie in painstaking and exhaustive analysis of a composition, and faithful observation of all the directions left by the composer? One might think so, yet nothing is more certain than that these factors, important though they be, do not suffice to ensure success. There must be something else, I thought, and this was a puzzle which constantly haunted me and eluded all my efforts to solve it.

The gifted Chinese author, Lin Yutang, has given us a fascinating picture of a music lesson in the time of Confucius. We see, just as in our own traditional methods, the student proceeding slowly and painfully from the reading of the notes, through the intricacies of beat and rhythm, to performance with musical expression, and finally—at long last —arriving at the understanding of the message of the composition.

When I read this, I seemed to rediscover my youth, with the processes, long since discarded, that I employed for musical study. The puzzle now seemed to take on a different aspect. I decided that the solution was to reach an understanding of the music and give it a definite characterization at the very beginning, not the end, of study of a composition. This involved acceptance of the somewhat paradoxical proposition that nothing could be properly studied unless it had first been learned. It meant that in the construction of my edifice of musical interpretation, I must start at the roof and work downward to the cellar. It meant that instead of polishing the technique before attempting the details of expression, this process must be completely reversed, since technical effects necessarily vary with the constantly changing line of musical expression. It meant a whole lot of things besides, but what it mainly signified was that I must never, never study in the way that Confucius did; that, after all, was not unlike the process employed by my illiterate student who practiced his piece on the white keys only in the belief that the black keys formed part of the expression, which must on no account be introduced until everything else had been completely mastered.

A considerable effort was required for me to break away from ingrained habits of study and to make up my mind to spend no time on small details until I had mastered the whole musical content of a piece. Sometimes I imagined that every one of the markings on the page was screaming at me not to pass it by, but I had to shut my ears to these pleadings, determined as I was to allow nothing to interfere with my understanding of the main structure of the composition.

As I grew more accustomed to this analytical method of study, it became apparent that many of the markings in question were only superficially related to the music. They did not form an integral part of the work and occasionally represented nothing more than subconscious mannerisms of the composer. One example of this is Beethoven's almost invariable practice of using slur marks in piano music as they would be employed to indicate bowing for stringed instruments. The markings of most other composers display personal peculiarities to an equal extent, and while these are occasionally helpful in revealing what we call the style of the writer, it seems to me that they are, as a general rule, not nearly as important as many people hold them to be. Experience has taught me that the average composer's written indications are sometimes, but not always, right, whereas his verbal directions for performance (supplementing those already written) are almost invariably wrong.

It cannot be denied that it is one thing to compose and another thing to interpret and perform a composition, even one's own. How frequently, at orchestra rehearsals, is the spectacle to be witnessed of a composer begging for the realization of effects he has imagined, but which are totally impracticable, after which the conductor, with a display of the most courteous deference, proceeds to show him how the sense of his music can best be conveyed to the listeners! And, needless to say, exactly the same thing takes place, as a rule, between the composer and the soloist or the group of chamber-music players. Personally, although I have sought every opportunity of consulting a composer prior to playing his music in public, it is only very rarely that I have derived any benefit from his suggestions. I feel sure that this must be the usual experience of all instrumentalists who have the habit of conscientious analysis of the music they play. The training of singers, on the other hand, is seldom directed toward independent interpretation, and it is customary for them to receive guidance in this field from the composer or from a professional coach. They are consequently exempt from the perplexities I have attempted to describe.

Let me, at this point, insist that nothing I have written here is to be construed as a suggestion that the composer's indications are ever to be ignored. On the contrary, every single marking should be scrutinized with the most minute and reverential care. However, it involves no disrespect to the composer to recognize the fact that some of these markings are far more important than others, and it should be a vital point in our study to learn to distinguish between those which are inherent in the music and those which have been superimposed later upon a finished product. The fine gold is revealed when the dross has been separated from it.

It is noticeable that this process of sifting is particularly successful when carried out by eminent conductors and performers who protest that they do neither more nor less than what the composer has indicated. It can only be said that they deceive themselves strangely. They cannot possibly know the exact intentions of the composer for the simple reason that musical notation permits only of relative, and not of absolute, directions for performance, and must therefore be regarded as an approximation which no two people can interpret in precisely the same way.

How loud is "forte"? How soft is "piano"? How fast is "allegro," and how slow is "adagio"?

Beethoven was overjoyed when his friend Maelzel gave him the first metronome. "This will permit me," he said, "to leave a precise indication of the tempo of my compositions." Did he mean that the tempo was to be exactly the same throughout whenever he set a metronome mark at the beginning of a piece? I submit that there is no positive answer to this question. It will finally resolve itself into the kind of absurdity that Moszkowski was fond of quoting. "How long is a quarter note?" he was asked by a lady. Politely, he replied that it depended upon the music, some quarter notes being long and others short. "I meant to say an eighth note," said the lady. "How long is that?" Moszkowski patiently repeated his explanation and assured her that the duration was entirely relative. The lady was not discouraged, but annoyed. "I seem to be unable to express myself properly," she said. "I mean, of course, a note that is *really* short. Perhaps I should have said a sixteenth note. How long is that?" Moszkowski felt that the matter had gone far enough, and told her that a sixteenth note was indeed very short. "At last we have it," said the lady with great satisfaction. "Now, Professor, won't you be so very kind as to play me one?"

There is another question to which it is almost equally hard to find a precise answer. I can present this best by offering a concrete example.

Is the Funeral March in the Eroica Symphony intended to convey the impression of a slow procession with two steps to the measure, or of a march with more movement, four steps to a measure?

Beethoven's indication is two-four, yet it is generally conducted as four-eight, and this almost invariably necessitates a speeding up of the tempo in the middle section. Conductors with whom I have discussed this point generally evade the issue by the statement that it is better, for technical reasons, to beat four in a bar and that a slight increase of speed in the middle section is not only permissible, but will pass unnoticed. I totally disagree with this, believing that Beethoven, unique in so many ways among composers, knew exactly what he meant when he wrote duple or quadruple time signatures.

Here is a personal incident illustrative of this: A number of years ago, while I was in San Francisco giving concerts, I received a telegram from the Victor Company enquiring if I would make a phonographic record of the Moonlight Sonata on my return to New York. My first impulse was to accept immediately, but a second thought made me hesitate. Was the first movement not too long and too slow to be recorded on a twelve-inch disk (the largest size)? I played it through and it took just over five minutes. The limit was four minutes and forty seconds. I tried it faster and did not like it. I thought of making a cut . . . horrible! I thought of playing it in two sections . . . equally horrible! I did not reply to the telegram, and wandered disconsolately into the Public Library (not having the Sonata with me), in order to see if the sight of the page would offer any kind of solution. The edition was an unfamiliar one, and the time signature—two-two—was so unusual that it caught my eye at once. I had never seen anything but the ordinary common-time signature, and I had never played it or heard it played otherwise than with four distinct pulsations to the measure. The unfamiliar time notation intrigued me, and I returned to ask the librarian if he had another edition. He found two, one of which was similar to what I had studied from, and the other marked "alla breve." I made further inquiries and discovered an old edition at the home of my friend Oscar Weil, which gave a time notation that I had never before seen, namely: four-four. By this time I was thoroughly perplexed. What had Beethoven written, and why these differences? In the meanwhile, I tried the effect of the first movement with two instead of four pulsations to the measure. This obliged me to play it faster, although the rhythmical effect, on the contrary, was slower, and the more I played it the better I liked it this way. I could not decide what to do, but I remembered that I had, in my library at home, a facsimile of the composer's manuscript (which I had never examined carefully), and also a copy of the first edition. Since neither of these was available in San Francisco, I determined to wait until I returned to New York, and telegraphed the Victor Company to that effect.

When I reached home, I could hardly wait to consult these authentic sources. I dashed to my bookcase and pulled out the first edition and the facsimile of the manuscript. The time signature was "alla breve" in the printed first edition, but the manuscript! . . . *There was no first page!* The original from which the facsimile was taken is carefully preserved at the Beethoven Museum in Bonn, and nobody knows how or when the first page was lost or stolen. The result is that all editors, ignoring the evidence of the first engraved edition, have considered themselves justified, ever since, in making any time notation they choose. This is a great pity, for no musician who has once been released from traditional and unreasoning obedience to the printed page can possibly doubt that Beethoven knew exactly what he wanted when he indicated two beats to the bar in the first movement of the Moonlight Sonata. And Beethoven was right, of course.

I made the phonograph record in four minutes and thirty-seven seconds, and have never since reverted to the slow tempo, which today seems an absurdity to me.

I have related this incident at length because it illustrates at the same time the futility of blind respect for the text and the importance of certain authentic indications. In this particular instance, understanding of the composer's intentions came to me with the force of a sudden revelation, but it has not changed my opinion that the composer, as a general rule, cannot be regarded as the most reliable guide to the interpretation of his music. The best proof of this is that in those rare cases where the composer is a fine executant and plays his music as well as it can be played, it is not difficult, if the performance is compared with the printed page, to find literally hundreds of details where the two fail to correspond.

There are plenty of instances where the composer's express indications have been completely disregarded by common consent. I will offer a single example of this, taken from Chopin, who was not only a composer of extraordinary genius, but a splendid pianist who undoubtedly knew exactly how his music should be played; yet it will be admitted that the Etude in E major, Op. 10, is never played exactly as it is written and probably never will be played in that way.

In the first place, although the time signature is two-four, it is almost impossible to resist the impulse to break this rhythm up into four pulsations to the bar, that being in fact the way it usually sounds. A comparison with the slow movement of Beethoven's Sonata Pathétique (two-four) will show that Chopin, in all probability, intended the piece to be played as if written four eighths to the measure.

In the second place, the middle part of the Etude, marked "poco piú animato," is almost invariably played twice as fast as the first part, and this seems musically correct. I have yet to hear a performance which does not substitute thirty-second notes for sixteenths at that point. These thirty-seconds continue until the arrival of the dramatic climax which ends the section, and then revert to their former value of sixteenths, thus rendering the subsequent "tempo primo" indication totally superfluous.

But this is not all. The dynamic markings are questionable throughout, the slurs are inadmissible from the standpoint of musical phrasing, and it is hardly too much to say that none of these markings are of value in building up an artistic interpretation of this piece, while on the other hand there is unfortunately much which, if strictly followed, will distort its musical contour.

I realize that parts of the foregoing may convey the impression of an essay or a lecture on the art of musical interpretation, but it is nothing of the kind. Everything I have written represents my own personal struggle and my efforts to discover a formula for study which would enable me to be not only a good artist but a good teacher as well. It seems to me that I have been, all my life, between Charybdis and Scylla: the confused and dangerous whirlpool of the composer's inconsistencies and the rock of my own personal interpretation—both equally treacherous. Have I succeeded in steering a middle course? Have I been shipwrecked?

Strange to say, I do not know. But one little incident which occurred when I was a young man in Paris comes back to me every now and then.

I was turning the pages for Paderewski during a rehearsal of a Brahms trio that he was to play with his friends Gorski and Salmon. A discussion arose regarding a diminuendo that Paderewski wished to replace with a crescendo. "Cela ne va pas," objected the cellist, supported immediately by Gorski. "Brahms has distinctly written 'diminuendo' here for all three parts." I can still hear Paderewski's impatient reply: "Il ne s'agit pas de ce qui est écrit. Il s'agit de l'effet musical." (The point is not what is written, but what the musical effect should be.)

I remember thinking at that time that it was quite proper for a genius such as he was to take liberties which must be denied to the ordinary man. Later on I came to feel that the ordinary man who fails to realize what lies in the music beyond the printed indication is just . . . an ordinary man.

Fifteen

THE STORY IS TOLD OF AN EASTERN MONARCH WHO, IN THE fullness of his days, determined to learn all that was known of the history of mankind. He sent for his wise men and instructed them to prepare such a history. At the end of five years, they brought him a hundred large volumes. "This, Sire, is the history you demanded!" The king, astonished, exclaimed: "By Allah the merciful! I cannot read all these volumes. They must be condensed into a smaller compass."

Five more years elapsed, and two of the wise men, each bearing a volume, appeared before the king. "O Commander of the faithful!" they said, "your desire is fulfilled. Within these two volumes will be found all that is known of the story of humanity." The king, now old and feeble, replied: "These two volumes must be further condensed. Time will not allow me to study them."

The wise men sadly departed, and after another long lapse of days a single old man appeared at the Court. He produced a small scrap of paper. "O King!" he gasped painfully, "I am the last of those who set out in search of the history of mankind. This paper tells all that has ever been learned:

"MAN WAS BORN, HE SUFFERED, AND HE DIED."

The celebrated Captain Jack Bunsby, if he had heard this story, might conceivably have delivered himself of his favorite oracular pronouncement: "The bearings of this observation lays in the application on it." Is there any connection between these memoirs and an old Oriental tale? None whatever, gentle reader, unless you wish it, in which case you are at liberty to share my thought that everything which is really essential in the life of one individual could very well be summed up in a simple phrase, no longer than that which ends the Eastern fable.

As I approach the end of my personal narrative, I feel more and more inclined to condense it for the reason that few happenings nowadays have the spice of novelty or seem worthy of being recorded. My thoughts and my actions are, in the main, guided and shaped by patterns which were molded long ago. The strange, uncanny sense of familiarity with new faces, new scenes, and rather particularly with new music, occurs with ever growing frequency, and nothing seems to happen any more *for the first time*. "Plus ça change, plus c'est la même chose." And possibly that is why a beneficent Providence has arranged for gradual decay of the faculties with advancing age. It may not be an unmixed evil when one can no longer see or hear with the same acuteness as before. Very likely the mistiness which now veils the outline of these sense impressions serves also to soften what would otherwise be intolerable repetitiousness and monotony.

Consequently I intend to make no effort to recall with distinctness the events of yesterday, which so often seem far more remote than those of half a century ago. Memory, in the long stream of human consciousness, may be compared at the outset to a limpid and narrow brook, flowing swiftly over objects which appear plainly through the clear water. Later on it overflows its banks, the water is muddied, and the current runs slower. Finally, the movement becomes quite sluggish and nothing is to be seen beyond a few loose, disconnected fragments which float on the surface. My memory of yesterday's events is also slow and sluggish, and it is only rarely that I discover amid the flotsam and jetsam anything that seems worth saving. Here, for example, comes drifting along, lazily, a small bundle labeled:

HAVANA, A GREEN CIGAR, A HAT, AND A BOTTLE OF RUM

There is nothing about music in this story, but if I had not been a professional pianist, engaged to give three recitals in the city of Havana, it never could have been told. It begins with two lapses of memory. I cannot recall the year of my first visit to Cuba, and I cannot recall the name of Georges Barrère's flute pupil who received me so kindly when I arrived. But this amiable gentleman plays the most important part in the tale.

The month was April, and it was terrifically hot in Havana. I wanted to see everything in that beautiful city, and he was willing to take me everywhere. Toward noon on the first day, slightly overcome by the heat, I proposed a drink. He looked at his watch.

"At five minutes past twelve you can have your drink," he said. I did not understand. We were not in England or the United States, and there were no regulations against drinking at any hour one chose.

"I want my drink now," I wailed.

"At five minutes past twelve," he replied sternly.

And at that precise hour he drove me up to a palatial building which, he explained, housed the main offices of the world-renowned distillery firm, Bacardi and Company. At the entrance stood Señor Bacardi in person, receiving his friends in accordance with what I learned was his daily custom, for the noonday cocktail. I was introduced to this courtly gentleman, who, following the customary Spanish polite assurances that his house was at my entire disposal, invited me to inspect what he was pleased to call his little counting house.

The sight of an apparently interminable array of desks and typewriters with hundreds of people working busily at the task of keeping other hundreds supplied with Bacardi rum was amazing. But I could not examine all the details with the attention they deserved, for I was terribly hot and tired and I longed unspeakably for a cool drink.

My host must have observed signs of distress on my face, for he suddenly struck his forehead in remorse (as he said) for forgetfulness of the duties of hospitality and proceeded to conduct me to a large and handsome paneled room where a number of people were seated around tables in luxurious armchairs, sipping cocktails and conversing with great animation. A pleasing tinkle of ice being vigorously agitated in cocktail shakers partially attenuated this buzz of conversation, and I observed a generous-sized bar set up on one side of the room, behind which two white-clad men were engaged in the process of mixing drinks. It was immediately apparent that the sole mission in life of these two men was to quench the thirst of Señor Bacardi's guests, for their entire energies seemed to be set forth in the astonishing skill and rapidity with which they shook up the cocktails.

One of these cocktails was set before me. It was in a long,

thin glass reminiscent of the French "flute," formerly reserved for drinking champagne, and this glass was covered with powdered ice like the beard of Santa Claus. I lifted it to my lips. . . .

O friends, topers, epicureans, sybarites, voluptuaries, connoisseurs, tasters to the gods of Olympus, never say that you know the heavenly bliss of absorbing a Daiquiri cocktail unless you have experienced its gustatory effect on the tongue and palate in the Bacardi private barroom in Havana with the thermometer at ninety degrees in the shade!

Time stood still in those first few seconds of ineffable rapture. But I was not permitted to finish the cocktail, for Mr. Bacardi laid a restraining hand on me.

"Please," he said, "drink no more."

Recalled to the commonplaces of daily life, I looked at him in pained surprise.

"What! not finish this?" I cried. "I want a second one immediately after."

My host smilingly replied: "A second one you shall have, amigo, and a third and a fourth, up to a twelfth cocktail shall you have, *but not of the same kind!* Today you must learn that Bacardi rum is the most versatile and accommodating of all liquors. It mixes with everything and imparts the glory of its tropical sunshine to each combination. Come, amigo, courage! You have a dozen other experiences to live through."

I did not have twelve cocktails, I am sure. But if a slightly hazy memory serves, I must have had seven or eight, after which my host asked me to declare which one was the most delicious.

My answer, delivered sententiously and with the deliberate care required by the circumstances, was to the effect that all the drinks were wonderful but that none of them had succeeded in recapturing the ecstasy of my introduction to the first, the Daiquiri cocktail.

"How is it made?" I inquired.

The reply was in the form of a flowery compliment.

"That, caballero, you should never be told, for if you took away the recipe for the Daiquiri cocktail, you might also deprive us of the hope of welcoming you again. Permit us to keep the secret which will bring you back to us."

I bowed my acknowledgment and protested that nothing, in any event, should prevent me from returning to Havana.

"In that case, amigo," said my host, "I need not hesitate to tell you the great secret. It is in reality very simple."

He dropped his voice and continued in confidential tones.

"First the glass," he said. "Ice cold, and after the moisture forms on it, dip it into powdered sugar. Then two parts of Bacardi to one part of lime juice, sweetened to your taste."

There was a momentary silence and he then resumed.

"That is all, except for the shaking, which must be long and energetic. That is positively all. But . . . ," and his voice suddenly rose almost to a shriek, while he clasped his two hands together, "I implore you—a GREEN lime. In the name of the Mother of Heaven—a GREEN lime, not a yellow lime. If you cannot find a green lime," and his excitement abated with a dropping of his voice, "you may try the juice of a lemon. But of course it is not the same," he ended with a kind of weary sigh expressive of a disillusioned perfectionist.

Shortly after this conversation, I took my leave with suitable expressions of gratitude. My friend then took me to visit an equally impressive establishment, that of the great cigar manufacturer Cabana. It was tremendously interesting to see the various processes of cigar manufacture. I remarked that I had never smoked a green cigar and expressed my desire to try one. They smelled so wonderful.

My friend laughed and asked me if I thought I could stand the effect. Being a very experienced smoker, I saw no reason why I should not try. I was given a freshly rolled cigar, which tasted more delicious than any other tobacco I have ever smoked. But in a few moments I grew deathly sick and passed out in a dead faint. There were further consequences after I recovered consciousness, and I was so weakened that I accepted my friend's invitation to take some rest at his home. A little coffee soon revived me, and I happened to mention my desire to acquire one of the fine straw hats which were everywhere to be seen. My friend started, and looked intently at my head.

"What size?" he said.

I told him, and he immediately ran out of the room, returning in a few moments with an unfinished straw hat which he clapped on my head. It fitted, and he immediately began to dance about the room, crying out, "I have the head! I have found the head at last!" I took off the hat and examined it. It was a perfect example of the finest sort of straw weaving.

"What does this mean?" I said.

"It means, my dear friend," was the reply, "that the hat is yours. How happy this makes me! For two years I have been looking for the right head!"

I protested that I could not possibly think of accepting a gift of such value from him.

"Nonsense!" he answered. "It never belonged to me and you will have no hesitation in accepting it when I give you my solemn assurance that it was stolen!"

I was aghast.

"Stolen!!"

Roaring with laughter, he said: "That is what I told you. And now you shall hear the whole story."

It appeared that my friend, some years before, had been Cuban consul in San Francisco, where his duties involved commercial relations with many Spanish-speaking countries. A man with Cuban credentials called at his office with a request for introductions to certain Californian firms as well as to business houses in Central and South America, where, he said, he was on the point of establishing important trade connections. He was told to return to the office a few days later, after the necessary inquiries had been made and his references checked. In the meanwhile my friend took some trouble to render him a small service, the nature of which I have forgotten. The following day the man returned, saying that business compelled his immediate departure from San Francisco. He expressed his thanks for the courtesies extended to him and placed a package on the Consul's desk, saying, "Here is a small mark of my appreciation," after which he left the office so hurriedly that nobody thought of delaying him, neither was he seen again. A few hours later my friend received a cable message from Cuba to the effect that this man, whose description was given, was expected to call on him and should be immediately handed over to the police as an internationally known swindler and thief. I forget what reason my friend gave for feeling so sure that the hat contained in the package left on his desk was stolen, but I do remember that he told me that the police refused to take it away.

As a result, that hat, he said, had been in his possession ever since. Since it was too large for his own head, he had made up his mind that the first person whose head fitted the hat should relieve him of the burden.

The end of the story is that I accepted the gift; I had it finished and made up with a suitable band and ribbon, and I have worn it each summer since that time.

No, there is nothing about music in the tale of my first trip to Havana. There is a record of my having given three piano recitals there. But my only recollection of these events is that the physical effort of playing in that tropical heat without clothes suited to the climate caused me acute discomfort and a sensation I had never before experienced, namely, the feeling of my coat becoming heavier and heavier on my shoulders as it absorbed the weight of the water that was literally streaming from every pore in my body.

A number of kind friends came to see me off when I left Havana after a most delightful visit. At the moment of boarding the steamer, Señor Bacardi appeared, bearing a package which he placed in my hands with cordial expressions of friendship. The parcel contained two bottles of Bacardi rum marked with the number 1873. I wondered, and I still wonder, if he knew that 1873 was the year of my birth and if he had selected liquor bottled in that year as a specially delicate attention.

But I have never heard of vintage rum, and the year following, when I returned to Havana, I did not see him.

Another package of reminiscences comes floating toward me over the waters of memory, and I shall label it:

TROUSERS, TAILORS, AND SCIATICA

In Paris, one of my first extravagances, as soon as I began to earn a little money, was to call on Paderewski's tailor and order a suit of clothes. This tailor was one of those sartorial artists whose greatest pleasure is to see other artists wearing the clothes they have designed for them. This man had a large clientèle among musicians, and there was nothing he would not do to oblige them and to give them an individual style. His establishment was on the Boulevard des Capucines, near the Opera House.

Since I came with Paderewski's recommendation, he received me with special courtesy and assured me that I should never, never have occasion to go to any other tailor after he had once settled upon my patterns. Then he started to study my figure and, for some reason which was never explained, decided that I must wear trousers which were very wide at the bottom, so that the feet were partially covered. Although there was a reaction at that time against the previous fashion of tight-fitting nether garments, I thought that he went too far in the contrary direction with me and was making me conspicuous. I mentioned this several times, but I never could prevail upon him to alter his pattern. Throwing out his hands with a deprecating shrug, he invariably replied: "Mais, Monsieur, que voulez-vous? C'est votre genre." (It's your style.)

My New York manager, who was a natty dresser, was quite shocked by the width of my trousers when he first saw me, and he begged me to dress like an American gentleman. But a pair of trousers in New York cost as much as a whole suit in Paris and I said I would not and could not pay the price. He said that the trousers I was wearing gave me a "chunky" appearance (a word I had never before heard). He was delighted when James Huneker, in a newspaper article, once described me as "chunky," thus apparently confirming his judgment, but I did not care. I even suggested that it might not be a bad thing to advertise me as the "chunky" pianist, in order to distinguish me from other pianists who were not chunky.

Meanwhile . . . Pablo Casals will never forget what happened in São Paulo. We were rehearsing late, oblivious of the clock, and suddenly realized that we had only ten minutes left to reach the auditorium for the announced hour of the concert. Off flew the day clothes and we pulled on our clean evening shirts in frantic haste. Black shoes: where were they? Collars, ties, studs, everything dashed into place with feverish speed. Into the box with Pablo's cello, have I got all the music, yes, let's be off. But Pablo still had his trousers to put on, and his trousers were rather tight. Setting his jaws and introducing his feet, he pulled violently. Cr–r–r–ack!! The toe of his right shoe ripped right through the trouser leg, laying it open from the knee down to the bottom. There was no time even for consternation over this hideous mischance. Ring the bell, rush to the door and yell desperately —"Chambermaid! Chambermaid! Hurry here, for God's sake! Come at once! Bring a needle and black thread! Hurry!" The girl came flying, and in three minutes Pablo's trouser leg was whipped over in a manner that would have done credit to a sailmaker or a meat packer.

The concert started only fifteen minutes late, and if anyone noticed anything peculiar about the right trouser leg of the cellist, he never mentioned it.

A pessimist has been defined as a man who wears both a belt and suspenders; I say he is one who also carries in his vest pocket a couple of mechanical trouser buttons which can be snapped on in case of emergency. "Tout arrive," says cynical France. Anything might happen, whispers a malicious fate, and almost everything seems to have happened to me at some time or other. The buckle of my belt has broken, my suspenders have given way, seams have burst open, and buttons have dropped off. Suspenders broke on me once, while I was playing the Tchaikowsky Concerto in Monte Carlo. It did not matter as long as I was seated at the piano, but when I rose at the end to bow and retire from the stage, I felt it incumbent upon me to swell myself out as far as possible—like the frog in the fable—so that with the artificial tension thus induced, I might be able to stave off the

[283]

impending disaster. I succeeded, and from the shelter of the side wings I sent out a frantic whispered appeal to the men in the orchestra: "Au secours! In the name of heaven, get me a safety pin! Mon pantalon dégringole!"

It is hard to explain why a mishap to clothing should cause the cruel embarrassment that all of us have probably experienced at least once in our lives. It is even more curious to reflect that the general desire to assert one's individuality by some original detail of attire is constantly counteracted by the feeling that one must, in the main, be dressed like everyone else. How terrible it is to appear wrongly clad! Nothing can excuse this, and there is no defense against the ridicule it excites, whatever the cause may have been. I have known many people (why hide it? I am one of them myself) whose lives have been temporarily poisoned through no graver reason than that they have worn a tuxedo with a black tie at an evening party instead of the expected swallowtail with a white tie.

I repeat that I have always been one of the unwilling slaves of this kind of conventionality, and I writhe retrospectively even now at the recollection of solecisms of which I was guilty in days when, it may be admitted, such things took on a greater degree of importance than they do now.

On one occasion I was invited to a garden party at the palace of the Ministry of War in Paris. General Picquart was the Minister, and he was my good friend. It was a warm and beautiful day, and I put on my new light suit together with my new hat, a soft felt with a wide brim. I felt very elegant until I saw, on entering the gardens, that all the men were dressed either in stiff military uniforms or in formal, black clothes with high silk hats.

My first tendency, I recall distinctly, was to laugh secretly at them and to hug myself with the thought that I was the only one there who was comfortably dressed; but that feeling did not last long. I was weighed down by the unspoken criticism of the large group of "correctly" dressed people, and I realized that I was a pariah. My numerous friends, including the Minister himself, did their best, I am sure, to spare me any feeling of mortification, but despite their tactful kindness I could not help discerning a faint tinge of amused tolerance in their attitude, and that completed the crushing effect of my *faux pas*. There was only one thing to do. I sought out the refreshment tent, consumed a quantity of ice cream, and went home.

Gabrilowitsch, I remember, at one of our two-piano recitals, had failed to change from blue to black trousers. It was useless for me to tell him that it did not matter and that I could see no difference. He knew I was partly color-blind, and he was terribly upset. He insisted on using the piano which had the bass side turned to the audience throughout the evening, saying that it screened him better than the curve on the other piano. It was our custom to change over from one piano to the other during the performance, but he would not do so, and when we came out to bow, he refused to advance, as usual, to the edge of the platform, but took shelter behind the piano, merely inclining his head in response to the applause. Of course, I had to imitate him. Ossip was one of the musicians who frequently suffered from trouser trouble, and this has been amusingly related by Clara Clemens in the biography of her distinguished husband.

Gabrilowitsch and I had the same tailor in New York. This man, like the Paris tailor previously described, had a large circle of musical customers. He was very fond of music and always begged for concert tickets, in the front row whenever possible, so that he could watch the arrival on the stage of his coat with the man inside. He made every effort to catch the eye of the wearer at that moment, and made a slight gesture which he hoped would be seen and imitated, namely, that of pulling at the lapels in order to bring the coat into perfect position. The coat was his artistic creation, part of his very self, and it was absolutely essential that it should set exactly right. "Mr. Bauer," he said to me once after a recital, "my coat looked just like an angel on you."

All his customers were prevailed upon to give him signed photographs with suitable words of admiration for his tailoring abilities. His prices were exorbitant, and I remember writing on the picture I gave him: "Costly thy habit as *my* purse can buy."

Very different was the tailoring adventure undertaken by Fritz Kreisler and myself in Madrid, where we once spent a week giving a series of sonata recitals. Fritz had a shabby traveling suit and a grand-looking fur-trimmed overcoat. I had a shabby overcoat and a new suit. One of our colleagues, visiting us at the hotel while we were rehearsing, showed us his suit, which he said had been turned inside out by a Madrid working tailor who specialized in that particular operation. The suit looked splendid, and Fritz and I decided to entrust this tailor with the shabby suit and the shabby overcoat for a similar transformation. Two days later the work was done, and both suit and overcoat looked like new. But when Fritz put on his suit, he presented an indescribable sort of twisted appearance. It was impossible to say what was wrong, but he simply did not look natural. And then he discovered that he would have to button his vest and coat from right to left instead of in the usual way, from left to right. While he was struggling with this problem, I put on the overcoat, and found, to my fury and disgust, that I, too, was expected to button from right to left. The tailor, in reply to our remonstrances, said that nobody minded that kind of change and nobody would notice it. When we referred to our friend's costume, which, although turned, continued to be buttoned in the usual manner, he simply shrugged with one word: "Double-breasted." That was the answer, of course. Fritz's suit and my overcoat were both single-breasted, and it had never occurred to us that the button-holes would be on the wrong side after the clothes were turned.

Friends, take warning by this experience of two poor musicians. Do not have clothes turned unless they are double-breasted. And even so . . .

I don't know how long Fritz wore his funny-looking crooked suit, but I used my overcoat for quite a long time and developed a first-rate left-hand technique for buttoning it.

Mention of Fritz Kreisler reminds me of the sciatica from which I have suffered for many years. I was always happy to play with him, not only because he was a great artist, but because he gave me no trouble if I had a backache. Fritz has always acknowledged applause by an inclination of the head and, as far as I can recall, he has never bent over from the hips as Paderewski, for instance, was wont to do. Kreisler's attitude was very nice indeed when I had a stiff back and we took a bow together.

A painful attack came on during one week when I had a two-piano recital with Myra Hess and a joint recital with Albert Spalding. Myra was most considerate when I begged her to refrain from what Casals used to call "le geste désespéré," a low obeisance with deprecatory outflung arms, and she bowed charmingly from the head only in order to accommodate me, since I could not bend over at all. Albert promised to do the same thing, but habit proved too strong for him, and after the first sonata out went his fiddle and his bow to the entire length of his arms, leaving me to make my stiff bow in agony though in determined emulation. He admitted that he had been carried away by the bow and violin, and for our subsequent recalls to the stage he left them in the hands of André Benoist, whereupon our respective bows were models of ensemble performance.

At this time my tailor was a man recommended by Rubin Goldmark, who was very particular about clothes, but did not care to pay high prices. The new tailor satisfied me completely. He, too, was pleased to have customers who were public performers, but he did not care for music, and his main preoccupation was to make well-cut clothes feel easy and comfortable.

He was always very friendly, and he displayed great concern about my sciatica, which, for a time, compelled me to wear a steel corset. This was almost a grievance to him. "I try to make you comfortable in your clothes," he complained, "and you have to go and get that machine to make you uncomfortable. How can I cut trousers to fit properly over this hard metal edge?" He was in perfect despair. Finally he addressed me solemnly: "Mr. Bauer," he said, "it won't do. You are not treating yourself right. Don't go to those machine makers. They do you no good. Mr. Bauer, take my advice. Go to a doctor. Doctors are clever men. A good doctor will give you a pill and that will cure you. Believe me, Mr. Bauer, that is the proper thing to do. Go and see one of these clever doctors." I told him that I would follow his advice and limped out. The following week I returned for a fitting, still limping painfully. "Aha!" said the tailor, "you promised to follow my advice, but you did not do so. Believe me, Mr. Bauer, one of those clever doctors would have given you a pill and today you would be cured." "I did see a doctor," I replied rather impatiently. "I saw two doctors, and they both told me to keep on wearing the steel corset. They have done nothing else." There was a momentary silence, and the tailor stared sadly at me. At last, shaking his head in a melancholy fashion, he said, "I never had any faith in doctors. Believe me, Mr. Bauer," he continued earnestly, "they are all fakes and humbugs. Every one of them: fakes and humbugs. They take your money and they don't cure you. Swindlers, I call them. No friend of mine should ever go to see a doctor."

No other package of recollections appears, so I shall return to the present and to the task I have undertaken to edit all of Schumann's piano works.

How does it happen that I am engaged on this editorial work? It is over forty years since Carl Engel, then associated with the Boston Music Company, came to me with the proposal that I should revise and correct the errors to be found in every existing edition of Schumann's works. I agreed with him that this revision was certainly desirable, but I declined the offer, feeling that I was insufficiently experienced to undertake such a task. However, the offer was never withdrawn, and so it came about that a generation later, with Carl Engel president of the great publishing firm of Schirmer, I started on a task, now almost completed, which I hope will prove helpful to performers and teachers.

I have just finished correcting the G minor sonata, with the restoration of its original finale and the inclusion of the youthful song "Im Herbste," which inspired the slow movement. I have written a preface which tells of the circumstances under which the piece was composed, and I have spoken of Henriette Voigt, the lady to whom the composer dedicated the Sonata. He wrote the words "I am a poet when I think of you" and signed his name over a tremendous crescendo mark intended to symbolize his constantly growing affection for her.

I had laid down my pen, musing on the personality of this fascinating lady, which must have been highly characteristic of the manners of the eighteen-thirties, when suddenly the thought of that "sempre crescendo" caused my mind to fly off at a tangent. Those two words, together with mention of the period during which the genius of Robert Schumann was in its fullest flower, reminded me of the Dutch musical society "Sempre Crescendo" which was established by students at the venerable University of Leyden in the year 1831. The original membership of this organization (greatly extended since) consisted of an orchestra formed exclusively of students desirous of studying and performing the masterpieces which they loved. From the time of its inception the society has given an annual series of public concerts, and I was invited to play at one of these.

It has of course been abundantly evident that my narrative has throughout been conspicuously empty of dates. This could not be helped. I have never kept diaries or records beyond a certain number of programs casually laid aside, and I have nothing to refer to except my memory. Only the fact that a certificate of honorary membership in "Sempre Crescendo" has been preserved in a dusty attic enables me to state that I played in Leyden in the month of March, 1898.

I was already well known in Holland at that time, and on my arrival in the ancient city I was received by a committee of students from Sempre Crescendo with every mark of respect and honor they could devise. I played with the orchestra and was presented with a laurel wreath. A banquet followed the concert, and the president of the society conferred the honorary diploma upon me with a flowery oration and great ceremony.

The hour was late when the banquet ended, and I prepared to retire to my quarters at the hotel. A suggestion to that effect was met by pained and indignant protests. It transpired that the committee, before fixing the date of the concert, had ascertained from my manager that I had no engagement on the day following, so, they said, there was no possible reason why I should not spend the rest of the night talking and drinking with them at the University Club. This, they assured me, was a sacred tradition at all Sempre Crescendo events. I yielded, and enjoyed their company very much.

At six o'clock in the morning they took me to the train and I returned to my headquarters in Amsterdam, where I went at once to bed and slept for the rest of the day. When I awoke I was conscious of a faint odor of laurel and discovered that I had been sleeping on top of the wreath which had been presented to me the previous evening and which I had deposited on the bed when I came in, worn with fatigue, that morning. I remembered then that the Honorable Secretary of Sempre Crescendo had been most assiduous in collecting my belongings at the railroad station in Leyden and had flung in the laurel wreath just as the train was moving off.

This incident, unimportant in itself, serves as introduction to an account of the part played by laurel wreaths in my career years later in Holland. Dutch audiences used to be considered stolid, if not apathetic, and I have written of my feelings of cruel discouragement when I first played there. They applauded very little, and a "toegift" (encore number) at a concert was the exception rather than the rule. If they liked an artist, they kept on attending his concerts; if they did not like him, they stayed away. There was no manifestation and no excitement. What was it that caused these sedate and self-contained people to change their manner and their attitude at musical performances, so that they became, in course of time, perhaps the most demonstrative audiences in Europe? I have no answer to this question.

But I can vouch for the fact that while audiences in other countries still considered it sufficient to greet an artist, however celebrated, with a round of perfunctory applause as he came on the stage, the Dutch public had decided that the only proper way to welcome him was to rise as one man when he appeared. And they did this everywhere. In addition, one frequently heard subdued sounds of approval during the performance. Nobody ever thought of leaving the hall until several "toegifts" had been given and received, and it became quite customary for groups of young people to gather around the exit door from the stage to hail the departing performer with shrill shrieks of delight. A certain naïve awkwardness in these proceedings was sometimes inexpressibly touching, for the concert giver was made to feel that he had succeeded in awakening musical sensation which had lain dormant until then. Finally—the laurel wreaths! In speaking of them, words almost fail me. The intention was so complimentary, so kind and so serious, and the effect was (to me, at least) so unfortunate, so absurd and such a horrible nuisance! What was one to do with the darned things? A tour in Holland involved from twenty to thirty concerts, and sometimes two, or even three, laurel wreaths were laid on the stage at each performance. There were no formal presentations and, more often than not, the wreaths were on the stage before the performer appeared—sometimes on the piano, sometimes on the chair, and sometimes propped up in a manner which compelled the performer to rearrange them before he could start the concert. And this little act had to be accomplished with suitable simpering obeisances, while the public stood and applauded. With every feeling of retrospective gratitude to my kind Dutch friends, I look back on these experiences with something like horror. An intolerable, dreadful nuisance.

The wreaths were of all sizes and weights, some of them woven around a straw center, suitable for funerals, others woven around a heavy twisted wire, obviously intended for monuments. At first I thought I would keep the ornamental ribbons which bore my name as well as that of the donor (generally a musical organization), but I soon found that this would not serve to identify any particular occasion, since the letters of the name, instead of being printed on the ribbon, were made of ornamental paper loosely stuck on, so that they soon fell off and became mixed together in inextricable confusion after being packed in my trunk.

I had recourse to innumerable expedients in order to dispose of these wreaths, which accumulated daily, with each concert. Some I carefully picked to pieces, depositing the remains in my waste basket. Others I left in closets, between mattresses, or in any place where I thought they might stay concealed until it was too late for the hotel baggageman to run after me with it at the moment of my departure. The thing was a constant worry to me.

One day in Amsterdam I was positively awestruck to see an immense wreath, about five feet in diameter, leaning against the piano before I entered on the stage. As usual, I set it aside. After the concert, it was brought to me. My name was on the ribbon, but there was no indication of where it had come from. It was too large to go into the cab. The concert hall attendant pointed out, however, that the wire circle was jointed and fastened with a small bolt. He loosened this, and the wreath, folded into a semicircle, seemed just about large enough to fit the toenail of the Statue of Liberty on Bedloe Island, but it was squeezed with some difficulty into the cab with me.

In my hotel bedroom I contemplated the monstrous thing with dismay, wondering how on earth I should get rid of it.

The next day I was in Rotterdam, and as I walked on the stage I nearly fell over in consternation. There, leaning against the piano, was the same colossal wreath. After the concert was over, one of my Amsterdam friends appeared in the artists' room.

"I came to your room to fetch you so that we could travel together," he said, "but you had already left. The maid showed me this wreath, saying that you ought to have taken it with you, so I brought it along."

There was nothing to be done. The Rotterdam concert was the last of the tour, and I had to leave for Switzerland the following morning. I took the wreath back to the hotel, folded it up, and packed it tightly down into an old chest, used to contain wood logs for burning, which stood at the fireplace. The next day found me in the train, a free man unencumbered by wreaths of any description.

Several weeks later I was home in Paris. In my room I found an enormous round tin box. It contained the laurel wreath. There was a note from my janitor explaining that he had gone to the Custom House to fill in the necessary declaration for importation from a foreign country. The note contained the list of his disbursements to obtain delivery of the box. There was also a letter from a florist in Rotterdam who had been requested by the hotelkeeper to pack and forward the wreath to me. Enclosed was his bill, together with a request that I should kindly return the empty box to him, carriage paid.

Coda

PEACE IS OVER MY SOUL. I HAVE RETIRED FROM PUBLIC LIFE.
I am never going to practice the piano any more. Gone—
and how willingly dismissed!—is the searing feeling of
ambition to succeed, gone the qualms of stage fright, the
vain and silly satisfactions of applause, the humble abase-
ment before the shades of the composer and the artificial
shams of refusing and at the same time humoring the ubiquitous autograph hunter; gone also the tedium of travel,
the hideous fatigue of submitting to journalistic interviews,
all the same and all equally stupid; gone the resentment
against critics who failed to discover genius in everything
I did and whose writings, consequently, could not be "used"
for advertising propaganda—finally, God be praised, gone
the feeling that I must pile up enough money to live in
idle luxury whenever I chose to quit. The wars and the taxes
have taken care of this last item, and I am still at work, my
interests being now entirely bound up with matters of
musical education.

The story of my life would be incomplete if I omitted mention of my activities at the moment of writing, for, after all, the present does exist, if only as a very short link between the past and the future. Fate has been kind in allowing me to continue to devote my energies to the art whose faithful servant I have been throughout my life.

I am connected with two schools of music. Both of them lie very close to my heart, for they are built on artistic principles of the highest order. Janet Schenck, the founder and director of the Manhattan School of Music in New York, studied with me years ago in Paris, and her wise and inspired leadership has resulted in an institution which stands second to none. In Hartford, Moshe Paranov, director of the Julius Hartt School of Music, is also a former pupil of mine, a musician of remarkable gifts and inexhaustible energy who, within a few short years, has developed a small school into the most important and the most artistic institution of its kind in the state. In addition to my work at these two schools, with which I am proud to be associated, I have temporary relations with many colleges and universities throughout the country.

I have now done what I set out to do: I have faithfully recorded a number of the happenings in my long career which have left their mark on my memory and on my character. Without concealment or disguise, I have also attempted to convey to my reader, for better or for worse, something of an impression of my personality and of the manner in which I have reacted to the conditions which surrounded me. I have tried to explain that actions and events of half a century ago seem today far more vivid than those of last week, and in doing so I have likened memory to a clear stream which flows rapidly at its outset, then spreads slowly over a broad area. My eye sees today an unbroken green expanse which reason tells me covers a bottomless swamp of things forgotten or purposely consigned to oblivion. If I were to set my foot on it, I might sink down and become suffocated. In any case, the waving grass over it which looks so serene and pretty would be disturbed by my footprints. So I shall leave well enough alone.

Stay! What is this slimy, loathsome creature that comes crawling from the marsh toward me? It appears to have several heads. . . . it cannot be! . . . Yes, it is! . . . it is nothing less than the Hydra.

"Foul monster!" I say. "What brings you here? What have I to do with you?"

The obscene creature grins at me with its nine mouths.

"You must not forget me," it snarls. "I have attended you throughout your whole life. *I am your nightmares!*"

I shudder.

"Look at me!" whines one of the heads. "Each time your memory failed you in a dream, I was there, ha, ha!"

I writhe convulsively.

Other heads chime in: "All those dreams of having to play a concerto without ever having studied it were my doing," one chatters. "Yes," says another, "and then you started to improvise marvelously to the amazment of the audience, and you decided that you would in future play none but your own compositions." "Not so bad," comes another voice, echoing my unspoken thought, "until the piano gave out and people started to laugh at you for moving your fingers without bringing forth a sound."

Ruthlessly, the other voices take up the tale: "How many times did you come too late for the concert? *We* kept back the trains, caused the taxicab to break down, and brought you finally to a cold dark hall with freezing fingers. You had to play something fast and loud to bring the audience back, for they had already left. We made the piano slide away from you as you were playing. We broke the strings and the leg of the piano stool so that you came down with a dreadful bang! Then we helped you rise from the ground with dignity, fastened wings to your shoulders, and you flew away, above the heads of the scoffers, saying, 'Now I'll show them what I can do!' "

"All this is nothing to what we all did in Indianapolis," booms a deep voice. "That was a nightmare all right! The orchestra started the Concerto before he was there! What a joke! Ha, ha! Ho, ho!"

The word rings in my ears: Indianapolis! No nightmare was ever more terrifying than the real experience I once had there at a concert. Here is the story:

There was a time when I was a favorite in the capital of Indiana. I played several times in a season, and for several seasons in succession. I was engaged to play Beethoven's Emperor Concerto with the local orchestra, which was directed by a very competent young German-American conductor. In those days, Indianapolis, like most western cities, was strongly influenced in its musical development by German culture, the "English" hotel and the "English" opera house to the contrary notwithstanding.

The date of the concert happened to fall on my birthday, April 28. Everything went well at the rehearsal. The hour of the concert came, and after the opening orchestral number I walked onto the stage to play my Beethoven concerto. The moment I appeared, the orchestra let loose with the mighty E-flat chord which starts this great work. As this sound burst on my ears I was immediately petrified by a feeling of the most intense terror I have ever experienced. A nightmare had suddenly materialized into being. How many times had I dreamed that the orchestra had actually started the Emperor Concerto while I was frantically struggling to get into my clothes and to reach the piano stool in time for the opening cadenza! How often have I awakened in a cold sweat of agony because I did *not* get there in time! Here, by some miraculous or diabolical intervention, the dream had come true—there was nothing to differentiate between the illusion and the reality, and I stood there spellbound, thinking that I had gone insane.

How long this state lasted I cannot tell, but it seemed like a lifetime before awareness of my surroundings returned to me and I was able to realize, amidst applause and waving of handkerchiefs, that the orchestra was extending to me, in the form of this sustained E-flat chord, the German compliment of the "Tusch" or flourish, intended for ceremonial occasions. The kind people had arranged to celebrate my birthday and wish me "many happy returns" in this fashion. However, I was totally unnerved by this correspondence between nightmare and reality, and my subsequent performance of the concerto was very shaky in consequence. The local newspaper reported the following morning that Mr. Bauer was "obviously moved by the cordiality of the welcome extended to him by the large audience."

This experience was fortunately unique in my life. Although I have had similar dreams since, none of them ever came alive in this horrifying manner. There were plenty of other dreams too which just escaped being regular nightmares, since they usually took the form of an obsession, an interminable repetition of some musical phrase which had no discoverable ending. One of these obsessions has pursued me since childhood, when I first heard the Eroica symphony. "This is the key of E-flat," the music tells me, with the two opening chords. "Here we are and here we stay!" say the cellos, grandly proclaiming the tonality of the noble melody for the subsequent four measures. Suddenly, with a frightful shock, the picture changes. There is a terrifying dissonance. The music is moving off to some other place. Where? What comes next? Wait! Oh, wait! It is unbearable! But the breathless syncopations force me onward and away until desperately I seize upon a chord which leads me home again.

Silly, sentimental twaddle, is it not? Just the kind of thing that people write when they know nothing whatever about music. Nevertheless, that is my feeling and it will not change. Wait! Oh, wait! while I explore the mystery and determine for myself, if I can, what comes next. Doubtless my childish reaction to this musical phrase has built up in me a fervid longing for a certain kind of dramatic interpretation which I have never heard. I wish I could hear it, although I freely admit that the whole thing is a kind of obsession.

Only last week, a similar obsession pursued me in a dream. This time it is not the Eroica, but a graceful waltz, the name of which I cannot recall. Here it is:

The question is the same: What comes next? For pity's sake, *What comes next?* Why am I dragged away so ruthlessly from the key—from my home? Is this worth thinking about or not? Has music, by any chance, some kind of connection or analogy with life as we know it, and do we feel impelled to put the same questions to both in order to attain understanding—interpretation? More than one philosopher, more than one poet has attempted to trace such a connection, and this should perhaps be the aim of every musician. "Others may reason and welcome," says Browning.

In any case, it is on this question: "What comes next?" that I propose to conclude the story of my life.

Says Marcus Aurelius: "Soon, very soon, thou wilt be ashes or a skeleton and either a name or not even a name. But name is sound and echo."

I had occasion recently to telephone to a large music store where there was every reason to believe that I was well known. The clerk took careful note of my order and then asked my name, which I had already given him.

"Mister Harold Bauer," I said carefully, thinking he had not heard me the first time. "Yes, Sir," he answered respectfully. "How is it spelled? B–O–W– . . . ?"

Index

[305]